AFRICAN AMERICANS

IN THE

INDUSTRIAL AGE

African Americans
IN THE
Industrial Age

A DOCUMENTARY HISTORY, 1915–1945

Edited by Joe W. Trotter
and Earl Lewis

Northeastern University Press
BOSTON

Northeastern University Press

Library of Congress Cataloging-in-Publication Data

African Americans in the industrial age : a documentary history,
    1915–1945 / edited by Joe W. Trotter and Earl Lewis.
        p. cm.
    Includes bibliographical references (p.   ).
    ISBN 1-55553-257-8 (cl. : alk. paper).—ISBN 1-55553-258-6
    (pbk. : alk. paper)
        1. Afro-Americans—History—1877–1964—Sources. I. Trotter,
    Joe William, 1945– . II. Lewis, Earl.
    E185.6.A255   1996
    973'.0496073—dc20   95-45279

Designed by Liz Doles

Composed in Galliard by Coghill Composition Company, Richmond, Virginia.
Printed and bound by Maple Press, York, Pennsylvania. The paper is Maple
Antique, an acid-free stock.

MANUFACTURED IN THE UNITED STATES OF AMERICA
00 99 98 97 96 5 4 3 2 1

To African Americans who helped to make the Industrial Age and to our mentors at the University of Minnesota,

CLARK A. CHAMBERS

ALLEN F. ISAACMAN

LANSINÉ KABA

RUSSELL R. MENARD

JOHN MODELL

STUART SCHWARTZ

ALAN SPEAR

CONTENTS

ACKNOWLEDGMENTS

We wish to thank the Department of History at Carnegie Mellon University and the University of Michigan for making this book possible. Generous research support enabled us to employ several able graduate and undergraduate assistants on the project. At Carnegie Mellon, we owe a special debt to graduate assistants Lori Cole (Ph.D. 1994), who carefully keyed the documents into the computer and even shared key sources from her own research on Pittsburgh, and Donald Collins, who helped to proofread the documents for accuracy. Carnegie Mellon undergraduate assistants Jennifer Geller, Aimee Sealfon, Sharon Metcalf, and Beverly Goines also provided essential clerical and library research for the project.

At the University of Michigan, we are indebted to Angela Winand and Marya McQuirter for their expert help as research assistants, and to Barbara Berglund for help in preparing the index. We also benefited from the ongoing enthusiasm, interest, and questions of students in our graduate and undergraduate courses in U.S. and African American urban and social history. Our colleague Robert Jefferson at Wayne State University and editors Nancy Toff and Paul McCarthy of Oxford University Press warrant special acknowledgments for their timely and generous assistance. And Earl Lewis wishes to acknowledge the financial support of the Center for Afroamerican and African Studies at the University of Michigan.

As always, we are indebted to our wives, Jayne London and LaRue Trotter, for encouraging and at times demanding the completion of this book. For their careful and patient editorial work, we also wish to thank director William Frohlich and the editorial staff, particularly Ann Twombly, at Northeastern University Press. Finally, for introducing us to the joys and perils of historical research, we respectfully dedicate this book to our mentors at the University of Minnesota.

PREFACE

Over the past three decades, African American history fully emerged as a field of scholarship in the United States. Under the impact of the modern Civil Rights and Black Power Movements, scholars revisited virtually every aspect of the black experience from the African background through the mid-twentieth century. Studies of slavery, emancipation, and the segregationist order proliferated. At the same time, a growing number of studies documented the mass migration of rural blacks to the nation's urban centers. By the early 1990s, research on urban blacks had gained increasing parity with scholarship on slavery, emancipation, and the rise of Jim Crow during the agricultural era.[1]

As scholarship on the black past escalated, interest in the collection, interpretation, and publication of primary documents on the black experience also increased.[2] Documentary collections on African American life

---

1. See Earl Lewis, "To Turn as on a Pivot: Writing African Americans into a History of Overlapping Diasporas," *American Historical Review,* 100 (June 1995): 765–87. Kenneth W. Goings and Raymond A. Mohl, eds., "The New African American Urban History Parts I and II," special issue, *Journal of Urban History,* 21, nos. 3 and 4, (March and May 1995). For a brief review of the African American field see also Joe W. Trotter, "African American History: Origins, Development and Current State of the Field," in Earl Lewis, ed., special issue, *Magazine of History,* 7, no. 4 (Summer 1993): 12–22.
2. Only a few documentaries on the black experience were published before the 1960s. These included James M. Gregory, *Frederick Douglass: The Orator* (Springfield, Mass.: Willey Co., 1893); Ernest Davidson Washington, ed., *Selected Speeches of Booker T. Washington* (Garden City, N.Y.: Doubleday, Doran, 1932); Carter

had roots in the late nineteenth and early twentieth centuries. Early documentaries stressed the writings and speeches of outstanding black men. As early as 1893, for example, James M. Gregory, professor of Latin at Howard University, published the speeches of Frederick Douglass. According to historian John Blassingame, Gregory's *Frederick Douglass: The Orator* was one of the first serious attempts to acknowledge the value of African American documents.[3]

During the late nineteenth and early twentieth centuries, however, most scholars concurred with the opinion of the prominent Southern historian U. B. Phillips. Writing at the turn of the twentieth century, Phillips maintained that existing documents on the black past were biased, unreliable, and invalid accounts and should therefore be ignored by historians.[4] It was more than 25 years later that E. Davidson Washington published a volume of speeches by his father, Booker T. Washington. Another ten years passed before the pioneer black historian Carter G. Woodson edited a four-volume documentary on the social reformer and minister Francis J. Grimké. In subsequent years, historians Herbert Aptheker and Philip S. Foner helped to broaden the base of such studies beyond the speeches of

---

G. Woodson, ed., *The Works of Francis J. Grimké* (Washington, D.C.: Associated Publishers, 1942); Herbert Aptheker, *A Documentary History of the Negro People in the United States: From Colonial Times Through the Civil War* (New York: Citadel Press, 1951), subsequent volumes followed in 1969, 1973, and 1974; Philip Foner, ed., *The Life and Writings of Frederick Douglass,* 4 Vols. (New York: International Publishers, 1950–1955). Documentaries of the modern civil rights and post–civil rights era emerged in two overlapping waves, one extending from about the mid-1960s through the early 1970s and the second covering the period from the mid-late 1970s to the present. For useful summaries, see James M. McPherson et al., eds., *Blacks in America: Bibliographical Essays* (Garden City, N.Y.: Anchor Books, 1971), 12–13; Dwight L. Smith, ed., *African American History: A Bibliography* (Santa Barbara: ABC-Clio Press, 1976); and Meyer Weinberg, ed., *Racism in the United States: A Comprehensive Classified Bibliography* (New York: Greenwood Press, 1990), 133–34.
3. John Blassingame, *The Frederick Douglass Papers,* Vol. 1 (New Haven: Yale University Press, 1979), lxxiii.
4. For a recent study of U. B. Phillips's racial views, see John H. Roper, *U. B. Phillips: A Southern Mind* (Macon, Ga.: Mercer University Press, 1984). Also see John Blassingame, ed., *Slave Testimony: Two Centuries of Letters, Speeches, Interviews, and Autobiographies* (Baton Rouge: Louisiana State University Press, 1977), xvii.

black elites and carried the black documentary genre into the 1950s and 1960s.[5]

The first major outpouring of black documentary studies emerged during the mid-1960s and extended through the mid-1970s. These studies represented a mix of single- and multi-volume works that covered relatively short as well as long periods of time.[6] Despite some diversity in chronological coverage and format, however, most of these studies were bound by a common interpretive framework. Edited or co-edited by scholars with strong ties to the modern Civil Rights Movement, most of these studies emphasized the ideology, politics, and problems of interracial cooperation and institutional integration in American society. Leslie Fishel, Benjamin Quarles, Gilbert Osofsky, August Meier, Elliott Rudwick, Francis Broderick, and others all edited or co-edited important volumes in this genre. In his documentary, *The Burden of Race* (1967), historian Gilbert Osofsky put it bluntly: "This is a study of the way Negroes and whites have lived together in America over the last 350 years. It has often been a sad relationship and sometimes a brutal one."[7] Similarly, in his *Negro Social*

---

5. E. D. Washington, ed., *Selected Speeches of Booker T. Washington;* Woodson, ed., *The Works of Francis Grimké;* Aptheker, ed., *A Documentary History of the Negro People in the United States;* Foner, ed., *The Life and Writings of Frederick Douglass.*
6. Milton Meltzer, ed., *In Their Own Words: A History of the American Negro, 1619–1966,* 3 Vols. (New York: Thomas J. Crowell Company, 1964–1967); Leslie H. Fishel, Jr., and Benjamin Quarles, eds., *The Black American: A Documentary History* (Glenview, Ill.: Scott, Foresman and Company, 1967); Mortimer A. Adler, Charles Van Doren, and George Ducas, eds., *Great Documents in Black American History* (Chicago: Encyclopaedia Britannica Educational Corporation, 1969). Studies from the first wave included Howard Brotz, ed., *Negro Social and Political Thought* (New York: Basic Books, 1966); Gilbert Osofsky, ed., *The Burden of Race: A Documentary History of Negro-White Relations in America* (New York: Harper and Row, 1967); William Loren Katz, ed., *Eyewitness: The Negro in American History* (New York: Pitman Publishing Company, 1967); Joanne Grant, ed., *Black Protest: History, Documents, and Analyses, 1619 to the Present* (New York: Fawcett Press, 1968); Albert G. Blaustein and Robert Zangrando, eds., *Civil Rights and the American Negro: A Documentary History* (New York: Trident Press, 1968); John H. Bracey, Jr., August Meier, and Elliott Rudwick, eds., *Black Nationalism in America* (Indianapolis and New York: Bobbs-Merrill, 1970); August Meier, Elliott Rudwick, and Francis L. Broderick, eds., *Black Protest Thought in the Twentieth Century* (Indianapolis and New York: Bobbs-Merrill, 1971).
7. Osofsky, *Burden of Race,* xv.

and Political Thought, 1850–1920, Howard Brotz emphasized the integrationist imperative: ". . . there has been one overarching question, whose comprehensive character has affected all the others, and that question is whether the Negro could look forward to a future as a citizen of this republic. Was color prejudice of such a magnitude and of such a fixed character that the Negro was not assimilable?"[8] Other documentaries of the period also revealed the impact of the Civil Rights Movement on their conceptualization. They also frequently focused on the struggle for black manhood. In his introduction to the Encyclopaedia Britannica's collection *A Taste of Freedom* (1969), historian Earl E. Thorpe explained that "[t]he central theme of Negro history is the quest for freedom, equality, and manhood."[9] In their *Great Documents in Black History* (1970), George Ducas and Charles Van Doren also suggested how the struggle for black manhood stood at the core of the first major outpouring of black documentary studies: "By all odds, any book of this decade that addresses itself to the significant documents of black history should probably begin with . . . a voice that the contemporary black revolution can identify with as it raises anew the question 'Are we men?' If in fact black people are men, then they are persons—capable of and entitled to a proper social relationship with their white counterparts, who are certainly no more than men!"[10] While the racial interests of black women were served by the growing emphasis on black manhood, women and gender issues represented key blind spots. The experiences of black women only slowly found expression in these studies, although Gerda Lerner's influential study probably found a wider audience and had a greater effect on historians than many volumes emphasizing manhood.[11]

A second wave of black documentary studies extended from the mid-1970s through recent times. Whereas earlier studies accented black-white interactions, ideology, and politics, the new studies were more specialized chronologically and topically. They also reflected the growing influence of

---

8. Brotz, *Negro Social and Political Thought,* 1.

9. Thorpe, "Introduction," *The Negro in American History, Vol. III: A Taste of Freedom, 1854–1927* (Chicago: Encyclopaedia Britannica Educational Corporation, 1969), ix.

10. George Ducas and Charles Van Doren, eds., *Great Documents in Black American History* (New York: Praeger, 1970), x.

11. Gerda Lerner, ed., *Black Women in White America: A Documentary History* (New York: Random House, 1972).

the new social history, which emphasized the history of the working classes and the poor. Historians Ira Berlin, John Blassingame, George Rawick, and others produced important social history documentaries on the experiences of blacks during slavery, the Civil War, and the emancipation era.[12] Historians Robert Hill, Philip Foner, Ronald Lewis, and others produced important documentaries on the black nationalist leader Marcus Garvey and the Universal Negro Improvement Association; the black labor leader A. Philip Randolph and the Brotherhood of Sleeping Car Porters; and numerous other facets of the black worker's experience.[13] At the same time, the new generation of scholars produced multi-volume works that deepened our understanding of influential black leaders. John Blassingame, Louis Harlan, Herbert Aptheker, and Claybourne Carson edited multi-volume studies on Frederick Douglass, Booker T. Washington, W. E. B. Du Bois, and Martin Luther King, respectively.[14] Once again the number

12. George P. Rawick, ed., *The American Slave: A Composite Autobiography* (Westport, Conn.: Greenwood Press, 1972–1979); C. Peter Ripley, *The Black Abolitionist Papers* (Chapel Hill: University of North Carolina Press, 1985–   ); and Ira Berlin, Joseph P. Reidy, Leslie Rowland, Barbara J. Fields, Thavolia Glymph, Steven F. Miller, and Julie Saville, eds., *Freedom: A Documentary History of Emancipation*, Vols. 1–3 (New York: Cambridge University Press, 1982–1990).

13. Robert Hill, ed., *The Marcus Garvey and Universal Negro Improvement Association Papers* (Berkeley: University of California Press, 1983–1987); Philip Foner and Ronald L. Lewis, eds., *The Black Worker: A Documentary History from Colonial Times to the Present* (Philadelphia: Temple University Press, 1978–1984); and Joseph S. Wilson, *Tearing down the Color Bar: A Documentary History and Analysis of the Brotherhood of Sleeping Car Porters* (New York: Columbia University Press, 1989).

14. Blassingame, ed., *The Frederick Douglass Papers;* Louis Harlan and Raymond M. Smock, eds., *The Booker T. Washington Papers* (Urbana: University of Illinois Press, 1972–   ); Herbert Aptheker, ed., *The Correspondence of W. E. B. Du Bois* (Amherst: University of Massachusetts Press, 1973–1978); Claybourne Carson, Ralph E. Luker, Penny A. Russell, and Louis R. Harlan, eds., *The Papers of Martin Luther King, Jr.* (Berkeley: University of California Press, 1992–   ). Although most of the studies discussed above are multi-volume works, important single-volume studies were also published. See Willie Lee Rose, ed., *A Documentary History of Slavery in North America* (New York: Oxford University Press, 1976); Blassingame, *Slave Testimony;* Thomas R. Frazier, ed., *Afro-American History: Primary Sources 1970* (revised ed., Chicago: Dorsey Press, 1988); and Mulaika Adero, ed., *Up South: Stories, Studies, and Letters of this Century's Black Migrations* (New York: W. W. Norton, 1993). Moreover, some of the multi-volume studies discussed

of volumes on individual black men outnumbered those that explored the intricacies and intimacies of black women and their experiences. There were a couple of notable exceptions and in some instances social historians integrated the studies of men and women.[15]

As suggested by the recent proliferation of black documentary studies, *African Americans in the Industrial Age* complements existing volumes. It focuses on the development of the black community between the two World Wars and treats the period as a significant watershed in the development of black America. More specifically, we emphasize the process by which African Americans helped to transform themselves into a new urban people during the industrial age. We place the experiences of black workers at the core of our concern, emphasizing their movement from the rural South and resettlement in the major urban centers of the nation. Although we accent the experiences of black industrial workers, we also document dimensions of race and gender relations as well as the interconnections between the lives of black workers, the black middle class, and black elites. In other words, the documents also show how people struggled over definitions of race, class, and gender—illustrating, for instance, the extent to which these facets of black life were social constructions as well as realities in the lives of numerous Americans during the industrial era.

In detailing how individuals constructed their lives, the documents succeed in doing several other things. First, they force us to think about the processes by which African peoples made themselves into African Americans. More important, we see how words and concepts such as community, identity, and race functioned as other than abstractions. For instance, through efforts to secure decent housing, avoid lynching, or vote, a collective memory was created that shaped what it meant to be black. This sense of a shared history in turn aided those who built communities in post-1915 Detroit, Atlanta, or Milwaukee. Second, the documents reflect the myriad ways in which African Americans lived beyond the stare

---

above are now being abridged into single-volume works. See, for example, Ira Berlin et al., *Free at Last: A Documentary History of Slavery, Freedom and the Civil War* (New York: New Press, 1992).

15. See, for example, Dorothy Sterling, *We Are Four Sisters: Black Women in the Nineteenth Century* (New York: W. W. Norton, 1984); and Bert J. Loewenberg and Ruth Bogin, eds., *Black Women in Nineteenth Century American Life: Their Words, Their Thoughts, Their Feelings* (University Park: Pennsylvania State University Press, 1976); Rose, *Documentary History of Slavery;* Blassingame, *Slave Testimony.*

of white America. In their own communities, among their own friends and relatives, they could relax and be totally themselves—at least for a while. Third, the documents highlight African Americans as multipositional actors—i.e., individuals shaped by race but not solely defined by race.[16] As a result we are reminded of a broader humanity, of men and women who laughed, loved, cried, and felt pain, men and women who lived life as fully as possible. And fourth, the documents remind us of the uneven effects of industrialization and proletarianization. We are at once invited to acknowledge and then critique dichotomies such as rural-urban, industrial-agricultural, and southern-northern.

Our documentary history builds upon a growing body of primary sources. Unearthed by a variety of scholars working on various aspects of black life during the industrial era, collections of oral interviews, manuscripts, newspapers, photographs, and social surveys provide key documentation. In addition to numerous sources in state and local archives, this volume draws upon records at the National Archives and the Library of Congress; Departments of Labor and Justice and various New Deal agencies; the president's Fair Employment Practices Committee; the National Urban League; and the National Association for the Advancement of Colored People, to name a few. Under the general editorship of August Meier, John Bracey, the late Elliott Rudwick, and others, many of the most useful primary documents at the Library of Congress and the National Archives are now available on microfilm at university libraries.[17]

This book is divided into four major parts. Each part is in turn divided into major topics. Part I, the largest section of the book, covers World War I and its early aftermath. Selections illuminate the dynamics of black migration, the role of work in the process, and the impact of black

---

16. For a fuller discussion of multipositionality, see Earl Lewis, "Invoking Concepts, Problematizing Identities: The Life of Charles N. Hunter and the Implications for the Study of Gender and Labor," *Labor History,* 34 (Spring–Summer 1993): 292–308.

17. See August Meier and Elliott Rudwick, *Black Studies Research Sources: Microfilm from Major Archives* (Bethesda, Md.: University Publications of America, 1990); Deborah Gray White, "Mining the Forgotten: Manuscript Sources for Black Women's History," and Robert L. Zangrando, "Manuscript Sources for Twentieth Century Civil Rights Research," both in *Journal of American History,* 74, no. 1 (June 1987): 237–51; Joe W. Trotter, review of James R. Grossman, "Black Workers in the Era of the Great Migration, 1916–1929," in *Journal of American History,* 74, no. 4 (Mar. 1988): 1390–1401.

population movement on wartime and early postwar class, race, and political relations. Part II documents the experiences of African Americans during the nation's economic recovery and the expansion of a consumer-oriented society during the mid- to late-1920s. It shows how economic prosperity was unequally distributed and often occurred at the expense of black communities.

The collapse of the economy during the Great Depression is the subject of Part III. Documents in this section illustrate the persistence of racial inequality, despite the benefits of much-needed New Deal social welfare programs, and offer life histories of African Americans under the impact of hard times. These stories demonstrate the ways in which African American men, women, and families experienced, as well as responded to, the depression. By allowing African Americans to tell their stories within the larger context of their own family and community histories, these documents also show aspects of change and continuity in the lives of African Americans from the late nineteenth century through the late 1930s.

Finally, Part IV documents patterns of racial discrimination in defense industries, military service, and the institutional, cultural, and political life of the nation during World War II. This section also illuminates the rise of new demands for socioeconomic and political justice, as reflected in the work of the federal Fair Employment Practices Committee and the launching of new black publications like the *Negro Quarterly* and *Negro Story*. In addition to brief headnotes that enable readers to identify key features of each document, we begin each section with a brief introduction that discusses the major changes in African American life during the period and places the documents within a larger historical context. The introductory essays and short annotations also aim to link the various parts of the book and place specific issues within a broader conceptual as well as historical framework.

Editors' Note

Several editorial decisions guided our effort. First, we retained the original spelling in all documents, except where a correction (indicated by brackets) was necessary for clarity. The designation "sic" does not appear unless it was part of the original document. Occasionally, however, we insert in brackets missing words that we believe clarify the author's intent. Second, in several cases, we have reproduced excerpts rather than the entire document. In such cases, we acknowledge with ellipses (. . .) where original material has been deleted. Third, we use headnotes at the beginning and citation notes at the end of each document. Since the headnotes and citations include the names of authors, titles, dates, and sources of our documents, we do not duplicate this matter in the text itself. Finally, much of our documentation comes from the microfilm collections of University Publications of America, and we have included reel and frame numbers in our citations. Since our selections from these sources are usually a component of a much larger body of documents, we wish to encourage students to use our citations in conjunction with the published index of specific collections.

CHAPTER I

World War I and Its Early Aftermath, 1915–1921

A. INTRODUCTION

Historical Context

World War I opened up new opportunities for African Americans in the nation's major industrial centers. For the first time in the nation's history, African Americans broke the agricultural "job ceiling" and entered the industrial sector in rising numbers. They gained jobs in iron, steel, automobile, meatpacking, and other mass production industries. Black urban-industrial workers averaged between $3 and $5 per eight-hour day compared to little more than $0.75 in southern agriculture and no more than $2.50 per 12-hour day in southern cities. An estimated 500,000 blacks left the south for northern and western cities between 1916 and 1920. At the same time, the proportion of southern blacks living in cities increased from about 21 to 25 percent, while the proportion of all African Americans who lived in cities rose even higher, from 27 to nearly 35 percent of the total.

A variety of factors helped to stimulate black population movement. On the one hand, the key socioeconomic and demographic factors included the labor demands of war industries, the curtailment of European immigration, the exploitative sharecropping system, the boll weevil, and destructive storms and flooding, which devastated large portions of southern agriculture. On the other hand, social injustice, racial violence, disfranchisement, and the intensification of the segregationist system reinforced the economics of black migration. More importantly, however, African Americans played the pivotal role in their own movement from rural to urban America.

Southern blacks developed elaborate kinship, friendship, and com-

1

munity networks. In a variety of social and institutional settings—churches, barber and beauty shops, fraternal orders, and clubs—they gathered and shared information about urban conditions and carefully debated the pros and cons of life in cities before making their move. Thus, they were not merely pushed and pulled by forces beyond their control. They deliberately planned their actions and helped to shape their own experience in the industrial phase of American life. Still, African Americans frequently described the movement north in biblical terms such as "Promised Land," "Flight from Egypt," and "Land of Hope."

Unfortunately, as African Americans entered cities in growing numbers, they faced new patterns of inequality. The discriminatory policies of employers, labor unions, and urban institutions relegated African Americans to the bottom of the urban economy. African Americans occupied the so-called "Negro jobs," low paying, heavy, and dirty work for black men and domestic service positions for black women. Employers expressed the view that blacks were particularly suited for such work, while white workers described their black counterparts as a "scab race" and justified their exclusion from labor unions. At the same time, municipal governments allotted growing sums for the expansion of health, education, and social welfare institutions, which employed rising numbers of white

women, but almost uniformly excluded black women or relegated them to unequal status in all-black institutions.

As African Americans faced limits on their lives at work, they also confronted restrictions on where they could live and the institutions that they could patronize. Racial violence erupted and segregated neighborhoods emerged. New zoning legislation, racially restrictive real estate covenants, and numerous informal patterns of discrimination ensured that African Americans would occupy the poorest dwellings in or near the vice districts, where ordinary conveniences were often nonexistent. Efforts to contain the rising black urban population produced growing interracial tensions, which culminated in bloody riots in East St. Louis (1917), Chicago (1919), and other major cities during this period. In Chicago, 38 persons lost their lives, 500 received serious injuries, and property valued at an estimated $250,000 was destroyed.

As the nation subordinated African Americans at home, it also relegated them to the bottom of the military establishment. Black servicemen served in segregated and unequal units, usually in the U.S. Army labor and service battalions, which provided support to their white counterparts. Blatant social injustices notwithstanding, African Americans resolved to "close ranks," support the war effort, and place their own grievances on hold until the nation achieved victory on the battlefield. Some 367,000 African Americans served in the armed forces during World War I.

Despite loyalty to the nation's defense effort, urban blacks soon resisted the unjust conditions in their new environment. As their numbers increased, for example, black workers helped to create the cultural foundations for the new urban gospel and blues, the economic basis for the rise of a new business and professional middle class, and the demographic foundations for the emergence of new black political and Civil Rights movements. African Americans captured the spirit of their own new possibilities by calling themselves "New Negroes." Initiated during the war years, these developments in American and African American urban life would gain fuller fruition during the 1920s.

Documents

This section focuses on three major issues: 1) diverse viewpoints on the origins and meaning of black migration; 2) the role of work; and 3) the

A panel from Jacob Lawrence's 1940–41 series, **Migration of the Negro.** *Courtesy of the National Archives.*

relationship between work and community. Subsection IB enables us to compare and contrast a variety of viewpoints on the causes and consequences of the Great Migration. Selections include the views of a broad cross-section of government and nongovernmental officials; blacks and whites; elites and workers; northerners and southerners. Some documents suggest that the Great Migration was a blessing and that the south should have been happy to get rid of its "race problem." Others also argue that black migration was a blessing but for different reasons. In the latter view the exodus was an opportunity for African Americans to gain full citizenship rights and escape an oppressive past. Still others argued that the migration undermined the prosperity, growth, and progress of the south by depriving the region of a cheap labor force. Thus, the documents also show how some Americans hoped to encourage the black exodus, while others campaigned to stop it.

Subsections IC and ID provide perspectives on work in the migration and resettlement of blacks in major cities. Subsection IC illuminates the networks that African Americans used to get jobs, the obstacles that they faced, and the strategies that they devised to fight racial inequality in the work place. These selections allow us to examine how black men and

women relied on an elaborate network of kin, friends, and community institutions, as well as labor agents hired by railroads and industrial firms, to obtain information about the urban labor market and make their move. Subsection ID highlights the connections between work and residence. Documents enable us to assess patterns of racial discrimination in the housing market and the process of residential segregation of blacks and whites. This section includes brief contemporary social surveys of specific cities, including Cleveland and Columbus, Ohio, East St. Louis, Illinois, and Atlanta, Georgia.

B. BEGINNINGS OF THE BLACK EXODUS: RACIAL, REGIONAL, AND GOVERNMENTAL PERSPECTIVES

1. *"Why Stand Ye Idle?: The Migration from the Negro Viewpoint." Letter to the* Biloxi Herald, *ca. 1916. Emphasizes the growing volume of the black exodus, and suggests the need for social reform, higher wages, and better race relations as deterrents for black movement out of the south.*

To the Herald: A few months ago, I stood at the Y and M. V. station where a crowd of colored people had gathered to bid farewell to one of their number who had decided to try life in Chicago. On the surface there was nothing unusual in this gathering of Negroes; but any one standing near might have heard enough to convince him that they had come not alone to say goodbye to their departing friends, but to prepare the way for their own departure a few weeks later. I believe every member of the party, after wishing the friend good luck, called out, "Look for me in the Spring." These Negroes in question were of the industrious, law-abiding type and hence, the most useful to the section they proposed to leave.

I have been called to the same station many times since then to take leave of my own friends; and, upon every such occasion, I have seen such

---

Graduates of Morehouse College and Atlanta University in Georgia, Wilbur and Ardie Halyard symbolized the New Negro Movement when they migrated to Milwaukee in 1923 and founded the Columbia Building and Loan Association the following year. Courtesy of the late Ardie Halyard, Milwaukee.

---

troups of other Negroes going north as to leave no doubt in my mind of the sincerity of the intention of the Negroes generally as expressed by that first group. In the last few months, Negroes of all classes have been leaving the city and county, and in such numbers as to cause serious alarm. Business establishments are affected, professional men are losing patronage, and property in tenement districts is depreciating in value; yet no concerted effort for ascertaining the reason for their leaving and reaching a rational, practical, and workable plan for inducing them to stay has been attempted by those to whom the welfare of this community means most. This seeming indifference has prompted the question stated in the caption of this article.

I would suggest that the salary scale be raised so that a Negro laborer may supply himself his wife [unclear] his little ones with the bare necessities of life.

If it required $1.25 for the daily sustenance of a man a year ago, it

requires at least twice this amount for him to live just as well now. A 10% or a 20% increase in salary will not meet the 100% increase in the cost of living, and such a condition represents the most favorable that this vicinity has yet afforded.

Better educational facilities for Negroes would do much to arrest the northward movement of those who are rearing children.

This state of mind is, as a rule, prophetic of what is to follow. Some have said to me at the station, "I would not leave but I have children and I want them to have better opportunities."

Give the Negro an equal chance in the courts of this community.

In this connection, it may be well to note that in many instances the reporters themselves do much to upset the contentment of the Negro. Frequently, details of the court proceedings are purposely drawn out with needless exaggeration in order to give a humorous color to the grave matter of crime, and to hold up the criminal [N]egro to the ridicule of a public all too ready to laugh lightly at serious matters. Such exaggerated reports do not deter crime in the criminal [N]egro, and they are discouraging to the better class of Negroes.

SOURCE Charles S. Johnson, "Migration Study," National Urban League Papers, Research Department Series 6, Box 86 (Manuscript Division, Library of Congress), (hereinafter cited as CSJMS). Note: These documents formed the basis of Emmett Scott's study, *Negro Migration during the War* (1920; reprint, New York: Arno Press, 1969).

2. *"Causes of the Migration, From the Viewpoint of Southern Negroes." Article in the* Atlanta Independent, *2 Dec. 1916. Stresses white mistreatment of blacks as the cause of the migration and criticizes black leadership for covering up black dissatisfaction as the major cause for movement north.*

To our minds the fundamentals underlying the movement of black folk from the South to the North is not far-fetched. Any student of economic, social and political conditions, who is willing to admit that the Negro is a human being, possessing the same capabilities, aspirations and ambitions common to the human family, has the answer at hand.

We have read and studied with much concern the many reasons submitted by both white and black leaders in the South in answer to this grave question. To our minds none of them have been candid enough to face the

With all their belongings lashed onto their car, a Florida family prepares for the long journey north. Courtesy of the Library of Congress.

truth; to stand the Negro up as a man in the economic and politic struggle for existence and treat him as a man. The white writer has attempted to show everything else except the real causes for the movement. He has submitted every reason except the real one underlying the unrest among the laboring black folk in the South. He has not asked himself a single time the question, "Am I not responsible for the unrest and uncertainty and migration of the Negro"? "Is not the treatment he is receiving as a social, economic and political factor in the southern equation responsible for the unrest and movement?"

The white man's pride and belief that the Negro is not entitled to the same treatment that the white man is, is responsible for his failure to look the facts in the face and explain to his black brother that he is a part of the conscience, the thought, the tradition and character of the South, and is therefore a part of the economic, social and political equation, and entitled to just such consideration as his worth and character merits.

The black man, knowing as well as the white man the real fundamentals underlying the unrest, has been evasive and too cowardly to meet the issue squarely. He has apologized and tried to make the white man believe that he was satisfied with the conditions obtaining, and that there was no real cause for the movement north or elsewhere. The Negro leader, in this instance, has not been fair to himself; he has not been manly. He has undertaken to please the white man at the expense of his own manhood, character and usefulness. In fact, the Negro leader's position has been cowardly, mercenary and vacillating. The white man's position has been evasive of the truth and he has sought ulterior motives rather than to meet the facts and figures.

The Independent's position on this question is plain. We are not in favor of wholesale migration any more than we are in favor of wholesale immigration from foreign lands. So far as we are concerned, we are going to stay in the South, for the reason it is our natural home and we have faith in its possibilities and the final triumph of our rights as citizens. We are not going to run away anywhere. We are going to stay here and struggle it out. We believe that the Southland belongs as much to the Negro as it does to the white man; that in common with every other nationality he contributes to the worth and character of the nation.

This being our position, we will not hesitate to recite the fundamentals underlying the black movement North. In the first place, the Negro is a human being and citizen; has aspirations, ambitions and intelligence in common with every other man. He knows that he has been the chief political question in the South for a quarter of a century, and that the trend of legislation in every southern state has been to reduce the Negro to a serf, to unman him and to decitizenize him, to take from him every social, economic and political right enjoyed by other citizens. Therefore he has reached the conclusion that the law is not intended for his protection, but for his degradation and undoing.**********************************

The same press that is now so solicitous of the Negro's welfare, has been industriously preaching for a quarter of a century the displacing of Negro labor on the farms, in the shops and in the factories with white pauper labor from Europe. There has been no disposition on the part of white citizens or the government to encourage Negro farmers or to offer them ample protection and advantages for the education of their children on the farms. In education he is discriminated against, his teachers are poorly paid. He is packed into double sessions. He is driven from the shops and denied every economic and industrial advantage that the conscience of social justice demands.

In politics, the white man has tried to assume unto himself the entire governmental fabric through the abominable white primary, in which all white men are called together to enlist under a white banner to the exclusion of every black man in official affairs. Every white man, without regard to his intelligence or his worth morally or materially, is invited to vote, to have a voice in the government; but every Negro is excluded and denied the right to vote, regardless of his intelligence or his moral and material worth. He is taxed in common with the good and bad white man who is permitted to vote, but denied the voice of representation in the government that exacts the taxation. Hence, the student of social conditions is not at a loss for the answer why Negroes migrate North, where they are paid better wages, permitted to vote and to have a voice in the selection of their representatives.**********************

The movement from Georgia has been most largely from those counties where mob rule prevails, where Negro men and women have been mowed down by white mobs without interference from the law. In the counties of Early, Randolph, Calhoun, Decatur, Worth and Lee the exodus has been the greatest—and in each of these counties Negroes have been strung to limbs and riddled with buck shot upon mere suspicion, and the strong arm of the state has made no effort to apprehend and bring the lynchers to justice. Our governor sat idly by and looked on the cold blooded murder of his citizens without any protest or offering a reward for the apprehension and conviction of the murderers, who are only waiting for other black victims to kill. How can the white man expect Negroes to live in a community where life and property are not regarded? Give the Negro ample school facilities, encourage him in farming districts to buy homes, open all the vocations to his livelihood, grant him his right to vote and stop taxing him without representation, and there will be no black movement North. The white man has the remedy in his hands, and all that is necessary for its application is the principles of Godliness and humanity, the Negro cowards who are apologizing and offering excuses to the contrary notwithstanding.

SOURCE CSJMS.

3. *"Causes of the Migration, From the Viewpoint of Southern Negroes." Article in the* New York Age, *22 Mar. 1917. Lists grievances articulated by black men as cause of the migration and suggests social improvements in the south as inducements for blacks to stay. A southern newspaper, the* Houston Observer, *21 Oct. 1916, made the same point.*

New York Age: Below is a list of grievances mentioned by southern colored men:

1. The "Jim Crow" car, product of the separate coach law that compels Negroes of every description to ride in one compartment of a railway coach, denies them the privilege of sleeping and dining cars, and in the case of street cars, obliges them to stand while seats are vacant on the possibility that some white passenger may get aboard.
2. The denial of the right of franchise, enforced usually by intimidation and mob methods.
3. The lack of equitable administration of school funds so that Negro children may be properly educated. At present Negroes pay their proportion indirectly in their rents, yet Negro schools receive in some cases less than 30 per cent of their just deserts, compelling Negroes to bear the added burden of supporting the many small colleges so well known among them.
4. The segregation laws forbiding their residing outside of designated areas, thus leaving no room for natural expansion and forcing a fictitious value upon property rented or sold to them.
5. The generally neglected condition of streets, car service, street lighting, and other public utilities in Negro neighborhoods.
6. The denial of the privilege accorded others in public parks and places of amusement. "For Whites Only" is a sign frequently seen in the South.
7. The abuse of Negroes by police officers, even attempts at explanation being usually regarded as resisting an officer, and as such rewarded with beating.
8. Lack of legal redress for insults offered to their women folks, and the generally prejudiced attitude of the courts.

9.   The insulting and embarrassing treatment accorded the Negro patrons in many stores. A brutally frank statement often heard is "We don't serve niggers."

10. The remarkably low scale of wages offered to the Negro for his labor.

Houston Observer: Some are decrying this exodus and scoring the Negroes for doing what they believe to be best for them. Every man ought to make an effort to improve his condition. But there is a reason why these people are leaving the South in such numbers and going to the North.
* * * * * * * * * *

The Negro has proven his worth to and in the South and the South should accord him the same privilege and opportunity that is granted to other citizens of the community. The educational facilities should be as thorough, modern and efficient as those for other races. The sanitary conditions of the Negroes should be as thorough, modern and efficient as those for other races. The courts should prosecute, not persecute, him on the merits of the case and not because his skin is ebony-hued.

He should be given full protection of the law, whether guilty or innocent. His women ought not to be subjected to the insults forced upon them by men of a different race. Their children should have playgrounds, parks and other places of amusement and recreation. He should be paid more than $1.25 and $1.50 per day for his work, ranging from 9 to 12 hours and in some instances from "can to can't."

When he prospers in these small communities, he should not be hated and disliked by his neighbors, but should be complimented and encouraged to continue his onward march. He dislikes and despises the terms "nigger," "darky," "coon," etc., that are applied to us here.
* *

Take some of the sections from which the Negro is departing and he can hardly be blamed when the facts are known. He is kicked around, cuffed, lynched, burned, homes destroyed, daughters insulted and oftimes raped, has no vote nor voice, is underpaid, and in some instances when he asks for pay receives a 2 × 4 over his head. These are facts. If he owes a bill he must pay it or his body and family will suffer the consequences. But if certain people in the community owe him, he must wait until they get ready to pay him or "sell out." In some settlements, if his crop is better than the other fellow's, his early exit is demanded or forced. When such conditions are placed and forced upon a people and no protest is offered, you cannot blame a race of people for migrating.

SOURCE CSJMS.

4. *Letter, J. W. Phelts, Macon, Ga., to* Macon Telegraph, *10 Oct. 1916. Complains of low wages, mistreatment, and exploitation at the hands of the white Georgians and requests improvements in wages, living conditions, and race relations as key to curbing the black exodus.*

I am a law-abiding citizen of Georgia, honest and true to his white fellow-citizen of the south for more than three hundred years, and about two hundred and fifty years of slavery. We has made the white man what he is to-day and are still making him stronger in wealth. The white man has always been with the negro in the south and knows just what he can do on the farm. He toils from morning until night in the fields of cotton and corn, and everything his boss tells him to do he tries hard to do. And I must say to our white citizens of Georgia that what we need is higher wages for our work and better treatment.

I am making $1.25 a day and other common laborers are making the same. Every one in Macon is very well acquainted with the high cost of living. Flour has gone up to $10.00 a barrel and I understand that it is going still higher to about $12.00 a barrel. That would make 24 pounds cost $1.50 and meat 20 and 25 cents a pound. House rent is higher and we have got to pay more money for clothing. It has been proved that the Negro is the best laborer on the globe, and for that reason the Negro deserves better pay. We are punished with unwritten laws constantly, which ought to be prevented. Just make this question a personal one and there won't be any such thing there as an exodus northward.

SOURCE CSJMS.

5. *Letter to the editor,* Atlanta Constitution, *ca. 1916. Remarks on the many letters received from blacks asking advice on the desirability of moving North; links the contemporary movement with past movements, including back-to-Africa movements, and encourages blacks to "think well before you pass over 'Jordan.' "*

Editor Constitution: For the past two or three weeks I have been receiving two and more letters daily from colored people in all sections of Georgia asking my advice as to the advisability of the colored people leaving the state in large numbers, as they have been leaving for the past six months.

I have endeavored to reply to them all and give them what I thought best advice, namely, not to leave in large numbers; and to be slow in moving until they were sure that they would get all that were promised in the way of wages.

I remember hearing my mother tell of the exodus of the colored people years ago to Kansas and other points west. It was followed with much suffering. I remember very well of the great movement of our people to Africa some years ago; many of them practically gave away their lands and other property. Many died on the way and thousands died in that far-off strange land. Now comes the great movement to the north, and I have been informed that within the past six months over one hundred and ten thousand have gone north, west and east. That there will be some suffering and sacrificing goes without questioning. I hope it will not be as severe as it was in the previous movements of the race.

No one can question the right of a free man to move to any part of our country or to any other country where he thinks he can better his condition; but those who know should give this man proper advice so that in executing his rights he may not make a mistake. I think it a mistake for our people to sell and practically give their earnings of years just on a hearsay that they will be given large salaries and great advantages in some other part of the country. I would say to all of my people who are thinking of leaving to think well before you pass over "Jordan." My heart is in sympathy with my restless people. They need encouragement and advice daily from their friends—white and colored.

SOURCE CSJMS.

6. *"Voice from Afar:* Buffalo Express *Speaks Truth Concerning Real Conditions." Article in the* Buffalo Express, *14 Apr. 1917. Criticizes the* New York Herald *and federal officials for suggesting that the Great Migration was a plot engineered by the Germans to undermine the U.S. war effort.*

The New York Herald is moved to this bit of sarcasm: "Having discovered that the European War is to have its great final battle on the west or east front or at Salonica, in Mesopotamia, in Egypt or at sea, if it is not going to end in a stalemate, the New York Tribune now finds that millions of Negroes in the South are plotting a rebellion against the United States. They probably will advise Mr. Wilson to let the erring Senegambian sisters go."

There's the trouble. The South won't let the Negroes go—North to get better wages and living conditions—and will jump at this chance to have them coerced into staying.

It is not unlikely that German agents have been working among southern Negroes to induce them to revolt. Some of those German agents are silly enough for anything. Almost any other race but the Negro would have risen in revolt long ago against the treatment they have received in our southern states. But as the *Buffalo Commercial* points out: "That tale of German efforts to stir up the Negroes of the South is one of the most ridiculous which has been heard so far. We have had no better fighters in the American Army than our colored troops, and, after all, the true test of a man's devotion to his country is his willingness to give up his life for it."

The *Tribune* quotes a Negro editor as complaining of the treatment that his people have received from the Wilson administration. That complaint is general—and justified. But the same man is made ridiculous when he is made to say: "The only way, in my opinion, that President Wilson can get many Negro recruits for the army is to appoint Theodore Roosevelt Secretary of War. Then the colored men would flock, sure of a square deal." The only comment needed is that Theodore Roosevelt was the President who directed William H. Taft, as Secretary of War, to issue the infamous Brownsville order against the 25th (Negro) infantry.

Roy Nash, Secretary of the Association for the Advancement of Colored People, puts the case squarely when he says: "Although they are bitter against the Wilson Administration, the great mass of the colored people will be absolutely loyal to the United States in war." Slowness in recruiting he blamed on the attitude of the administration which has made it plain that the colored man is not wanted in the army. "There are now only four army regiments which are open to Negroes," he said, "Our association recently sent a letter to Franklin Lane, Secretary of the Interior, asking him to use his influence in having two new regiments of artillery and two of infantry opened to colored soldiers. If the army were open to Negroes on an equal basis they would flock to the colors."

The great danger is that the South will use this story as a pretext for further oppression of the Negro. The black migration to the North was bringing southern employers, at least, to their senses. Now federal officials are quoted by the Associated Press as using the weird reasoning that the alleged pro-German plots "are believed to be allied closely with the recent exodus of southern Negroes in large numbers to northern industrial centres."

Let the friends of the Negro be on their guard.

SOURCE CSJMS.

7. *"If 2,000,000 Negro Wage Earners Should Actually Come North." Article in the Springfield, Mass.,* Republican, *Nov. 1916. Predicts "profound disturbances . . . in the world of labor" if two million blacks migrate North, which it doubts will happen.*

If 2,000,000 Negro wage earners should actually come North—which may be seriously doubted—profound disturbances, of course, would be caused in the world of labor. The economic effect on the South would be disastrous to a degree because the South has no other labor supply, while in the North trade unionism might react violently against the low-priced, unorganized labor going with a much-increased Negro competition. There are almost boundless social and industrial possibilities involved in a very extensive redistribution of the labor supply of the United States, in case European immigration on account of the war continues to fail the country for some years to come; but enough has been said concerning the present conditions to show why the organized labor of the North in this year 1916 is displaying unusual restlessness and even militancy. It is being played upon by forces of the most stimulating nature—first, the steadily increasing cost of living; second, the tremendous business prosperity with its great profits which labor wishes to share; third, the scarcity of labor and the exceptional opportunity that is afforded for more firmly establishing unionism and collective bargaining. Should Negro competition with labor in the North become at all formidable, unionism would probably fight all the more zealously for the control of the 'labor market.'

While the outlook in the immediate future for quiet in the labor world is not very promising, it is well to bear in mind that underlying forces are at work which neither capital nor labor can fully control, and that this epidemic of strikes is nothing but the manifestation of organized labor's jealous care for its own interests in a period particularly disturbed and over-wrought by reason of world-wide economic stresses and strains. It is a time when to an exceptional degree, both employer and employed need to employ the processes of frank understanding and conciliation with the one purpose of doing justice.

S O U R C E   CSJMS.

8. *"The Real Lesson." Article in* New York Evening Post, *Oct. 1916. Suggests that the "real lesson" to be derived from the migration is that "the South . . . must revise its whole attitude towards the Negro if it would keep him."*

The real lesson in this situation for the South is that it must revise its whole attitude towards the Negro if it would keep him. It has not yet learned how to treat free labor; this was the burden of an official report to the Italian Government which put an end to the efforts to land Italian immigrants at Charleston, and other cities with the Italian Government's sanction. It must learn that well-educated, intelligent and contented labor is the best, whether white or black; that a mass of unhappy, ignorant workmen retards economic development, whether in America or Europe or Asia; that if the Negro is the basis of the South's prosperity that prosperity will be enormously advanced by giving to the Negro the rights and privileges of all other citizens. For thereby the economic desires of the masses will be stimulated, with the result of greater and greater steadiness of effort and habitation, and the starting up of innumerable new enterprises to cater to the economic demands thus created. It is not the cheap Negro who is keeping out the white laborer, the Columbia *State* to the contrary notwithstanding. It is the stigma still attaching in the southern public mind to certain forms of labor, and in addition the absence of many of the desirable things of life, such as good schools, good roads, good government, and many other things that make life rich and happy, even for the poor, that is doing the mischief.

SOURCE CSJMS.

9. *"To the Northern Negro the War in Europe Has Been of Immense and Unexpected Advantage." Article in New York* New Republic, *24 June 1916. Argues that the migration represents "the Negro's chance, the first extensive widening of his industrial field since emancipation."*

To the northern Negro the war in Europe has been of immense and unexpected advantage. It has shut out the immigrant, who is the Negro's most dangerous competitor, has doubled the demand for the Negro's labor, raised his wages and given chances to him which in the ordinary course would have gone to white men. If immigration still lags after the war, or is held down by law, the Negro will secure the great opportunity for which he has been waiting these fifty years.—

The Negro asks for little. A half century of the contempt and exclusion which we call "freedom" has taught him to be modest. He does not look to the big prizes of life, but is content with the common things, the right to walk unnoticed and uninsulted through the streets, the right to live where his purse permits, the right not to be robbed by landlord, tradesman and employer, and last and most fundamental, the right to earn a living at the work for which his skill and intelligence fit him. Yet, because the immigrant has given us all the labor we need and has made the black man superfluous, we deny these rights to the Negro. He becomes the bellboy, elevator-boy, Pullman porter, the obsequious tip-receiver. Debarred from lucrative occupations, he receives low wages in the occupations into which he is forced; debarred from living in most neighborhoods he pays exorbitant rents in the districts into which he is crowded.

We cannot understand the problems of the Negro in the North unless we constantly bear in mind this fact of industrial opportunity. The northern Negro has the right to vote, the right—and duty—to send his children to school, and technically at least, many civil and political rights. We do not put him into Jim Crow cars or hold him in prison camps for private exploitation. Nevertheless the pressure upon him is almost as painful, though not so brutal or debasing, as that upon the southern Negro.

If the northern Negroes increase in numbers while their opportunities widen and increase, they will be less dispensable, and more able to make terms. It is the Negro's chance, the first expensive widening of his industrial field since emancipation.

To just what extent the northern Negro will grow to his new opportunities, it is impossible to predict. On the average he is probably not yet so efficient or so tenacious as the white man. He must combat certain racial virtues and vices. Yet from what we know of how ability responds to opportunity, and of how the Negro has advanced under almost impossible economic and social conditions, we cannot but draw hopeful conclusions.

SOURCE CSJMS.

10. *"Necessity Compels a Fair Consideration of the Negro's Right to Employment." Article in the* Guardian, *11 July 1916. Emphasizes the desirability of black workers over the dangers of continuing waves of foreign workers.*

The decrease of immigration, the shortage of labor, and the imperious need of finding new sources of supply suggest the possibility that employers may turn their attention to that vast reservoir of human energy now lying half latent in the colored people of this country. There are millions of them quite as energetic, trustworthy and capable as the immigrants from every tribe and nation in the southeast of Europe. Forty or fifty years ago a shoe manufacturer in North Adams, Mass., imported some Chinamen to supply the need caused by transferring the making of shoes from the shop to the factory. The experiment would have been successful had it not been for the evident dangers of opening the dikes and letting in a human flood more dangerous than an irruption of the sea in Holland. In the case of the colored workers, no such danger exists. The supply is here, and it would improve the health of the nation to have it fully utilized.

At length necessity compels a fair consideration of the Negro's right to employment. Let the work go on.

SOURCE CSJMS.

11. *"Treatment." Letter from Rev. Richard Carroll, Columbia, S.C., to* New York Age, *22 Mar. 1917. Calls migration "a Godsend," but affirms his willingness to stay in the south "to fight it out."*

To the Editor of the New York *Age*: The injustices, discriminations, treatment of Negroes in prison and on chain gangs, lynchings, inadequate school facilities, poor housing conditions and other things in the South are deplorable and I feel it keenly. The condition of my people is a burden on my heart daily. For twenty years I have delivered lectures to both races, speaking in white churches, as well as in colored churches, before assemblages, such as white conferences, synods, conventions, associations, etc. Every speech I have made to the white people has been an appeal to them to give the Negro justice and the same treatment accorded to white people. I believe I have accomplished some good. For the last year the migration fever has been on. Some of the readers of your paper, I suppose, believe that I am opposed to the migration of the Negro to the North. I am in favor of the Negro going like other people wherever he pleases and wants to and anywhere but hell if he can better his condition. I have said for twenty years and I say now, that if the Negro could get justice and his rights in the South, this would be the best country in the world for the majority of our people. I have never catered to white people nor to colored people. I have spoken what I thought was right and just.

Any man who will come to South Carolina or any man in South Carolina that wants his bravery and courage tested, I will give him a chance. If anyone will stand up and say to the white people, face to face, what I have said or will say, make the same speeches, say the same words, I will give him $100 board and railroad expenses while on the journey and in South Carolina. I made this offer several times in South Carolina to Negroes who misunderstand me. I will also go with him anywhere in the state, even to Senator B. R. Tillman's home. It is all very well to stand off and call some of the Negroes in the South cowards. Such men as B. J. Davis, editor of the Atlanta Independent, John Mitchell, editor of the Richmond Planter, W. T. Andrews, editor of the Watchman and Defender, Sumpter, S.C., and a few others know what it costs to speak out in South Carolina. I am not boasting, neither am I boasting for the men I have named. $100 reward is no joke. If there is anybody who wants to take the chances some of us are taking, call on me. The money is on hand.

This migration business is a Godsend. It will be better for us all. I hope the Negroes who go North will not return and that none will go unless they know there they are going and what they are going to do. I hope the sunny south will be redeemed. God reigns! The mills of the gods grind slowly but they grind exceedingly small. Any way, I am willing to fight it out on this line if it takes a lifetime.

SOURCE CSJMS.

12. *"Report of Sermons on the Great Migration," on Rev. H. H. Proctor, in* Atlanta Constitution, *16 July 1917. Emphasizes need for better treatment of blacks to discourage the migration.*

Rev. H. H. Proctor gave the third of his series of sermons on problems growing out of the war last night at the First Congregational Church, colored, dealing particularly with the Negro exodus from the South to the

North. After giving the social basis of the movement he told what the white people could do to arrest the movement and what the Negroes could do to secure here what they seek by emigration.

"In a word," he said, "the Negro is seeking a man's treatment. Here the black man has a white man's expenses but too often a black man's income. In matters of public concern, he too often has a black man's opportunity with a white man's responsibilities. To arrest this migratory movement, let the white give the black simply a square deal, based on the Golden Rule.

SOURCE CSJMS.

13. *"Letters of Southern Negroes Published with a View to Discouraging the Exodus." Migrant from Lowndes County, Ala., writes from Pittsburgh to Cincinnati* Enquirer, *28 Feb. 1917. Asks old landlord to hold his place; complains of cold weather in Pittsburgh.*

Here are some of the lines from a Negro formerly of Lowndes County, Alabama, to his landlord of a year back:

> I want you to save me my same place for me, for I am coming back home next year, and I want my same farm if you havent nobody on it. When it is cold here you can't get out of the door. I wish I was round that old gully now, for it is naturally too cold here for us anyway. When I get home no one will never get me away any more.

SOURCE CSJMS.

14. *Letter from R. Taylor to Prof. A. T. Atwater, Rome, Ga.,* Enterprise, *21 July 1917. Urges blacks to stay south unless jobs and housing are secured elsewhere.*

Dear Sir: Please publish this letter. Those who came from the South to this city are making good.

This city has a population of 500,000, for which 40,000 are colored and they find employment in shops, mills and foundries. The colored people are not Jim Crowed here, but are admitted to the public parks and other places of interest. Color don't cut any ice here. We have not had any summer weather yet, there is a continual cool breeze which makes it pleasant during the day; the nights are real cool.

The greatest trouble that the newcomer is having is to find somewhere to live. So many have come until one cannot find a house very easily. Houses rent from $20.00 to $30.00 per month. I would not advise anyone to think of coming North unless you are prepared to take care of yourself until a job is secured.

Mr. Editor, I thank you very much for publishing my former letter. Please continue to send me the Enterprise as I am lonesome without it. I hope you a continued succes in all of your plans.

SOURCE CSJMS.

15. *Letter from Rev. I. N. Fritzpatrick, an old black Georgian, pastor of St. Peter A.M.E. Church and president of the Law and Order League, Atlanta, to* Atlanta Constitution, *30 Aug. 1917. Urges blacks to remain in the south because it is their "best home, because he is better known and better understood by the southern white people, who have grown up with him and by many considered as one family."*

Editor Constitution: I delivered the annual sermon of the Atlanta district conference of the A.M.E. Church in the city of Atlanta a few days ago. When the minutes were read the following morning, on motion to adopt, one of the preachers of the Conference rose up and asked me why, in my sermon of the day before, I advised the colored people to remain in the South. I told him I would answer this question through the columns of the *Constitution*.

I now re-iterate my statements with emphasis, without fear of successful contradiction. Having traveled extensively through portions of Great Britain, Europe and Africa, and throughout the states, and having come in contact with different nations and races, I feel competent to advise my people for their best interest. I know that the South is the Negro's best home, because he is better known and better understood by the southern white people, who have grown up with him and by many considered as one family. The northern people do not know these intrinsic ties. The southern people (white) know the indiosyncracies of the uncultured Negro and, with such sympathy, will make allowances for his shortcomings and defects.

I know that many of my race have been lynched, but let the Negro strive to remove the cause leading up to this infraction of the law, as well as to condemn the act of lynching. Let the good, law-abiding Negro separate himself from the criminal classes and seek to expose and apprehend such villains and turn them over to. . . .

[page missing]

SOURCE CSJMS.

16. *Letter to Montgomery* Advertiser, *1 Feb. 1917. Exhorts whites to help blacks through hard times and urges blacks to stay on their land in order to drive the price of food down to affordable costs.*

Editor: During this wet weather, I have been talking to different people of the county. Most everybody I talked to has a mind to go off on public work. They tell me some places are cleaned up, not a family on the place; some places nothing but women and children and their children are crying for bread. I have been talking to some of them. I told them have they one time thought that they were running up the price of the bread and meat on themselves; some told me they had not thought about that, but the merchant man and the land owner just would not let them have anything, and they are going where they can make the dollar. And some of them are making it and coming back under the doctor. That could be helped by our white friends by helping us through these hard times. I want our white friends to look at our condition on both sides. If there are one thousand farms laying out, if there are a thousand mules to feed, there are about two thousand people to feed. Just the same there are more people than that gone off, but I am just saying this to give you a little idea what I am talking about. This will throw up the meat and meal another year still higher, because there ain't no one to raise it. I was talking to a gentleman who had been off and he said meal was three dollars a bushel where he came from. You see that it would be better for us to stay here and raise seed corn, peanuts and peas, sugar cane, potatoes and raise hogs and cows and chickens. I think that we could do very well. It would be better for us to stay home because we are used to this climate. There is not a family that is no more compelled to go than I was.

SOURCE CSJMS.

17. *Letter from E. W. Cooke, superintendent of the Snow Hill Institute, Ala., to the Montgomery* Advertiser, *11 Jan. 1917. Criticizes movement north, emphasizing the crowding of boxcars, death on the railroads and in the mines; expresses belief that "our people in masses are not prepared to leave this part of the country."*

Editor: Please, may I have the space to say a few New Year words on this unsettled question of Negro exodus? Since my letter of November 1st, I have been made to know some things that I had not up to that, been published; such as the box car crowding, death on the roads and in the mines of the places where our people are engaged to work. On receiving a letter from Mr. W. A. Wadsworth of Prattville, Ala., in a friendly and fairminded way, he expressed the real deplorable condition under which most of our people had to live and work after leaving here. Since then I have met with some who have come back. I heartily agree with him that it is not the going that we so much oppose, but the manner of going and the mode of living after going, are the facts that make the inner man revolt.

Then, too, the coming back to take less jobs than some of them had before leaving and therefore receiving less pay and consideration than if they had not gone. As Mr. Wadsworth has further said: "If those who go will stay, then it will be better for those who remain." Races, like crops, need thinning out and so that the others that are left can thrive more vigorously and be more productive. I still contend that our people in masses are not prepared to leave this part of the country, from the fact that they do not know conditions and will have to do much suffering before learning the same. There are three things the unlearned and uneducated Negro has not learned and which very much handicap us in working with the class of people that look upon these as being very essential to success. They are accuracy of work, quickness of work and continuation of work. The average unlearned Negro works down here about eight months in the year and uses the other four for what he calls a good time, and then at the end of the year holds that the white man has changed his account. He did change it, but the Negro was the cause, for he was feeding the Negro his mule as well as his family, sometimes families when the Negro was frolicking or stepping off to see somebody. When he is at work he loses three days in the week at his best. He takes Saturday to get ready for Sunday, Sunday is his all day, Monday he gets in late and has as his excuse his wife was sick last night or he had such a cramp in the stomach that he thought he was going to die, so it takes him that day to get right for the next. Lots of times he hasn't been home more than one hour before reporting to work. Thus his account got changed. I think we have a dance they call the "slow drag." This fittingly expresses the kind of work that class of Negro has been doing. Not "slow drag" dancing, but "slow drag" farming. Left without intelligent guidance he exhibits no interest in neither stock or tools, and is thus a constant worry and expense to the employer. This kind of service will bankrupt a nation, to say nothing of the South. One only has to look around the fields and the homes of this class to observe that no accuracy is displayed.

I am glad to see that the churches are taking a prominent part in helping to intelligently direct our people as to what is best to do, but I feel that the church should also impress the fact and insist upon it being one of the fundamental principles of religion, that "an honest man is the noblest workman of God," and should place more emphasis on economy and living at home. Gathering up the fragments is a great part of Scriptural teaching. I believe that it is the schools' duty to co-operate with the State to make its citizens through the boys and girls, by making them industrious and self-supporting. It is all right to teach a man to know how to increase his desires, but to leave off teaching him how to supply these desires, we have only a half man. In other words, we have been too largely consumers and not producers of our many needs. I am glad to say, however, that the young men who have come out from these institutions of learning are not those who are crowding themselves off to other places to get jobs. For the most part they are finding a way or helping to make one. Therefore, the Negro should be encouraged educationally, so that whatever he does will be done intelligently.

Now since the springtime is near at hand, I feel that the white people should bestir themselves and have as many acres of land cultivated as possible; for every acre of land that is idle is fifty dollars or more taken from their bank account. Land that is not cultivated is like machinery lying idle and is a constant expense. Since this change has come, the white man should help to pick the best and most desirable colored citizens and make provisions for them to stay where they are. I say desirable, because there are many desirable ones and all of us will be delighted to see these remain. The white people can do this by having meetings and devising plans and means by which the colored man can see his way clear, and he will be too glad to enter into the race of partnership with the spirit of work and its return. I do not believe in the mob idea of keeping the Negroes away from the trains, for that is but little better than the box car method of taking them North; but to talk to him as man to man such as no one knows like the white man, how to reach the Negro's heart for after all you can do more with him through his heart than any other way. It is a fact that the white man is most easily reached through his pocket book, but if you want to use a Negro, it must be done through his feelings.

When we have chosen this better class of people, the manly thing then to do is to stand squarely by our choice and see that justice and fair play be given in proportion as they measure up to the responsibility and requirements; hence we will have a better land, more thrifty people, and safer homes. Mr. Wadsworth is thoroughly right when he says that the Negro is not looking for social equality. There is no respectable Negro that would have his social life changed by external force, for he delights to have the other man stay out of his functions. In many cases, his leaving this section is purely for the want of encouragement and the want of needed advice. Let some of our best white farmers be made president and officers of the Farm Bank Association and use this money in ways that will save the farms. Then, they can both advise and do. Now is the time for the "Solid South" to act.

Some are constantly writing to us and others are coming to ask what is the best thing to do. We have, in nearly every case, made them see that they should "cast down their buckets where they are." If the white people will get together in money matters and devise plans to lead us, we are no less disobedient than heretofore, and will be sure to follow. It is useless to discuss the evils of either race, for "there is so much good in the worst of us, and so much bad in the best of us, that it hardly behooves any of us to talk about the rest of us." We all must allow the great Shephert of the Universe to lead us into green pastures, besides the still waters in the valleys of the Sunny South.

SOURCE CSJMS.

18. *"Attitude of Southern White Men to the Migration as Expressed in Southern Papers." Article in* Times Picayune, *15 Dec. 1916. Emphasizes the beneficial results of black migration's spreading the black population evenly throughout the nation, and indeed reversing black majorities in states like Louisiana, South Carolina, and Mississippi.*

We are getting some additional information about the emigration of Negroes northward because of the demand for more labor due to the deficiency caused by the check of immigration from Europe. It is not to be wondered at that with this additional information the question presents many new angles. There was a disposition on the part of the United States Department of Justice some time ago to believe that the movement of the Negroes was of a political character; and that thousands of them were being paid to go North to help the Republicans in close and doubtful states like Illinois, Ohio and others. Present reports indicate, as we thought, that there was very little of this done, for the movement continued after the election, although it has recently held up somewhat in consequence of the cold weather. The Negro does not like the cold; and it was an exceptionally bleak winter in the seventies that checked and killed the Kansas exodus movement of nearly forty years ago, which was deemed at that time so threatening.

Despite the attitude of certain extreme papers of the North that there was a broad conspiracy existing here to prevent the Negroes from leaving, the records show that many southern papers and people welcomed the movement believing that it would have a beneficial effect on the South by removing the Negro majorities in many districts and in at least two states, South Carolina and Mississippi. The problem of Negro majorities is rapidly working itself out. Louisiana, a state in which the Negro was more numerous a few decades ago, is white today by several hundred thousand, and will have a million more whites by the next census. South Carolina and Mississippi expect to report white majorities in the next ten years as they are drifting rapidly in that direction, and Negro emigration will help this condition along.

During the first months of this Negro movement northward, a number of South Carolina papers, led by the Columbia States, instead of expressing apprehension over these departures, shoed satisfaction that the state was getting rid of its excess of Negroes. At the convention of the Southern Commercial Congress in a session at Norfolk, Judge Francis D. Winston, of North Carolina, expressed this sane view of the situation in a resolution which declares that "The complete industrial, intellectual and social development of the southern states can be secured only when the Negro becomes a part of the citizenship of our sister states, and that we will encourage all movements tending to an equitable distribution of our Negro population among the other states of the Union."

It is not likely that there will be any serious objection to a declaration of this kind in favor of the more equitable distribution of the Negroes throughout the country as the question involved can then be better handled. No encouragement to the Negroes to leave the South will be held out, but there will be no effort made to keep the Negroes from going, beyond explaining the situation to them.

SOURCE CSJMS.

19. *Justice Department Documents, "Cannot Remove Negro Laborers from State, Says Assistant City Attorney F. M. Gerard." Memphis, Tenn., ca. Oct. 1916. On investigation of black migration; response to charges of southern Democrats that northerners encouraged black migration as a means of increasing votes for the Republican party.*

In corroboration of the rumors being passed around recently regarding the removal of carloads of negroes from Tennessee and other Southern states to the doubtful Northern and Middle Western states for the purpose of voting them en masse in the coming November election, a man is in Nashville to-day in the interest of taking away a carload of negroes to some point in Ohio, the place being understood to be Alliance, a town about eighteen miles from the city of Cleveland. Transportation for the negroes has already been arranged for.

Owing to the fact that there was some legal question involved, Mayor Ewing was in doubt as to the right to remove negroes from the city in such a manner and requested an opinion from Mr. F. M. Garard, assistant city attorney on the matter. Mr. Garard declared this morning that it had been his opinion that a law forbidding the enticement of negroes away from the state was in existence and his belief was corroborated upon an examination of the statutes of Tennessee. Mr. Garard said that he had found that there was a law which prohibited the enticement or taking away of negroes from this state if they were hired laborers at the time of their being taken away and so reported the law in the case to Mayor Ewing at a consultation this morning. Action in the matter had not been taken at a late hour this afternoon, but it was expected that Mayor Ewing would convey the information regarding the legal phase of the question to the parties interested in the removal of the negroes.

SOURCE James R. Grossman, ed., *Black Workers in the Era of the Great Migration* (University Publications of America, 1985) (hereinafter cited as *BWEGM*), Record Group 60, Department of Justice, Reel 20, frame nos. 0056, 0119, and 0047–0048.

20. *"Beginning of the Exodus of 1916–1917." Report of the industrial secretary, National Urban League. On the origins of the Great Migration in the recruitment of black women, men, and college students to work on New England tobacco farms and on the railroads of Hartford, Connecticut, and other cities; numerous testimonials of employers praising black workers for performing satisfactorily after a short period of dissatisfaction and complaints.*

The enormous proportions to which the exodus grew when once well under way, have obscured the inconspicuous incidents which mark its origin.

The earliest definite trace of the movement dates back to 1915 when the anxieties of the New England tobacco planters were felt in the New York labor market. Backed up against the infant prodigy munitions plants that sprang up over night, these planters had no means of holding their foreign labor against the tempting offers of 65 cents an hour. They rushed to New York and promiscuously gathered up 200 girls of the worst type, who straightway proceeded to demoralize the little town of Hartford. The blunder was speedily detected and they rushed back to New York and sought some agency which might assist them in the situation. The National League on Urban Conditions Among Negroes was importuned for help. Below are extracts from the diary of its representative's first trip:

> I reached Hartford at noon on the 15th of December, 1915 and immediately got in communication with the corporation. I found that the Vice President who had invited me to make the trip was snow-bound in Farmington, a suburb of Hartford; his telephone wire was down as a result of the snow storm; consequently, I could not have a talk with him. During the afternoon, Mr. ——, the manager, got in touch with me at the residence of Dr. Ball, a colored Methodist minister. I was directed to come out to the plant in Glastonbury, Station 18, in East Hartford, at which place I found Mr. —— awaiting me. We went over the following points:
>
> Mr. —— stated that the corporation has three plantations, one at Hazelwood, one at Titusville and one near the main factory that

at present Poles, Lithuanians and Czechs are employed as laborers; that these laborers are getting scarce because the war has attracted quite a number back to their countries; that the laborers are paid the unusual price of 65 cents per hour; that these firms are willing to guarantee that the work will last two years with prospects of good prices when the war is over. He stated that they had recently had an experiment with importing girls from New York; that they advertised from their New York office for girls and about 200 of the worst type came to Hartford and partly demoralized the town. He wants to be especially careful not to make a similar mistake. Mr. —— stated that he wanted it distinctly understood that he does not intend to cheapen his product or cheapen his labor; that he will pay colored people well. He stated that the company owns tenements on each farm which are rented at a very reasonable sum to laborers. He is willing to make an experiment in Hazelwood; he needs from 30 to 40 families and will employ an average of two members to each family; fifty families are needed, or at least 100 laborers. During the harvest season it is possible for men to earn $14 per week and girls can earn on an average of $11.50 per week. The pay-roll was inspected and Secretary saw that these prices were verified. One woman, working on piece work, earned $20 per week.

There are different seasons of employment. The rest of the year workers are paid at the rate of twelve and half cents per hour, making on an average of from $8 to $12 per week. During the month of May the workers are used to take weeds out of tobacco beds; in June they are used to string lathes, i.e., to string tobacco leaves with long threads. From this time on they are used in the curing sheds for about a month and from July 15th until August 1st is the only time they are not employed and this is considered their vacation period. Beginning with August until the last of September is the harvest season, at which time the prices are given by piece work.

When question regarding church and school facilities were raised he stated that he himself lived on Floydville farm; that he had a large family and that his children went to the same school with his employees' children; that there is a compulsory law that each child must get an education. Mr. —— stated very emphatically that he would under no conditions lower the wages; that he was willing to go into this proposition right away.

He stated that he wanted the Secretary to see everything first hand before taking up the proposition of getting in touch with families; that he was anxious to start an experiment at any rate and that he would take 12 families within the next few weeks; that he would pay the transportation of the families and the expense of moving their household effects and guarantee them immediate employment. He stated that he could use 50 men from now until the opening of the tobacco season in April; that these men could be used in clearing 100 acres of forest, clearing trees away, etc., and would pay them $2 per day. He wants a class of people from whom he can develop superior workmen. Mr. —— has had much experience with colored people, having come from Florida where he conducted a place of business and had in his employ nearly all colored help. He stated that he had been thinking of taking this step for a long time, but did not know just how to go about getting the proper class of people.

Mr. Floyd suggested that before steps are taken to get in touch with the people that the Secretary take another trip to Hartford so that he can see just what the entire proposition is like and be in a position to represent the matter plainly to the people who might be interested in coming to Hartford.

Report of Industrial Secretary's Trip To Hartford, January 9th, 1916.

Mr. —— informed me that at a meeting of the representatives of all of the tobacco concerns during the past week, the matter of their future labor supply and the possibility of using colored people in this industry was presented for consideration; he stated that quite a number of the men were intensely interested in this proposition; that one Mr. W. H. Whipple of the Olds & Whipple Company, has a son now in the South who is interested in educating colored people; that through Mr. Whipple's son plans have already been considered for bringing colored people from the South to work in their tobacco plants. Mr. —— stated that the Kaiser & Bosbery Company was likewise short on labor and would be interested in the importation of Negroes if the proposition could be worked successfully. He emphasized the fact that this proposition would not be philanthropic, but worked on a strictly business basis. Their purpose, he stated, is not to import Negroes in order to cheapen the labor, but rather to provide steady sources of labor.

Mr. —— stated that several men, prominent among the Poles, have informed him that they plan to return to Europe as soon as the war is over in order to ascertain what has become of their relatives and properties. The number of laborers is also getting fewer because many of the employees are now leaving this industry to go into the munition plants which offer exceptionally good wages.

During the harvest season, from July 10th to Sept. 15th, there is a great demand for extra help. Mr. Griffin stated that he could use 200 extra persons. Mr. Floyd can use 300, not to mention the number that can be used by other firms. Heretofore, help has been obtained in various ways.

If it were possible to get 1,000 young colored men who are accustomed to farm life, but who attend school, they could make from $1.50 to $3 per day during the harvest season. I suggested that I thought it possible to get such a number of young men, the only question being that of transportation. Mr. —— suggested that if a large number could make their way as far up as Norfolk, Virginia, that they could arrange for transportation from that point to Hartford. Mr. —— stated that one Mr. C. C. —— is now taking up the matter of cheaper transportation for colored labor. Mr. G—— is a Yankee. His parents came to America in 1635 and settled in this locality.

Within the next ten days, Mr. —— plans to take a trip to Florida in company with Mr. G—— to make investigation about a reliable class of colored people who are accustomed to this subsequent trip if they find that the people are suitable and can come to a colder climate. He stated that he would come through New York on his way South; that he would wire the Secretary of his coming and would like to go over the matter with an officer of the League, whom Mr. —— might suggest.

The material for this experiment was sought in the schools of Virginia, North Carolina, Florida and Georgia. More than 1,400 young students were transported to the State of Connecticut. The idea spread through New England and before the summer had passed, other firms there had adopted the plan. Statements of the result of the experience of several plants with this selected class of labor I append:

The Kaiser & Boasberg Plantation, Inc., East Windsor Hill, Conn. Sept. 12, '16

We have yours of the 5th inst. and are very pleased to say that the Negro students who have been sent us by your organization have been an unqualified success. They are such a success that we antici-

pate bringing up the student boys very early in the season next year
and employing them during the whole growing period.

H. F. Farnham (mgr.)

Clark Bros. Leaf Tobacco Growers,
Poquonock, Conn., Sept. 11, '16.

In reply to your letter of Sept 5th would say we are well satisfied with the colored help we received from the South, and we think
the boys are, as they want to come back next season.

Clark Bros.

Gurney Ball Bearing Co., Jamestown, N.Y.
April 12, 1917.

Of the men whom you sent to us, all are apparently satisfactory
to date excepting those whom you sent us from New York.

A. C. Davis, Works Mgr.

Deane Works, Holyoke, Mass.
Spt. 28th, 1916

Men making out fairly well; naturally a trifle slow and unaccus-
tomed to our ways, but this will wear off. We are watching them,
looking for equitable opportunity to advance any one worthy of it,
as we assure you we are anxious to do. The impression they have
made with us is good; outside of our plant we do not yet know, but
we hope they may remove any animosity that may exist against their
class; we have been trying to work them days, evenings, and Sundays
so as to keep them occupied and out of mischief. (Of course, they
get paid accordingly.) Kind of service they are rendering; probably
this is covered by the remarks above. Their fitting into the community; we are more hopeful in this connection than we were when you
called upon us, but we are not ready to definitely express ourselves.
However, things have gone with reasonable smoothness, although
this has required a good deal of diplomatic energy on our part.

Charles L. Newcomb, General Manager

THE TOBACCO PLANTATIONS AT HARTFORD.
A representative of the Age Visits this New Avenue of Endeavor to Negroes and Tells of Conditions as They Truly Exist.
Positions Open to Colored Help all the Year Round.

It was forthwith besieged with letters inquiring about the positions open. From Florida one writes:

> When Spring opens, we want to come North. We see through the columns of THE AGE very encouraging words for those who want work. We are enthused over this intelligence. Have been reading in THE AGE about employment offered at Holyoke, Mass., and in the tobacco fields of Connecticut. Let us know how we can get our tickets to come North, so we will be ready when the time arrives for our departure.

Before the middle of the summer of 1917, there were three thousand Negroes in Hartford; and these were not students. A correspondent in speaking of them said:

> I was talking to one the other day who is a carpenter and had lived all his life in one place until he came to Hartford last year. He spoke of a colored man "pushed into an auto, run out of town, riddled with bullets, brought back and thrown on the ground in front of an undertaking establishment as if he had been a hog. "

This statement is a fair gauge of the types who followed the students. They were, for the most part, Negroes whose motives for leaving were not wholly economic.

The next significant move after the promise of success in New England came from the Pennsylvania and Erie railroads. In the early summer of 1916, from Jacksonville, St. Augustine, Pensacola and other cities in northeastern Florida, the first train loads of Negroes were picked up promiscuously. They were at first organized into camps. The promise of a long free ride to the North met with instant favor and wild excitement ensued as the news circulated. Carloads of Negroes began to pour into Pennsylvania. When they had once touched northern soil and discovered that still higher wages were being offered by other concerns, many deserted the companies responsible for their presence in the North. Some drifted to the steel works of the same state; others left for nearby states. Letters back home brought news of still more enticing fields, and succeeded in stimulating the movement. Of the 12,000 Negroes brought into Pennsylvania by the Pennsylvania Railroad, less than 2,000 remained with the company.

Thus began in the year nineteen hundred and sixteen a flood of Negroes from the south which neither the dread of northern winds, nor the persuasion of their leaders, nor the intimidation of authorities, nor the withdrawal of facilities for travel, could abate until it had spent itself.

SOURCE CSJMS.

21. *"Negroes' Patriotism Praised." News release, U.S. Department of Labor, Information and Education Service, 6 June 1919. Positive comments on performance of black workers at a tannery plant in North Carolina; excerpts of letter to G. E. Haynes, director, Division of Negro Economics.*

Tanning plant executive gives great credit to colored employees for services in war and peace.

A striking tribute to the patriotism of Negroes and to their usefulness in industry is paid them by an executive officer of a large North Carolina tannery where 50 per cent or more of the help is composed of colored employees. The views of the tannery official are thus expressed in a communication sent to Dr. George E. Haynes, director of Negro Economics, Department of Labor:

> To say that the work of the colored men is satisfactory would be putting it mildly. We have always considered their work equal to that of the others and have paid them accordingly.
>
> Of the 52 employees from this plant who entered the service 22 were colored. Of these a number have returned and the pleasing part of their return was that they immediately came to us and went to work. We have tried not only to make room for those who were in our employ but also for a great number who were not in our employ before entering the service.
>
> There cannot be too much said of the colored men who stayed with us during the war. We purchased at the tannery $66,000 in bonds, notes and stamps, and when it is considered that the employees are 50 per cent colored, it is evident that the colored men stood right back of their colored brothers in the service. As we were 90 per cent Government producers, the colored man's work was the

foundation of victory and equal credit is due him for his services in the industrial field. His contribution to the Red Cross and other war work drives was very creditable; in the United War Work drive every man in the tannery donated a day's work, and in the Fourth Liberty Loan every man bought a bond.

The colored employees of the plant have recently formed a band which made its first appearance during the Victory Loan Drive.

SOURCE *BWEGM*, Record Group 3, U.S. Housing Corporation, Reel 22, frame no. 0575.

C. FINDING JOBS: STRATEGIES, OBSTACLES, AND PROTESTS

22. *"A Woman Writes for the Family." Letter from Biloxi, Miss., 27 Apr. 1917, to unnamed northern addressee. Disabled woman with a fractured ankle seeks work for herself and family; emphasizes "light work," use of 21-year-old daughter, and desire to "get out of this land of sufring."*

Dear Sir: I would like to get in touch with you for a pece of advise I am unable to under go hard work as I have a fracture ancle but in the mene time I am able to help my selft a great dele. I am a good cook and can give good recmendation can serve in small famly that has light work, if I could get something in that line I could work my daughters a long with me. She is 21 years and I have a husban all so and he is a fierman and want a positions and too small boy need to be in school now if you all see where there is some open for me that I may be able too better my condission anser my letter at once and we will com as we are in a land of starvaten.

From a willen workin woman. I hope that you will healp me as I want to get out of this land of sufring I no there is som thing that I can do here there is nothing for me to do I may be able to get in some furm where I dont have to stand on my feet all day I dont no just what but I hope the Lord willfind a place now let me here from you all at once.

SOURCE CSJMS.

23. *"A Widow and Children." Letter from Jacksonville, Fla., to* Chicago Defender, *29 Apr. 1917. Expresses knowledge of the* Defender *as an agency for helping men secure jobs, but does not know if the paper will aid women, particularly widows.*

My dear Sir: I take grate pleazer in writing you. as I found in your Chicago Defender this morning where you are secur job for men as I realey diden no if you can get a good job for me as am a woman and a widowe with two girls and would like to no if you can get one for me and the girls. We will do any kind of work and I would like to hear from you at once not any of us has any husband.

Now if you can get me a job with eny of the packers I will just as soon as I arrive in your city come to your place and pay you for your troubel. And if I cant get on with packers I will try enything that you have to offer.

SOURCE CSJMS.

24. *"From Alabama." Letter to* New York Age, *22 Feb. 1917. Woman seeks work in north as maid or children's nurse, although she had training in office work.*

Will you please try to get me work in your city or anywhere in the North as a ladies' maid or even as a nurse for children or for an invalid. I have a little girl about ten years old. I would like to bring her along if convenient. I would like for the party to send a ticket for each of us, which can be deducted from my salary until paid. If you can find work for me, it will certainly be appreciated. While I have my preference and am qualified to do office work, I am willing to take what you can find for the time being.

SOURCE CSJMS.

25. *"Labor Agents." Letter from Mobile, Ala., to* Chicago Defender, *28 Apr. 1917. Skilled mason, stone workman, and cement finisher seeks way to Detroit or any other northern city for himself, his wife (a seamstress), and his brother (a carpenter).*

Dear Sir Bro. I take great pane in droping you a few lines hopeing that this will find you enjoying the best of health as it leave me at this time present. Dear sir I seen in the Defender where you was helping us a long in secureing a posission as brickmason plaster cementers ston mason. I am writeing to you for advice about comeing north. I am a brickmason an I can do cement work an stone work. I writen to afirm in Birmingham an they sent me a blank stateing $2.00 would get me a ticket an pay 10 per ct of my salary for the 1st month and $24.92¢ would be paid after I reach Detroit and went to work where they sent me to work. I had to stay there until I pay them the sum of $24.92¢ so I want to leave Mobile for there. is there nothing there for me to make a support for my self and family. My wife is a seamstress. We want to get away the 15 or 20 of May so please give this matter your earnest consideration an let me hear from you by return mail as my bro. in law want to get away to. He is a carpenter by trade. so please help us as we are in need of your help as we wanted to go to Detroit but if you says no we go where ever you sends us until we can get to Detroit. We expect to do whatever you says. There is nothing here for the colored man but a hard time wich these southern crackers gives us. We has not had any work to do in 4 wks. and every thing is high to the

Motorized coal cars displaced mule teams in the transportation of coal from the mines. Here black miners lead a mule team in Fayette County, West Virginia. Courtesy of Ohio State University.

colored man so please let me hear from you by return mail. Please do this for your brother.

SOURCE CSJMS.

26. *"A Mother and Daughters." Letter from Moss Point, Miss., to unnamed addressee, 5 May 1917. A mother seeks cooking and washing jobs for herself and daughters, ranging in age from 13 to 16.*

Dear Sirs; Will you please send me in formation towards a first class cookeing job or washing job I want a job as soon as you can find one for me also I want a job for three young girls ages 13 to 16 years. Please oblidge.

SOURCE CSJMS.

27. *"Wary." Letter from Anniston, Ala., to* Chicago Defender, *26 Apr. 1917. Man expresses interest in migrating after satisfying himself that the paper would not "rob them [black workers] of their half loaf"; expresses the desire for work for his wife (a seamstress), his aunt (a cook), and himself (a janitor or common laborer).*

Dear sir: Seeing in the Chicago Defender that you wanted men to work and that you are not to rob them of their half loaf; interested me very much. So much that I am inquiring for a job; one for my wife, auntie and myself. My wife is a seamster, my auntie a cook I do janitor work or common labor. We all will do the work you give us. Please reply early.

SOURCE CSJMS.

28. *"A Widow of 28." Letter from New Orleans to* Chicago Defender, *7 May 1917. A young widow seeks live-in work for herself; she claims no living relatives and describes herself as "honest and neat and refined with a fairly good education."*

Gentlemen: I read Defender every week and see so much good youre doing for the southern people & would like to know if you do the same for me as I am thinking of coming to Chicago about the first of June. and wants a position. I have very fine references if needed. I am a widow of 28. No children, not a relative living and I can do first class work as house maid and dining room or care for invalid ladies. I am honest and neat and refined with a fairly good education. I would like a position where I could live on places, because its very trying for a good girl to be out in a large city by self among strangers is why I would like a good home with good people. Trusting to hear from you.

SOURCE CSJMS.

29. *"A Young Girl." Letter from Natchez, Miss., to unnamed addressee, 5 Oct. 1917. Stresses physical characteristics (hair, eyes, skin, teeth, weight, health) in looking for job as "body servant or a nice house maid."*

Dear Sir: Now I am writing you to oblige me to put my application in the papers for me please. I am a body servant or a nice house maid. My hair is black and my eyes are black and smooth skin and clear and brown. Good teeth and strong and good health and my weight is 136 lb.

SOURCE CSJMS.

30. *"Wants to Bring Quilts and Clothes." Letter from Corinth, Miss., to unnamed addressee, 30 Apr. 1917. Woman, 35 years of age, with daughter and six-month-old baby seeks job as cook, "housegirl," or nurse, but emphasizes, "I want to bring a box of quilts and a trunk of clothes."*

Dear Sir: I am a good cook age 35 years. I can bring my reccermendation with me my name is ——. I am in good health so I would like for you to send me a transportation I have got a daughter and baby six months old so she can nurse so I would like to come up there and get a job of some kind I can wait table cook housegirl nurse or do any work I am ready to come just as soon as you send the passes to us I want to bring a box of quilts and a trunk of clothes so you please send us the passes for me and daughter. Write me at once I am a negro woman. We will leave here Sat. if you send the passes if you are not the man please give me some infamation to whom to write to a negro friend.

SOURCE CSJMS.

31. *"As a Workman and Not As a Loafer." Letter from Atlanta to* Chicago Defender, *30 Apr. 1917. Stresses willingness "to do any kind of hard in side or public work," including cooking; emphasizes willingness to work in "city, country, town or state since you secure the positions."*

Dear Sir; In reading the Chicago Defender I find that there are many jobs open for workmen, I wish that you would or can secure me a position in some of the northern cities; as a workman and not as a loafer. one who is willing to do any kind of hard in side or public work, have had broad experience in machenery and other work of the kind. A some what alround man can also cook, well trained devuloped man; have travel extensively through the western and southern States; A good strong *morial religious* man no habits. I will accept transportation advance and deducted from wages later. It does not matter where, that is; as to city, country, town or state since you secure the positions. I am quite sure you will be delighted in securing a position for a man of this description. I'll asure you will not regret of so doing. Hoping to hear from you soon,

SOURCE CSJMS.

32. *"Better Freedom and Better Pay." Letter from Shreveport, La., to un-named addressee, 20 Apr. 1917. Emphasizes place "to obtain better fre[e]dom and better pay for the balance of my life"; describes skills as cook, barber, and steam worker.*

Dear Sirs I am writing you as to how and where I can go to obtain better fre[e]dom and better pay for the balance of my life as being a constance reader of the chicago defender the add in front cover frist colum refered me to you. If you can put me in touch of some one that I ma comunicate with as to the position I will be verry gratefull to you. I am a cook & barber also thoroughly acquainted with steam works hoping to hear from you will full particular. . . .
P S   I has a fair education.

SOURCE CSJMS.

33. *"Nothing Here for a Colored Man, Any More." Letter from Jacksonville, Fla., to* Chicago Defender, *9 May 1917. Asks for help in locating work in the north; is skilled as "farmer, sawmill man, a good cook"; wife is also "a first class cook and house woman."*

My dear Sir: In looking over the Chicago Defender why I come across your name in connections with —— of Chicago and thinking that you could do me a lots of good why I thought that I would write you asking of you to locate me with transportations with some one who are looking for a hard working honest and sober colored man.

Will do any kind of work. Am a farmer, sawmill man, a good cook. Also I have worked for quite awhile for expresse company here.

I am unable to pay my way to your city at present and any help extended me along that line will be more than appreciated by me. Am married, and my wife is a first class cook and house woman.

Now if I am not taking too much of your time why please let me hear from you at once as I would like very much to get out of the south as quick as possible for there is nothing here for a colored man, any more.

Please give my name to some one that needs a good man, who is willing to send transportation for me and wife, or my self. I probably can make some arrangements to get there in a few days.

Hoping to hear from you in a few days and thanking you for same afore hand.

SOURCE CSJMS.

34. *"Wage-Scale by Job and Days Worked of Black and White Miners, Birmingham District, 1913–17." Statistics showing racial inequality in the iron and steel industry.*

The Pratt Seam, the basis for the wage scale in the Birmingham Coal district. Rate per ton—

$$1913–47\cent$$
$$1914–57\cent$$
$$1915–67^{1}/_{2}\cent$$
$$1916–77^{1}/_{2}\cent$$

Basis now, December 13, 1917, 80¢. In some mines $1.00. About 26,000 workers in and around mines. Sixteen thousand coal diggers, 70% of them colored.

On December 13, 1917, a car load, fifty, men brought back from the North. The miners get larger pay than ever before. Many work only half time.

Pay Rolls.

Sipsey Mines, July 1917,—(Colored)

Pick Coal Miners.

Days Worked	Net Earnings.
20	$156.25
25	102.45
21	94.10

Contractors.

25	$142.10
25	140.15
25	139.10

Contractors Laborers or Helpers.

22	$104.65
25	100.30
25	99.75

24	96.05
23	90.45
24	90.00

Pay Rolls.

Sipsey Mines, July, 1917—(White).

Pick Coal Miners.

Days Worked	Net Earnings
25	$203.65
25	178.40
25	142.40
24	122.75

Contractors.

25	$209.25
25	197.45
25	163.65
25	160.95
25	150.46

Contractors, Laborers and Helpers.

25	$133.00
25	124.75
25	110.20

Mine Machine Runners Under cutting coal.

25w.	$208.25	
25w.	188.05	
25w.	141.55	w.—white
25c.	119.15	c.—colored
24c.	102.30	
25c.	92.45	

On November 1, 1917, the average earnings per day of 83 men, $4.65. Worked only ³/₄ of a day on account of shortage of cars.

SOURCE NUL Papers "Early Surveys—Migration Study Birmingham Summary." in CSJMS.

35. *"18 hundred of the Colored Race Have Paid To a Man $2.00 to be Transferd." Letter from Derrider, La., to* Chicago Defender, *18 Apr. 1917. Claims that 1800 black men paid a white labor agent $2.00 apiece for transportation to jobs in Chicago, but the man failed to deliver.*

Dear Sir   in regards of health and all so in need that I am riting you these fue lines to day to you. this few lines leves famly and I wel at the present and doe trus by the help of God these will find you the same. Now what I want you to doe for me is this wil you please give this letter to the Chicago Defender printers and I will bee oblige to you. I wood of back this letter to the Chicago defenders but they never wood of receve it from here.

I am to day riting you just a fue lines for infermasion I wil state my complant is this. now her is 18 hundred of the colored race have paid to a man $2.00 to be transferd to Chicago to work. he tel us that thire is great demand in the north for laber and wee no it is tru bee cors ther is thousands of them goin from Alabama and fla. and Gergia and all so other states and this white man was to send us to Chicago on the 15 of March and eavry time we ask him about it he tell us that the companys is not redy for us and we all wants to get out of the south. wee herd that this man have fould wee people out of this money. wee has a duplcate shorn that wee have paid him this money and if ther is iny compnys that wants these men and wil furnis transpertashion for us wil you please notifie me at wonce bee cors I am tired of bene dog as I was a beast and wee wil come at wonce. So I wil bee oblidge to you if you wil help us out of the south.

SOURCE CSJMS.

36. *"Fake Labor Agents." Letter from Live Oak, Fla., to unnamed addressee, 25 Apr. 1917. Shows a keen awareness of the techniques used to cheat would-be northern black migrants out of their money. "Listen there have been several crooks out saying they are getting men for difrent works in the north."*

Dear sir   I wish to become in touch with you. I have been thinking of leaving the south and have had severel ofers presented to me if only would say I would go and pay down so mutch money until a certain date but dont aprove of sutch. Know would be glad to have you relate to me wheather I can get a job in or near the city.

I am now working at a commission house. Listen there have been several crooks out saying they are getting men for difrent works in the north, all you had to do pay them $2 or $3 dollars and meet him on a certain day and that would be the last. Will you relate to me some of the difrent kinds of works & prices.

Nothing more, I remain. . . .

SOURCE CSJMS.

37. *"Distrusts Agents." Letter from New Orleans to* Chicago Defender, *22 Apr. 1917. Demonstrates distrust of labor agents: "I've got no confidence in some of these so called agents."*

Dear sir, with the greatest of pleasure for me to address you a few lines, concerning of labar as I was reading and advertisement of yours in the Chicago Defender stateing that those who wish to locate in smaller towns with fairly good wages and to bring their childrens up with the best of education will kindly get in touch with you. However if you are in a buisness of that kind it just fitted me. While I am a man with a very large family most all are boys and it is my desires to get in touch with some good firms to works. Kind sir if you are in that kind of position please let me hear from you at once I've got no confidence in some of these so called agents. Ill be to glad to hear from you at once.

38. *"Fake Agents." Letter from Mobile, Ala., to* Defender, *12 Apr. 1916. Discusses desire to leave and distrust of labor agents, including a preacher who took up a collection for movement north but skipped town at the appointed time.*

Dear Sir: While reading Sunday's Defender I read where you was coming south looking for labor I see you want intelligent industrious men to work in factories so I thought I would write and get a little information about it. there are a lot of idle men here that are very anxious to come north. every day they are fooled about go and see the man. pleanty of men have quit their jobs with the expectation of going but when they go the man that is to take them cant be found. last week there was a preacher giving lecturers on going. took up collection and when the men got to the depot he could not be found, so if you will allow me the privaledge I can get you as many men as you need that are hard working honest men that will be glad to come. I will send you these names and address if you will send for them to come. there is not work here every thing is so high what little money you make we have to eat it up. so if what I say to you is agreeable please answer this letter to . . .

SOURCE CSJMS.

39. *"Verbatim Statement of Ed Hardaway, Colored, Relative to Shipping to Virginia Coal Fields on Transportation and Conditions as He Found Them."*

Department of Justice files, ca. 1917. On black migration from Bessemer, Ala., to mines in Virginia and Kentucky; detailed description of life in company-owned towns and decision to leave.

I was in Bessemer on Saturday last year and met Mr. Frank Jones, who knew me, and he asked me to come and go with him on transportation. I asked him where to and he said Virginia. I asked him how much I could get and he said $4.00 or $5.00 a day. I asked him if they paid off and he said if you made it. I asked him if he would ship my furniture and he said he would send a wagon for the things the first thing Monday morning. I come home and told my wife and she said you are here now and you had better stay. I told her I thought I could do better and she said she was my wife and would follow me.

We went to Virginia, leaving here Wednesday night and got there Thursday at two o'clock. They put me in a house at $6.00 a month. They gave me $2.00 for grub to start with. I went into the mines on Friday to work. The first two weeks I loaded 75 cars of coal. I went down to the office to ask about my time. They said I owed $21.80. I said ain't I paid nothing yet. They said no. I said what about all that coal. They said I would have to see the company. I went on and worked two more weeks and got 62 cars the next estimate. Pay day was on Saturday and on Friday I went down to the office to see about my time. The Timekeeper told me I had no damn statement. I said I had loaded 62 cars. He said it was taken up for transportation and furniture. I told him I had the furniture I brought from Alabama with me. He said that was not worth a god damn and if I stayed there I would pay it.

I did not draw a penny and I worked for the Stonega Coal & Coke Company for three months at Imboden.

I went down in the mines on Tuesday morning barefooted and my wife was barefooted too. I told her to go see the Superintendent and see if he would give her a pair of shoes. I took two good pair of shoes away with me when I left here and wore them out on the coal. When you wanted anything you had to run the Superintendent down to get an order and if he did not feel like giving it to you he wouldn't do it. He would not give you over $2.00. My wife would go down to the office and stand around barefooted in snow knee deep to get an order. He would say he was going in the mines and would go in the mines and come back about twelve o'clock. If he felt like giving you the order then he would.

On Tuesday night I took Henry Morgeson and went in the mines. I stole my tools out and went to Imboden and sold them for $4.00 cash. Me and my wife then set out and walked across the mountains ten miles to Kentucky at the Pond Creek Coal Company. I asked them how coal was and they said it was all right. I went to work on Friday morning and went to the office on Friday evening after loading six cars to see about my time. The coal was three or four feet thick and had about a foot of rack in the middle. They told me at the office I had a balance due and I worked one month and three days and did not get anything out of them. I had $4.00 when I got there and I ordered me four gallons of whiskey and sold it and it brought me in $26.00. They said I owed them for furniture too and I told them I had the furniture I had bought from the Company I worked with in Alabama.

I then put my wife on the train and sent her home. They inquired where she was and I told them she had gone to Imboden after some of her things. I knew if they found out she was gone they would hold me.

One night they heard some of us were going to leave and the Sheriff come down to look for me. I saw him and hid and when the L. & N. train came in I ran out the back door and caught it.

I worked at Pond Creek for one month and three days and did not draw a nickel and the Superintendent would give me a little fat meat and bread to live on.

The Pond Creek Coal Company is worse than it is in Virginia. Every negro they get out of Alabama they put in the worse places. If they get killed they don't care. They will put them in the old robbed out places where men have been killed because they don't know any better.

Melvin Mimms, Howard Garris and Charlie Thomas from Red Mountain are there and want to get back here. The only way you can get away is to slip away in the night.

They had a Shack Rouster at Stonega who would come around with a big club. He would holler everybody out. If you told him you were not going that day he would come back with the Superintendent and Sheriff and if you told them you were not going that day they would come in your house and beat you and make you go.

There is not a man who left here on transportation that drew a nickel. On Christmas week they told us if we would work every day they would pay up. We all went to work and loaded six and seven cars a day and when Christmas come I went to the office and they shoved me out a blank envelope with nothing in it.

Mr. Frank Jones is working there and carries two big pistols. He is the Sheriff and Mr. Monroe Parker is the Coke Boss.

Sworn to and subscribed before me,
this, the 25th day of October, 1916.

_____

Notary Public Jefferson county, Ala.

SOURCE *BWEGM,* Record Group 60, Department of Justice, Reel 20, frame nos. 0179–0182.

40. *U.S. Attorney to Attorney General, enclosing newsclipping from* Atlanta Constitution, *1 Nov. 1916. On corrupt labor agent who took money and left migrants stranded in the city.*

Sir: I enclose herewith a clipping from the Atlanta Constitution of this date relative to the unrest among negro laborers.

I am informed that something like one thousand negroes congregated in Macon after having been taxed [$].50 each by some swindler who was taking charge of the movement recently under investigation.

This agent told a number of them to meet him in Atlanta or on the train between Macon and Atlanta. Some seventy five or eighty left Macon on Monday night, the 30th. of October, and paid fare as far as they were able. Approximately one half the number had to leave the train at a station fifteen miles north of Macon. The remainder came on to Atlanta and have been loafing around the streets here, looking in vain for the agent ever since. I have interviewed several of them in this city, but they are unable to tell anything. The fact is they were simply victims of the swindler who told them they could get employment with good wages in Detroit, and they appear anxious to go. Nothing of any value, however, has been obtained from them.

SOURCE *BWEGM,* Record Group 60, Department of Justice, Reel 20, frame no. 0038.

41. *Letter from Charlton G. Ogburn to Judge George T. Cann, president of Board of Trade, Savannah, Ga., ca. 1918–19. Requests information on black wage and turnover rates as a rationale for keeping black wages below minimum required by the National War Labor Board.*

Dear Judge Cann:—As you doubtless know, the National War Labor Board is now engaged in holding hearings to determine what shall be a minimum wage for the entire country based upon a minimum standard of American subsistence.

It would seem especially desirable for the welfare of Southern industries that the National War Labor Board in determining this minimum standard take into consideration special conditions affecting negro labor, not only the lower standards of comfort to which they are accustomed but their well-recognized tendency to "lay off" from work when their wages were much in excess of their needs.

I have discussed this phase of the matter with members of the War Labor Board and they were inclined to think this tendency of the negro was greatly exaggerated. The most forcible way in which to impress them is by actual statistics showing the actual number of days per week on the average negro laborers under the present prevailing high wages for war work do "lay off."

My recollection is that some Savannah manufacturers have been keeping accurate records from which these statistics could be made up. I believe a great service would be performed for Southern industry if the Savannah Board of Trade could favor the War Labor Board with such statistics. If this minimum wage be fixed at the high figure now contemplated without regard to the peculiar conditions of the negro, the effect will be somewhat disastrous upon the South.

s o u r c e *BWEGM,* Record Group 2, National War Labor Board, Reel 5, frame no. 0475.

42. *Affidavit of Henry Young, a southern black worker, 20 Nov. 1915. Discusses recruitment and mining conditions at Iboden, Va.; calls it "about the best place in the world to* STARVE TO DEATH.*"*

My name is Henry Young. For the past two years up until about six weeks ago I was employed by the Tennessee Company at Muscoda Mines. I was going up to Sloss Commissary one afternoon about six weeks ago and met Frank Jones, the labor agent, standing on the railroad track near Sloss depot. He asked me if I wanted to go to Virginia. I asked him what kind of work I could get. He said working in the coal fields. I then asked him what they paid. He stated they paid from $3.00 to $4.10 per day. He then asked me if anyone else up in the camp wanted to go and I told him that I didn't know. He told me to meet him at the livery stable on 3rd Avenue in Bessemer at 4:00 P.M. that afternoon if I wanted to go. I went on over to the stable and there were about forty waiting for Jones. We had a special coach on No. 4 train on the AGS that afternoon. There were twenty-seven men and one woman in the crowd. They carried all of us to Imboden, Virginia, and we went to work at Imboden Mines of the Stonega Coal & Coke Company. When they took us to the camps they put eight of us in three-room house and we had to "batch." The house was very small. The man who did the cooking had to work in the mines with the rest of us. I went to work the next morning after I got there. I went underground and took two rooms. Both the rooms I was running had water-tops, and was always falling. We had to walk in and out of the mine to our rooms which were about a mile-and-a-half from the surface. The third day I worked in there a big piece of slate fell from the roof and struck me, injuring my shoulder, arm and hand. The cars we had to load held about four (4) tons of coal and they paid us sixty (60) cents a car for loading them. We had to buy our powder and oil out of the sixty cents a car we got for loading it, so when we got through buying our supplies, etc, we cleared about ten (10) cents on each car we loaded. Four cars was the best I could load in a day, in fact nobody could load over four cars a day. I wasn't able to work the day after I got hurt, which was on Monday. I had tried to get away from there Sunday but the Company had guards watching us. Some of the boys got away Sunday but the guards caught them and hand-cuffed them and brought them back and put them in the mines. It was so foggy Wednesday morning that the guards could not see so I slipped away and "hoboed" to Louisville, Kentucky. I got a job in Louisville as "roust-about" on a steamboat plying between Louisville and Cincinnatti. They paid me $8.00 per trip. I worked at that job about three weeks and could not make any money at that job. It was so cold up there I could not stand it, so I caught a through freight to Birmingham.

I left Bessemer with $5.75, and when I got back I didn't have anything but a suit of greasy, dirty over-alls, which I had on. That place up in Virginia is about the best place in the world to STARVE TO DEATH. They didn't have any use for "Shines" up there.

(Signed)   Hy. × Young
[his mark]

November 20th, 1915.

SOURCE *BWEGM,* Record Group 60, Department of Justice, Reel 20, frame nos. 0149–0150.

43. *"Memorandum to Reinspection. Minneapolis Series #14, Chicago Series #119, and Pullman Company #2." Ca. 1919. Describes working conditions, pay, and treatment of black women employed by the Pullman Company.*

Series #14 . . . From the various sources of information the Agent is convinced that the toilet at the roundhouse is used exclusively by Mrs. Place who has one of the cleaners clean it for her use. The cleaners [at] both Pullman and Great Western use the outside privy at times. The Agent has not a doubt but what the women often use the toilets in the coaches. Apparently they never use the toilet in the roundhouse and are not expected to do so. From the discussion about colored people, it is apparent that Mrs. Place would not use the toilet should the colored women use it.

Because Mr. Place the foreman works with little or no supervision and because he has a personal interest in a toilet arrangement which keeps the best toilet for the exclusive use of his wife, there is no use taking up the matter of having all women use the roundhouse toilet, with him. The matter should be taken up with Mr. W. L. Parks, Federal Manager in Chicago, who should be requested to issue an order that the toilet is to be used by all women cleaners. Because the women are apt to think that the walk to the roundhouse toilet is too far away the W.S.S. should offer to have one of its Agents talk to the women at noon about using the sanitary toilet and keeping the yards clean. . . .

Chicago Series #119, Pullman Company #2. Four women count soiled linen as it comes from the cars, and supply the cars with equipment. Each car carries certain equipment described and listed in memo, Pullman Cleaners, Pittsburgh yards, Pittsburgh, Penna. As the supply is depleted, these women carry in small bags new supplies and replenish each supply box.

Two women sack the soiled linen. When it is brought into the store room, it is sorted, counted, and then sacked in large canvas bags ready to be sent to the laundry.

All of the above are colored.

One woman puts up the clean linen necessary for each car, using the printed list of the checker to know how much clean linen must be supplied to replace the soiled which has been removed.

One woman checks the clean linen left on the car, using form No. 254, see copy of form with memo, Pittsburgh Yards.

Two women are engaged in mending linen, Pullman curtains, blankets, and such. These women work by hand. The storekeeper said that a power machine had been ordered. The linen checker should be rated as a clerk, since all of her work is check-numbers on forms. The same work in the Pittsburgh yards is paid for at the clerk's rate, $87.50.

The others worked ten hours on Jan. 1, 1918, and should have received an increase under the Interpretation No. 1 to Sup. 7:

Those at 33 cents should now receive 38.2 cents
Those at 38 cents should now receive 40 cents

It is to be desired, however, that seamstresses may have an interpretation of their own.

The Pullman storekeeper complained that all of the employees in the yards had not been given the proper consideration under the wage orders.

Chicago Series # 151, C B and Q Cleaning Yards. The women work in groups of two, mopping, washing wood work, inside of windows, metal work etc. Men do outside work, head lining, icing, etc.

Thus the difference in the wage is justified. The Master Mechanic said that no cleaning yards in the city were paying the men the same as the women. This however, is not at present true. Agent called his attention to Interpretation No. Q, which he said he had not seen. Labor is not organized here.

The C B and Q has recently acquired a great deal of property in this locality and has extensive plans for enlarging the yards and improving the facilities.

Until recently, the women had only a small room in an old frame building. Now the offices and the locker rooms have been transferred to one of the buildings recently acquired, an old building, but very satisfactorily remodelled for the present use. On the second floor, the men and women have their locker rooms. The women's division is separated from the men's by a wall, and the approach will be screened in order to make it entirely private. New metal lockers have been installed. One toilet compartment is partitioned from the main room. Tables and benches are provided, and a long sink with hot and cold water. The room has windows on three sides.

Interview with Mr. F. X. Kaine, Pullman Supt. Richmond Va.

On January 27, after completing inspections of Pullman car cleaners at the yards of the R F & P, the Southern, and the C & O Railroads, the Agent called a second time on the Pullman Supt. She reported to him the adjustments asked for in the toilet and dressing room accommodations furnished by the Railroad Companies, and asked his cooperation in securing the improvements suggested.

The need for better method in cleaning cuspidors and disposing of the water was also suggested. Mr. Kaine was not particularly interested. He thinks the cuspidors in the Pullmans are cleaner than those of the coaches and do not need special care.

Clifton Forge, Va.

C&O
J. H. Callahan

Laundry	wangle feeders
	Shakers
Laundry Workers	Folders
	Press workers

There is no rotation of work [illegible] in this laundry, and nearly all the women work all day standing. The only exception is the folders, who have soap boxes on which they sit to receive the smaller pieces.

More comfortable chairs should be provided for this work, and for the feeders when handling small pieces. Relaxation should be supplied for all the women by planning a rotation of work.

No action by agent other than this report.

J. D. Potts, Gen. Pass. Agt., Richmond
(J. B. Parrish, Gen. Mgr., Richmond)
(G. W. Stevens, Fed. Mgr., "   )

There is no dressing room or locker space provided in connection with this laundry, and no place to eat or rest at the noon hour. Some of the women go home, but most of them bring lunch and eat it in the laundry, sitting on the tables for lack of chairs. (The Manager himself told the Agent that the colored women were not allowed to buy food at the lunch counter, and the reason given was that the colored men—the waiters—would give them bigger portions for their money than they meant to!)

The only washing facilities are those of the public waiting room (colored) at the station near by. This room has a good wash bowl with running water, but is not adequate for ten women released at one time, and has not the desirable privacy.

The station toilet is used by some of the women. There is also a toilet in the laundry building, which the Agent was told was designated for their use. This is at the end of the second story hallway reached by an outside stairway. To get to it the women must pass along the line of rooms occupied by the men of the hotel, some of whom (night workers) use the rooms by day. The men unquestionably use this toilet, as the door stands open and the corresponding toilet on the third floor, which was said to be the men's toilet is out of order and utterly neglected. The women say it has been that way since a fire on the third floor last summer.

The Agent considers that the location of this toilet makes it quite unsuitable for the use of the women, and that they should have facilities more complete and more private than those now available at the public waiting room. A special room for the use of these women and the three employed in the kitchen (see # 5) is much needed. Such a room should provide a lunch table with plenty of chairs or benches (preferably chairs with backs), locker space and privacy for changing their clothes, and adequate washing and toilet facilities.

The pay of all these women will be affected by the new wage provisions of Interpretation 21 of Suppl. 7., and should receive the minimum $70 with back pay to October 1919. Their present pay was fixed in accordance with G.O. #27, and the payroll shows back pay, which the Manager says was adjusted to Jan. 1, 1918.

(Note press workers still on piece work at 2 [cents]. The irregularity in the earnings is due partly to absences of the workers—most of them are married women with homes and children—but partly also to an irregular supply of work. One of the women said that a few days ago they got through their jackets on hand as early as twelve o'clock and then had to lay off. She said that when she could get two machines, which she can easily manage, she could do 150 or more jackets a day, but when all three workers were there she had only one machine and had to go slower.

SOURCE *BWEGM,* Record Group 14, U.S. Railroad Administration, Reel 11, frame nos. 0259–0260, 0192, 0194, 0155, 0162, and 0165.

44. *Complaint by Afred Milligan to War Labor Board, ca. 1918–19. Claims racial discrimination in discharge from his job as a grain handler at the Harvey Grain Company, Harvey, Ill.*

Mr. Milligan was discharged from the Harvey Grain Company, July 6th, 1918. His statement is as follows:

"Having worked at said place for one year, have only experienced trouble during the last two months that I was there. When I went to work at said place, there was no union of Grain Handlers ever mentioned. I also helped to build the place in which I was working.

On or about two months before I was discharged, all of the white fellows organized without our knowledge. After they were organized, they seemingly did not want us in the Union, and the delegate plainly told us that we would have to get off our jobs, and also went to the superintendent and told him to let us go. He refused point blank because we had been there for some time and did our work without a flaw.

This business agent appointed a man by the name of Herman to look after the interest of the Union on the job. After we saw that they were not going to ask us to join, we asked this man Herman to please bring us an application to join the Union which he promised to do. After every meeting night of their Union, I would ask him if he brought the application. He said that he would bring it after the next meeting. [H]e would give me the same "dope" after every meeting.

On the 6th of July, the real business agent of the Grain Handlers' Union came out and went to the superintendent and told him that unless he discharged us all of his men would strike on the 8th, which was the following Monday, a very busy day. The superintendent against his will had to let us go.

The Union official did not endeavor to get us out until the agreement was signed. In my estimation, there must have been a clause of discrimination in the agreement against us, because he said to me to my face that we could not work there because we were colored."

SOURCE *BWEGM,* Record Group 2, National War Labor Board, Reel 4, frame nos. 0962–0963.

45. *Letter from black baggage handlers and mail porters, Philadelphia Terminal Division, to National War Labor Board, 16 July and 11 July 1918. Protests racial discrimination in railroad wage settlement.*

7/16/18 Sirs: The undersigned Baggmen and mail Porters in harmony with others not on the list, appeal to you for consideration of our present wage. We claim it is not living wages. The wages were increased June 1, 1918. And when the notice of the increase: All baggman of the Philadelphia Terminal Division signed a petition stating not satisfied for no man could take care of his family. The petition was drafted and sent in to the Railroad Board we suppose. When we received notice from the Board that only men of two years' service and over would be considered. The largest part of the signers received no consideration at all as all we requested was equal rights. We colored baggman drew up this petition and asked our foreman to recommend the same to the rightful party. But he could not handle it as it starts on the subject of discrimination.

We, colored baggman of Philadelphia Terminal Division ask your faithful consideration and give to the rightful parties who can adjust such matters.

7/11/18 To Whom it may Concern: According to the high cost of living and maintaining our families, we the undersigned think that the present wages received, as insufficient to do so. We still request the 20% increase above the amount allotted to the colored baggagemen before the petition of June 15th was presented. And we also feel that in the latest pay increase (that of July 9th) that we were not at all considered and your body promised all of the working men "equality."

Respectfully yours,

E. A. Brank	Station Baggman
Richard N. Saunders	"
George Wilson	"
Samuel W. Adams	"
Wm. P. Newlin	"
Wesley J. Coffey	"
Edward Giles	"
James E. Rud, Jr.	"
Edward Pitt	"
Barney Frederick	"
Armstead Leay	"
James H. Brown	"
Charles H. El—?	"
William Summers	"

G. W. Garries   "
J. A. Hudson   "

S O U R C E *BWEGM*, Record Group 2, National War Labor Board, Reel 4, frame no. 0644.

46. *Letter from W. G. Bierd, president of the Chicago and Alton Railroad Company, to Mr. LaRue Brown, general solicitor, Division of Law, U.S. Railroad Administration, 6 Dec. 1920. Response to charges by black porters that they were entitled to, but denied, brakemen's wage rates.*

Dear Sir: I have yours of December 1st, with which you sent a copy of your letter of the same date addressed to Messrs. Pile and Goodrich, of 1810½ Main St., Parsons, Kans., on the subject of claims made by certain colored train porters on the Chicago & Alton Railroad, that they were entitled to train brakemen's rates of pay.

I feel certain that your position in this case is a correct one. These porters were never entitled to brakemen's rates of pay, which they later readily admitted, and proposed a fixed monthly salary which I had previously recommended to the Regional Director.

I fear this is clearly a case of these attorneys taking advantage of the situation and injecting themselves into this question because of the inexperience of these colored porters in handling matters of this kind. One of the points we tried to make clear to these porters was that they would only be used by other people that such other interested persons might secure a fee from them. I am sure these colored porters have been treated perfectly fair and right and that they now so understand.

If, as requested by you, any action is taken by the porters or by other attorneys in the way of suits, I will gladly notify you and our files and our officer's personal knowledge of this case will be subject to your call at any time.

S O U R C E *BWEGM*, Record Group 14, U.S. Railroad Administration, Reel 7, frame no. 0363.

47. *Interpretation No. 13 to General Order No. 27, U.S. Railroad Administration, 3 Apr. 1919. Calls for equal wage rates for black and white railroad employees.*

Article VI, General Order No. 27, reads in part:

> Effective June 1, 1918, colored men employed as firemen, trainmen, and switchmen shall be paid the same rates of wages as are paid white men in the same capacities.

QUESTION.—What is the intent of that portion of the above-quoted paragraph, reading "shall be paid the same rates of wages as are paid white men in the same capacities," on roads where white firemen are not employed?

DECISION.—Retroactive to June 1, 1918, the compensation and over-time rules for colored firemen shall be the same for all service as for the same services for white firemen on the minimum paid contiguous road.

SOURCE *BWEGM,* Record Group 14, U.S. Railroad Administration, Reel 6, frame no. 0385.

48. *Report by Oscar F. Nelson, investigator, U.S. Dept. of Labor, to H. L. Kerwin, Assistant Secretary of Labor, ca. 1919. Offers final report on discriminatory policies of the Chicago Grain Elevator Employees Union, not an AFL union; claims unable to do more than note practice of discrimination. No action taken.*

My dear Sir:—As a "Final" report in the above mentioned matter, I have the honor to submit the following:—

In accord with instructions, I called on Mr. John Riley, who is a colored man, engaged as an organizer for the A.F. of L. Mr. Riley informed me that the Urban League, a welfare organization among the colored people, had complained to him "that the Chicago Grain Elevator Employees Union had refused to admit two colored men to membership in its body." Mr. Riley recited "that the Chicago Grain Elevator Employees Union is not affiliated with the A.F. of L. and he had thereupon filed complaint with the National War Labor Board regarding such discrimination."

After discussing the matter thoroughly with Mr. Riley I called on Mr. W. E. Fuller, Pres. of the Grain Employees Union. Mr. Fuller admitted very frankly that the two colored men in question had made application for membership and that by a vote, taken in accord with their Constitution, had been rejected. He stated "that white men, applicants for membership, had also been rejected—that like every other organization, the membership by ballot decided the admission or rejection of all applicants."

I ascertained that the Chicago Grain Elevator Employees Union have a membership of 900—that the Union has a contract with all Grain Elevators in the Chicago District as to hours, wages and the employment of their members. That while it is not affiliated with the A.F. of L.—it is a substantial organization, known and respected by the other trades unions that come in contact with it. The Union has been organized since Nov. 1902.

After my interview with Mr. Fuller I again called on Mr. Riley and explained that there was nothing anyone could do to prevent the organization from deciding who shall or shall not be admitted to membership—that some Unions affiliated with the A.F. of L.—notably the Machinists Union, have provision in their constitution "that none but white persons shall be permitted membership." Mr. Riley assured me that he fully understood that it was impossible to do anything more than to let the Grain Elevator Employees Union know that the matter had been noticed and that had been accomplished by my interview.

source *BWEGM,* Record Group 280, U.S. Conciliation Service, Reel 1, frame no. 0170.

49. *Letter from Florida East Coast Railway Firemen to W. G. McAdoo, U.S. Railroad Administration, 28 Oct. 1918. Black firemen discuss wage discrimination on the Florida East Coast Railway.*

Dear Sir: We the undersigned, firemen of the Florida East Coast Railway, feeling that we have not received absolute justice in the application of your general order No. 27, hereby petition your honor as the head of the railways of the country for a square deal, assuring you of our best endeavors for efficiency in the work allotted us and our high appreciation of any effort you make in our behalf.

We beg to submit to you the following facts: All the firemen of the Florida East Coast Railway are colored men. They receive for their wages approximately forty-five per cent. of the wages paid to engineers. Some white firemen received fifty-five per cent. of the wages paid to engineers when they were employed. Your general order No. 27 has been applied to us upon an approximate basis of forty-five per cent. of the engineers' wages, which is contrary to the spirit of Article No. 6 of your general order No. 27. We feel that there should be no discrimination in wages on account of color. We all do the same work. We inclose herewith a schedule of the pay of firemen of the Florida East Coast Railway, and a schedule of the pay of firemen of the Atlantic Coast Line Railway for comparison.

You are a busy man, we realize, and your time must not be consumed in the consideration of nonessentials; we feel justified in making this appeal, however, on the grounds that 1, we must be able to withstand the enormous increase in the cost of living. 2, We are subscribers to all the Liberty Loans and certain amounts are deducted from our wages each month to pay the same. 3, We have authorized deductions from our wages to pay our subscriptions in the Thrift Stamp drive, and other war funds to which we are all subscribers. We therefore find it increasingly difficult to live upon our wages as reduced by the Florida East Coast Railway and in defiance to your order No. 27. We are certain that, if this company pay us according to the spirit of your order, we not only could meet the advanced cost of living, but could pay all our subscriptions to the several war funds with impunity. We beg to remain,

Yours respectfully,
FLORIDA EAST COAST RAILWAY FIREMEN

AUTHORIZED SIGNATURES.

First District.

Mose Gardner

L. Williams

W. Goor

G. W. Crawford

Will Thomas

C. Robinson

W. Ericson

SOURCE *BWEGM*, Record Group 14, U.S. Railroad Administration, Reel 7, frame no. 0462.

50. *Letters from Berry Tillman to W. S. Carter, director, Division of Labor, U.S. Railroad Adminstration, ca. Nov. 1918. He confirms that black firemen on the Florida East Coast Railway were paid lower wages than white workers for the same job; believes that the government will treat blacks fairly once facts are known.*

Dear Sir: I have your letter of the 4th inst. in which you request additional information pertaining to rates paid to firemen of the Florida East Coast Railway. I herewith submit the following:

While it is true that the Florida East Coast Railway employs only colored firemen, it is also true that when white men were employed as firemen, they were paid higher wages than the colored firemen. Colored firemen at that time were paid a rate of about 45% of the wages paid the engineers, while white firemen received 55% of the wages of engineers. After the dismissal of the white firemen because of a strike, the colored firemen continued to work for the same wages until a recent increase was granted. Now, owing to the fact that the firemen of the Florida East Coast Railway received lower wages than was paid firemen on other roads, when the increase was granted, a certain per cent. of increase was ordered, which did not bring the wages of the colored firemen of the East Coast Railway system on a par with the wages paid to firemen by other roads.

We believe that because all the Florida East Coast firemen are colored, the authorities of the road have taken advantage of that condition and as a result, the firemen of this road receive lower wages than do the firemen of any other first rate railroad in the south. We contend that in the absence of white firemen, whose rate of pay would at least equal that of firemen of other roads, we should receive the same rate of wages paid to firemen of other systems. I handed Mr. Glendenning a copy of the rates of wages paid by the Atlantic Coast Line Railway and the Florida East Coast Railway for comparison. If you will refer to those rates, you will readily see that the firemen I represent receive less per day and per mile than the firemen of the Atlantic Coast Line Railway receive, although the labor is equal and the costs of living the same.

We await with pleasure a revision of wages by the Board of Railroad Wages and Working Conditions, and would appreciate an established rate; but if we faild to contend for our rights in the present matter and get what really belongs to us, there would be no chance for us to receive the back pay for labor done at too low a rate.

Thanking you for the interest you manifest in our cause, I beg to remain. . . .

Dear Sir:

Your favor of the 18th instant received. We are pleased to note that our grievance has been referred to the Chairman of the Board of Railroad Wages and Working Conditions and thank you heartily for the interest you manifested in our behalf. Feeling that when the situation with us is fully understood by the authorities of the Government the wages of the firemen of the East Coast Railway will receive fair and impartial consideration, we beg to remain. . . .

S O U R C E *BWEGM,* Record Group 14, U.S. Railroad Administration, Reel 7, frame nos. 0466, 0471.

51. *Letter from James A. Green to W. G. McAdoo, director general, U.S. Railroad Administration, and affidavit of Alex Jones, 22 June 1918. Black workers complain of discriminatory pay scales and layoffs.*

Dear Sir: I realize fully that you and your office are very busy and have no time matters and I am truly sorry that I am forced to worry you but as the matter stands now It seem that get no releif. So I in my humble way have appealed to you. First, I am a colard man. I have employed by the International and Great Northern Ry. as porter & record clerk for the past ten years and during that time I have given all my time and best energy to my work and have been employed at a salary $60.00 sixty dollars per month since 1911. On Oct. the first my salary was raised 10 per cent or

$66.00 sixty dollars per month. On April 27, 1911 the Houston Belt and Term. taken over the I.G.N. and I am now employed by the Houston Belt and Terminal Co. at $66.00 per month under Mr. W. S. Clark as agent. I have lost no time have continued to work steady and In figuering the increase in pay that the government ordered or allowed to railroad Employees under government ownership my name was placed on the Terminal Co. pay compare with their office porter in the year 1915 which was $45.00 forty-five dollars per month and not allowing me any increase in pay at all. I appealed to you for justice and fairness and to consider my long continued service that I may get the increase that is rightfully due me. I respectfully refer you to Mr. J. P. Burruss Supt. of Terminals H.B.&T. Co. Also Mr. W. J. Werner, auditor I.&G.N. Ry for my record. Thanking you for any consideration shown me and I beg to remain your humble servant.

Affidavit/Letter: I, Alex Jones, fireman, residing at Savannah, Ga., being first duly sworn on oath depose and say that I have been in the railroad service for twenty-six (26) consecutive years, having been employed for two years as fireman on the Seaboard Air Line, and for twenty-four (24) years as fireman on the Atlantic Coast Line; that on February 21, 1919, I was pulled out of service at Savannah, Ga.; that on February 22, 1919, a call boy brought me a message to go to the shop; that on arriving there, P. H. Jenkins, road foreman of engineers, told me he wanted me to go to Florence, S.C. and fire with Mr. Artopee, and gave me a letter to that effect signed by Mr. F. P. Howell, master mechanic at Savannah, which letter I presented March 1, 1919, to the roundhouse foreman at Florence, S.C., who in turn presented it to E. J. Smith, master mechanic. The said Smith told me that he would not use me out of Florence, I asked him the reason to which he made answer that it was his own personal business. I then asked him for transportation to Savannah. He refused to give it to me. I asked him the reason for his refusal, to this he made no reply. I went to the Telegraph office of the A. C. L. and wired Mr. Howell that instructions given by him had failed to be observed and that I was also refused transportation back to my home terminal. I received no answer from Mr. Howell to this telegram. On March 4th., being still at Florence, I wrote to Mr. Willard Kells, General superintendent of Motor Power at Wilmington, N.C., stating the facts in the case; I received no answer from him until March 24, 1919, when he answered that he had investigated the case and now ordered me restored to duty at once. I was given a pass by Mr. E. J. Smith and returned to Savannah on March 25th. presenting my letter of instruction from Mr. Kells to F. P. Howell, mm, at the South overshops in Savannah; Mr. Howell, upon reading it said the letter was to me and not to him. Upon my insistence that I should be given employment as directed in the letter presented, he ordered me to see engineer Lundy Counsel, and if he agreed to accept me, that he would restore me to duty. I asked Mr. Howell if this procedure was in accordance with the regulations of United States Railroad Administration; if it was not my right under seniority rule to be placed to work without an appeal to the engineer. Mr. Howell replied, I instruct you to see the engineer. I did so, whereupon engineer Counsel told me to report back to Mr. Howell stating that he would accept me, and stated that he had asked for me three or four days ago, making his request to Mr. Jenkins, road foreman of engineers. I reported this to Mr. Howell but was not placed in position at this time. From March 25th. to April 3rd, 1919, I held frequent conferences with Mr. F. P. Howell, P. H. Jenkins, and Mr. Lamden, the last named being travelling fireman, seeking to be placed at work according to instructions issued by Mr. Kells. I was not given employment, however, until April 3, 1919. My pay was six dollars and thirty-nine cents ($6.39) per day, and I am now asking for pay from March 1st. to April 2nd., both days inclusive, this being the period of my suspension through no fault. . . .

SOURCE *BWEGM,* Record Group 14, U.S. Railroad Administration, Reel 7, frame nos. 0486–0487, and Reel 9, frame nos. 0737–0738.

52. *Letters from E. S. Hege, manager, Washington Division, U.S. Housing Corporation, to Louis Post, Assistant Secretary of Labor, 30 Oct. 1918, and Jeannette Carter to Secretary of Labor, 28 Oct. 1918. Detailed discussion of the case of a black woman discharged from her government job for refusing to accept a demotion and reduction in pay.*

10/30/18 Dear Sir: The accompanying papers are handed to me this afternoon by Captain Julius I. Peyser, Chief of the Housing & Health Division of the War Department, with the statement that you desire same forwarded to you with my comments.

Miss Jeannette Carter was appointed October 7, 1918, by me on the recommendation of Mr. Francis Mahoney as in charge of the colored women engaged on work of my office in soliciting and inspecting rooms for colored war workers, her salary being at the rate of $1400 per year, and she was removed by me from such position and assigned as an inspector at $3.50 per day effective as of the close of work on October 21, 1918, in accordance with a recommendation made to me by Mr. Carl Phillips, whose recommendation I understood you desired me to accept.

Miss Carter has refused or failed to take a new oath of office as a $3.50 per diem employee, apparently preferring to give out newspaper articles about herself; protest to a co-ordinate official (Captain Peyser) against my action; criticise Dr. George E. Haynes and Mr. Carl Phillips of the Bureau of Negro Economics; carry her fancied grievance to the ears of numerous local colored persons and sow the seeds of discord in the small working force of which she forms a part.

To my mind, Miss Carter is temperamentally *un*suited for any position connected with this office, and Dr. Haynes has papers and information to support this view, but I have refrained from dispensing with her entirely at the request of Dr. Haynes that the matter may go as it is going until early in November when he expects to bring here from St. Paul a colored man whom he thinks would make a good head for our Colored Registry.

Assuring you that I shall be most happy to afford promptly and fully any additional information you may desire regarding this case, and that I will be glad to carry out any wishes that you may have in the premises, I am. . . .

10/28/18 Sir: I beg to call your attention to a matter of personal interest to myself and in which I have a grievance which it is necessary for me to bring to your attention.

I am connected with the Department of Labor in the Housing Bureau, particularly looking after the interests of Colored people in the District of Columbia employed as war workers. I was appointed October 7, 1918, by Mr. Francis Mahoney of the Housing Bureau, on the recommendation of Mr. E. F. Kline, of the U.S. Labor Department Service, at a salary of $1400 a year. The appointment was given me, so I was informed because I had been working without pay with persons connected with this particular Bureau ever since our country entered the war. Those responsible for my appointment told me that they felt that I deserved the place for the services I had given, and I was made Director of this particular phase of the work for Colored people. I promptly began my duties in this office and was performing them to the satisfaction of the Department, when I received a notice from Mr. Hagge of the Housing Bureau, of which Captain Peyser is Chief, in the War Department, to the effect that I was removed from the position of Director by order of Assistant Secretary Louis F. Post, of the Department of Labor, which message came through a Mr. Karl Phillips, Secretary to Mr. George E. Haynes, of the Bureau of Negro Economics. This last named Bureau has attempted to place another Colored woman in my place as Director. I am therefore writing to protest against this unfair and unjust treatment. I have reasons to believe that Secretary Post has not ordered my removal or demotion and I make this appeal to you to be restored to the position which came to me without my solicitation. I hope you will give this matter some consideration.

I am sending herewith letters of recommendation which I hope you will read.

SOURCE *BWEGM*, Record Group 174, U.S. Department of Labor, Reel 14, frame nos. 0100, 0096.

53. *"Colored Women as Industrial Workers in Philadelphia: A Study Made by the Consumers' League of Eastern Pennsylvania," 1920. Shows that although black women remained disproportionately employed in domestic or household labor, they gradually gained access to industrial jobs during the period; suggests that black women preferred industrial over household work.*

This study has discovered no indication of any considerable number of colored women being employed before the World War, outside the domestic service and those industries included in the general term "public housekeeping." With the war came opportunities that brought a new day to this race. These opportunities were mainly due to three causes: (a) the industries were calling for workers, (b) immigration to the United States was rapidly decreasing, and (c) a large percentage of the male population of working age was being withdrawn for war service.

(a) The demand for workers was great because of Philadelphia's industrial position and the fact that the Federal Government operates here three establishments that have especially to do with the army and navy preparations, namely, Frankford Arsenal, the United States Navy Yard, and the Philadelphia Depot of the Quartermaster's Department, United States Army.

(b) While the industries were needing workers the immigration decreased in the whole United States as follows [U.S. Census Report 1910].

From 56,857 in 1914 to 7,114 in 1915
to 229 in 1916
to 274 in 1917
to 386 in 1918
to 333 in 1919

(c) The third thing mentioned a contributing toward a new day for the colored was the fact that, roughly estimated, the men who went into war service from Philadelphia numbered 85,000 [Estimate given by Philadelphi War History Committee], which meant just so many less workers at home.

It will be shown that the industrial labor supply was augmented to a considerable extent by colored women from domestic service, but in addition to this mere transference from one occupation to others, an actual increase in the colored population of the city at this time increased the total supply of colored labor. The census figures for 1910 showed 84,459 colored here in a total population of 1,549,000. To go a step further, 66,480 Negroes were fifteen years of age and over, and of this number,

35,790 were females of working age. The accompanying map of the city will show the distribution of Negroes in 1910 according to the ward section. [It is to be regretted that the figures of the 1920 census are not tabulated as this goes to press.]

The Philadelphia Year Book [Jackson's Philadelphia Year Book, p. 150] estimates that the Negroes in 1919 in Philadelphia number 125,000, or an increase of 48 per cent in nine years. [Mr. James H. Dillard writes in "Negro Immigration in 1916–17," U.S. Department of Labor publication, page 10: "A few days later I visited the Durham School in Philadelphia, a large public school for colored children. I thought that the new enrollment would probably afford some information as to new arrivals in that city. The principal had enrolled the new pupils on sheets containing 50 names, and he had been careful to enter opposite each name the place from which the pupil came. I took six of these sheets at random and found that one of them had 26 names of children who had been brought within the past year from various States of the South—Georgia, Alabama, Virginia, etc. The lowest number of names of recent arrivals found on any one of the six sheets was 21. In other words, among the new pupils there were between 40 and 50 per cent who were newcomers, and all these from the South."]

The fact that colored women were engaging in new and totally different lines of industry was noticeable. They were on Noble Street cleaning up after the track repairers and, in an interview while taking shelter during a rain storm, one woman said they were there because of the "almighty dollar." In a laundry they had been getting only $7 a week with a $2 a month bonus, and on the street work the wage was 30 cents an hour. On still another street they worked on the tracks with picks and shovels. They were also in evidence in and about railroad terminals, cleaning the outside of trains and replacing the night men who cleaned the waiting rooms. In office buildings they were replacing men as elevator operators.

"Use of negro woman labor to fill war workers; gaps," reads on caption.

"Negro women take places of men in industries; work as railroad track-hands, munition makers, inspectors and porters," reads another, which continues, "Negro women are repairing railway tracks, making explosives, and serving as porters and inspectors in many industries here taking the places of men who have gone to war or have entered other industries. Through a government agency . . . more than 300 of these women have been placed in positions within a week. ——, manager of the agency, says an average of 100 negro women a day apply there. Many of these women are at work at the Frankford Arsenal and other government plants about the city. Others are working as track-hands on the —— Rail-road."

"Ice women replace men here. Four women now handle the ice tongs at the —— Ice plant, replacing men who have gone to war. They have made good."

"Colored girls avoid housework. Y.W.C.A. is placing many in shops and factories, but few seek domestic service."

"Negro's chance coming at last. Stoppage of immigration due to war strips South of colored labor."

Newspaper advertisements such as the following frequently appeared:

"Twenty-five colored operators wanted with experience on double needle machine for government bed sacks—wages from $24.00 up."

One in authority reported that there were 500 women munition workers on the night force in the Arsenal; [No special records were kept by the government of the work done by colored women] a colored employment agency reported that many Philadelphia colored girls were in munition works in the neighboring towns that could be reached by trolley; an official visitor to a large number of garment and needle factories that were producing supplies for the government, observed colored women employees; and a study among the home workers for the Schuylkill Arsenal not only showed that the colored women took home shirts and other garments to sew for the army, but that they were often rated among the best workers. A hosiery firm (possibly anticipating a labor shortage) rented a hall in connection with a colored institution, and installed knitting machines under the supervision of a white forelady. Great difficulty was encountered in getting women to go there to learn, and it was said that those who did go were mostly southern Negroes who had never been in a factory before. This difficulty in recruiting might have been due to the very low wages given; a flat rate of $4.50 a week was offered while learning, after which 8½ cents a dozen pairs was given with a one-cent bonus on sixteen dozen pairs a day, and one cent on eighteen dozen. When this place was visited one girl was getting —— a week for eighteen dozen a day; another girl could make fifteen dozens, thereby getting $7. In a waste factory visited, colored women had replaced men, sewing up bales of the waste which necessitated continuous standing and working in unattractive surroundings, permeated with much dust, and, to quote the employer, were "doing work that no white women would do." In a shoddy mill some colored girls fed the picker machines for $11 a week. They had been doing it six months when interviewed and although working in a basement where there was much dust from the product, they were enthusiastic about factory work, particularly liking the regular hours with no night work and no

Sunday work. Realizing that many were entering the garment trades, an effort was made to ascertain their status, and its was found that at least fifty union shops had some colored workers. They were a new element and brought to the union many perplexing problems which will be discussed in this study.

Such, briefly, were the conditions when the armistice was signed: housekeepers were complaining that their domestic workers had deserted them for their husbands' businesses; it was a matter of much comment that colored women were working on the streets—obviously in positions that involved too much strain for women; the newspapers devoted space to assignments on the colored women workers and carried advertisements for them: factory inspectors noted them as innovations and the unions reported they were in their shops and even that they "had driven the whites from a few shops." With few exceptions, wages were low and were threatening to undermine fair and reasonable standards. A need was felt for more information on the subject, and the Consumers' League decided to undertake this study in order to present information that could be a help in clarifying public thinking.

The Chamber of Commerce expressed its interests in a letter to its members, saying "the League will attempt to discover the number of colored women who have worked in the industries of Philadelphia during the war and the number who are now employed, the nature and quality of their work, with the idea of discovering for what particular work colored women are best suited." and asked them to "co-operate with the Consumers' League to the fullest extent in furnishing information and affording facilities for gathering the necessary data in making this very valuable study." The League is happy to state that the majority of the employers called upon were most generous in their co-operation. The Waist and Dress Manufacturers' Association extended an invitation to visit all its shops. Among the organizations of the city that helped were the following: Armstrong Association, Public Schools, Department of Compulsory Attendance, Young Women's Christian Association, Unions, Society for Organizing Charity and Red Cross. To all of these, and to the friends who contributed time and money, and to the colored workers interviewed, the League extends its very great thanks. . . .

S O U R C E Archives of Pennsylvania Historical and Museum Commission (Harrisburg, Pa.). Bracketed material appears as footnotes in the original document.

54. *"List of Colored Employees." From employment manager, Pratt & Cady Company, Inc., to C. S. Johnson, director, National Urban League, N.Y., 13 Jan. 1922. Documents labor turnover among black workers by occupation, date of leaving, and reason for leaving.*

PRATT & CADY COMPANY INCORPORATED
MANUFACTURERS OF
VALVES, HYDRANTS, COCKS AND STEAMTRAPS
HARTFORD, CONN.

January 13th, 1922.

Mr. Chas. S. Johnson, Director,
National Urban League,
127 East 23rd Street,
New York, N. Y.

Dear Sir:—

I beg to apologize for not being able to forward the information which I promised in my letter of the 12th ultimo.

However, enclosed you will find a list of the colored employees in our employ during the years 1919–20 and 21 inclusive, together with their occupations and their reason for leaving. Letter "D" means discharged.

You will also find a separate list of our present colored employees.

Permit me to add that this list of ex-employees reflects the true conditions as they existed in our Plant.

Yours very truly,

PRATT & CADY COMPANY, INCORPORATED

PJS:M   EMPLOYMENT MANAGER

LIST OF COLORED EMPLOYEES
Jan. 5th, 1921

Adams, John	Core helper
Arnold, Love	Cupola Man
Banton, Elmore	Misc. Helper
Bryans, Wm.	Core Helper
Clark, Robert	Cupola man
Cody, Walter	Coremaker
Edney, Isiah	Oiler
Hall, Wm.	Melter
Harris, J.	Mach. Moulder
Jackson, F.	Tester
Jackson, Lonnie	Tumbling Bbl. oper.
Jackson, Willie	Moulder's helper
Jones, Ross	Seater
Levrett, L.	Cupola tender
Ross, Otis	Coremaker
Thomas, Henry	Trucker
Walker, Stephen	Flaskman

Willis, Jos.	Corehelper
Willis, Chas.	Furnace man
McIntee, E.	Core helper
McKenzie, W.	Sand Blast operator

NAME	OCCUPATION	DATE LEAVING	REASON FOR LEAVING
Adams, Rueben	Knockout man	5-28-20	Couldn't wash up at 4:30 P.M.
Allen, Charles	Furnace tender	D 6-9-20	Loafing on job
Allen, Geo.	Grinder	5-4-20	Left without notice
Allen, Will	Trucker	2-13-20	No reason given
Anderson, Herbert	Seater	2-6-20	Didn't take interest in work for the last two weeks he worked
Anderson, Wm.	Grinder	D 1-5-20	Lazy
Anthony, John	Core helper	12-19-19	No reason
Andrew, Nathaniel	Helper	5-21-19	Work too heavy
Anthony, Wm.	Yardman	D 3-7-19	Wanted overtime for Washington's Birthday
Arnold, Ernest	Core helper	D 5-6-20	Would do just so much work and no more
Ball, Norman	Grinder	2-2-20	
Banks, Gus	M. Moulder's Helper	10-9-19	Left without notice
Barns, Robert	Yardman	11-22-19	No reason
Bartlett, Jim	Trucker	11-14-19	Moved out of town
Barnett, Harold	Porter	9-8-19	Temporary position
Barlow, Sam	Boiler Maker's Helper	7-14-19	Noise from riveting hammer annoyed him

Bennett, Wm.	Nightman	6-11-19	Didn't show up in a week
Black, Leroy	Helper	6-12-20	Took a 3 weeks vacation and did not return
Black, Claud	Knockout man	5-28-20	Couldn't wash up at 4:30 P.M.
Blanding, Isaac	Helper	D 9-9-19	Too lazy to work
Biggins, Oscar	Mldr's. Helper	5-29-19	Absent without leave
Billington, Henry	Grinder	6-26-19	Not suited to our work
Bonner, James	Yardman	10-18-19	No notice
Brewer, Ben.	Yardman	1-6-20	Left—no reason
Brewster, Otis	Helper	4-3-19	Going South
Brown, Arthur	Porter	3-23-20	Dissatisfied
Brown, Fred	Grinder	D 12-12-19	Very stubborn
Brown, Chas.	Tester	D 9-9-19	Didn't want to work
Brown, General	Mach. Operator	2-25-19	Going South
Bukes, Wm.	Tumbling bbl. "	D 1-22-20	Absolutely no good
Buster, Terry	Trucker	D 9-15-19	Work too hard
Canry, Sherman	Trucker	D 2-6-20	Too old for trucking
Canty, Henry	Helper	12-19-19	Dissatisfied because he couldn't learn business in one day
Calmon, Moses	Nightman	7-14-19	No reason
Calloway, Melvin	Miscellaneous helper	5-29-19	Going South
Carter, Andrew	M. Moulder	2-20-20	Acc't of wages
Chalmers, Homer	Misc. helper	6-9-19	acc't of wages
Cogswell, Alvin	Knockout man	6-17-20	Wouldn't work faster
Coleman, Wm.	Knockout man	D 6-24-20	Wouldn't do as told
Colston, J.	Yardman	12-20-19	No reason
Cooper, C. H.	Grinder	4-21-20	Left without notice

Copeland, Luther	Corehelper	9-26-19	Going to work nights
Cox, Jefferson	Yardman	8-19-19	No reason given
Countryman, Jas.	Corehelper	5-3-19	Account of wages
Crump, Milton	Porter	D 4-1-20	Doesn't apply himself
Daniels, Judge	Yardman	2-21-20	Left without notice
Day, Mose	Mason's tender	D 2-6-19	Couldn't learn to prepare mortar
Davis, Harvey	Porter	5-19-19	Going to work on farm
Dixon, Chas.	Misc. Helper	10-25-19	Death in family
Dilworth, Edmund	Nightman	7-14-19	No Reason
Dowden, J. W.	Snagger Lac	3-7-19	Laid off
Ellis, Jos. J.	Yardman	9-20-19	Left—no reason
Federick, Walter	Porter	10-4-19	Going to Worcester, Mass.
Fletcher, Geo.	Grinder	4-21-20	Left without notice
Finch, Otis	Helper	6-9-19	account of wages
Frinch, John	Grinder	4-1-20	Left with notice
Frink, Theodore	Yardman	9-30-19	left without notice
Gay, Robert	Trucker	8-14-19	Work too heavy
Geter, Sherman	Corehelper	4-5-20	Work too heavy
Giles, Albert	Helper	4-8-20	Left without notice
Gilbert, Chas.	Trucker	D 3-12-20	Because of illness—excellent worker
Glover, Wm	Helper	3-2-20	Left—no reason
Givens, Jeff.	Yardman	4-19-19	left without notice
Green, Jas.	Assembler	6-30-20	left—no reason
Gurley, C.	Grinder	10-21-19	No reason
Halsey, Ed.	Misc. Helper	D 4-20-20	No reason
Hasty, Wm.	Flaskman	5-28-20	Going South
Harris, Payton	Knockout man	5-28-20	Couldn't wash up at 4:30 P.M.
Harris, Geo.	Helper	2-2-20	No reason

Harris, Dock	Misc. Helper	D 1-15-19	Had been breaking moulds
Hawkins, O. K.	Trucker	4-26-20	left without notice
Hawley, H.	Trucker	3-6-20	left to work elsewhere
Hayes, Olin	Gen. Helper	6-9-19	account of wages
Hawkins, Boyd.	Misc. Helper	1-11-19	left, no reason
Henderson, Wm.	Helper	5-15-20	left without reason
Hnderson, Thos.	Grinder	D 3-8-20	low in production
Henley, Emit	Tumbling Bbl.	7-19-19	working elsewhere
Heightower, John	Window cleaner	6-14-19	out 1 week. Didn't inform foreman
Hezkiah, James	grinder	D 1-23-20	does not apply himself
Hicks, Essie	Boiler-room helper	1-1-20	Approach of warm weather
Hicks, Bonnie	Trucker	D 11-25-19	arrested for shooting policeman
Hicks, Wm.	Yardman	D 9-17-19	left—no reason
Hicks, Elbert	Misc. Helper	5-29-19	absent without leave
Holoway, Elmore	Tumbling Bbl.	D 10-8-19	fighting in factory
Hodges, Octavious	Trucker	5-29-19	resigned
Howard, Richard	Corehelper	D 10-29-10	fighting
Holmes, Richard	Nightman	7-29-19	unsteady worker
Howard, Wm.	Nightman	6-25-19	Left—no reason
Hudgins, Jos.	M.M. Helper	12-19-19	leaving town
Jenkins, Alonzo	Corehelper	5-8-20	Left—no reason
Jacobs, Arthur	Helper		Left—no reason
Jenkins, Wm.	Helper	12-23-19	Work too heavy
Jameson, Jesse	Porter	D 10-25-19	Unreliable
Johnson, Wyott	Helper	12-27-19	Worked one day—no reason

Johnson, Dwelly	Nightman	7-29-19	Not steady worker
Johnson, Louis	Corehelper	D 2-4-19	Not steady and not to be depended upon
Jones, Essex	Snagger	D 5-28-20	Distruber
Jones, Wm.	M.M. helper	3-23-20	Left—no reason
Jones, Oscar	Sand Blast	D 2-2-20	Not steady
Jones, Chas.	M.M. helper	2-10-20	Left—no reason
Jones, Walter	Chipper	10-3-19	Leaving town
Jones, McClendon	Tumbling Bbl	10-6-19	Work too hard
Jones, A.	" "	7-25-19	Going South
Jones, Wilber	Helper	6-7-19	Resigned
Jones, Bert	Yardman	D 3-29-19	Went home without reporting to foreman
Kaigler, Henry	Yardman	2-7-20	Left without notice
Kane, Richard	Porter	1-16-20	Acct. of sickness
Kenn, Wm.	Trucker	D 5-6-20	Lazy, Wouldn't work
King, Marcus	Grinder	4-13-20	Recalled to Regiment in U.S.A.
Kimbrough, Chas.	Helper	2-2-20	Account of wages
Kirkland, Jos.	Trucker	3-31-19	Left of own accord
Lewis, Willie	Snagger	6-18-20	Gave no reason
Lee, Julius	Painter	D 5-26-20	Would not do his work
Lee, Leonard	Misc. Helper	2-2-20	Left—no reason
Lewis, David	Yardman	7-28-19	Dissatisfied
Lovitt, Clifford	Corehelper	9-5-19	Account of wages
Logan, I.	Clerk	D 8-16-19	Dishonest
Lumpkin, Allen	Helper	2-20-20	Left without notice
Mackey, Oba	Filer	4-30-20	Going to work on farm
Mackey, George	Grinder	4-30-20	Going to work on farm

Major, Wm.	Yardman	4-15-20	Dissatisfied
Mackey, Reuben	Knockout man	D 3-9-20	Would not do as told
Magoe, Willie	Porter	12-19-19	To work elsewhere
Martin, Jesse	Knockout man	6-25-20	Left—no reason
McCullough, Leonard	Furnace man	6-9-20	Continuous absence
McAlpine, F.	Grinder	8-21-19	Unreliable
McKenzie, Wm.	Sand Blast	4-29-20	Disliked job
McKinney, Major	Trucker	7-21-19	Resigned
Messick, Ellsworth	Painter	5-27-20	Wouldn't work
Murray, Cornellius	Corehelper	D 10-29-19	Fighting
Neal, L. N.	Yardman	9-27-19	Dissatisfied
Patterson, Hugh	Helper	6-20-19	Left—no reason
Patterson, J.	Furnace	5-29-19	Ill health
Pleasant, J.	Yardman	4-1-20	Gave notice
Pittmon, Fred	Yardman	3-24-20	Gave no notice
Pina, Manual	Helper	12-23-19	No reason (Portugese colored)
Phillips, A.	Yardman	7-15-19	No reason
Plater, Geo.	Nightman	D 5-22-19	Too slow
Porter, H.	Helper	12-10-19	No reason
Pope, Wm. D.	Grinder	12-24-19	No reason
Pounds, Chas.	Helper	8-5-19	No reason
Pruitt, C.	Tumbling Bbl.	D 3-22-20	Not steady workman
Reddick, W.	knockout man	5-28-20	Couldn't wash up at 4:30 P.M.
Reed, Wm.	Furnace	4-16-20	Moving to Chicago
Rembert, Jas.	Helper	D 1-10-20	Left—no reason
Reid, John	Helper	1-23-20	Left—no reason
Robison, Chas	Nightman	7-29-19	Doesn't work steady
Rutherford, Chas.	Furnace	1-14-20	Unable to satisfy him
Rushin, Wm.	Trucker	9-19-19	Work too heavy

Russell, J.	Yardman	7-16-19	Dissatisfied
Sanders, Jas.	Trucker	3-26-20	Reported sick 3 weeks. No word since
Sales, Lester	M. Helper	1-7-20	Left
Sailor, John	Tumbling Bbl.	8-4-19	Unreliable
Scott, Geo	Sand Blast	D 9-3-19	Absolutely no good
Sherard, J.	Trucker	6-7-20	Left without notice
Shepherd, B.	Helper	4-23-20	Left without notice
Shepard, Fr.	Trucker	12-20-19	Unreliable
Smith, Geo.	Knockout	4-23-20	Leaving City
Smith, Willis	Trucker	1-22-20	Left to go to dentist, didn't return
Smith, Chas.	Helper	9-20-19	Leaving to return to school
Smith, Doc-Emery	Helper	8-26-19	No reason
Smith, Russell	Nightman	6-6-19	Left—no reason
Steward, Walter	Mach. Oper.	6-23-20	Left—without notice
Steward, Randoll	Helper	6-15-20	Left—without notice
Stephens, Willie	Trucker	5-14-20	Went home sick—hasn't returned
Stephens, Sun	Helper	3-20-20	Left here sick
Stevens, Charlie	Yardman	9-22-19	Dissatisfied
Stuart, Thos.	Nightman	6-11-19	Left without notice
Sutton, John	Helper	1-12-20	Left—no reason
Taylor, Solon E.	Grinder	4-29-20	Not competent
Taylor, Ed.	Corehelper	4-13-20	Left—no reason
Terry, Jos.	Misc. Helper	1-23-20	Left—no reason
Terry, Lewis	M. Helper	11-10-19	Left—no reason
Thomas, Nelson	Misc. Helper	5-4-20	Left—no reason
Tinsley, Willie	Grinder	4-24-20	To work on farm
Thomas, Joe	Helper	2-16-20	Left—no reason

Tinsley, Cleveland	Misc. Helper	11-10-19	Left—no reason
Tinsley, Jim	Misc. Helper	1-11-19	Left—no reason
Troutman, M.	Porter	11-1-19	Wouldn't work
Trueblood, Alec	Tumbling Bbl.	D 10-8-19	Fighting
Traylor, Jos.	Porter	D 4-1-19	Insubordinate
Walker, Stephen	Flaskman	4-23-20	Account of wages
Wallace, Royal	Trucker	2-27-20	Left without reason
Wallace, Otis	Helper	1-27-20	Sickness
Walker, Mora	Yardman	12-22-19	Left—no reason
Walker, Isaac	Yardman	6-17-19	Left without notice
Ward, Jasper	Knockout man	6-25-20	More money at previous position
Webb, Herchell	Trucker	1-17-20	To take an inside job
Weaver, John	Yardman	12-6-19	Wages
White, Acy.	Knockout man	9-2-19	Unsteady
Williams, Allen	Helper	4-24-20	Working in Brickyards
Williams, Sidney	Misc. Helper	10-4-19	No reason
Williams, Davis	Knockout man	D 9-24-19	Didn't work steady
Williams, Henry	Helper	6-9-19	No reason
Willis, Jeffie	Helper	5-19-20	Short hours
Wright, Chas.	Misc. Helper	1-26-20	work too heavy
Wright, Lester	Nightman	7-3-19	No reason
Worrell, Delma	Misc. Helper	D 5-5-19	Refused to hurry
Adams, James	Trucker	12-24-20	Laid off
Arnold, Ellis	Trucker	12-18-20	Laid off
Bell, Arthus	Cupola man	D 11-24-20	Not suited to our work
Bell, Orden	M.M. Helper	D 11-17-20	Staying out without notifying
Belle, Harry	Furnace man	D 8-25-20	Refused to be transferred
Berry, Charlie	Tester	12-3-20	Stayed out without notice
Bolling, Wm.	Yardman	8-5-20	Left—no reason

Brewer, Jos.	Knockout man	7-28-21	Work elsewhere—full time
Bradley, Will	Porter	9-4-20	Left without notice
Brown, Jason	Porter	2-3-21	Removed on account of depression
Brown, John	Helper	11-2-20	No reason
Coleman, A.	Trucker	12-17-20	Laid off
Cooper, Geo.	Sand Mixer	8-24-21	Job done away with
Countryman, B.	Corehelper	1-25-21	Unsatisfactory
Daniels, Isaah	Grinder	8-27-20	Going south for good
Davis Alfonso	Painter	8-6-20	Left without notice
Delvatche, Almore	Helper	8-24-20	Refused to be transferred
Denkins, Theo	Trucker	8-24-20	Wished to get through
Dukes, Redther	Knockout	D 11-8-20	Lazy
Dupree, Albert	Moulder	8-5-20	Lacked experience to operate machine
Floyd, Joe	Knockout man	8-10-21	Left—no reason
Fordham, J.	Helper	9-7-20	Left—no reason
Gason, R.	Helper	12-17-20	Laid off
Gillens, Wm.	Helper	9-8-20	left without notice
Grays, Sam	Knockout man	7-30-20	Going South
Hart, Burning	Trucker	1-12-21	Business depression
Hasty, Frank	Corehlper	2-28-20	Left—no reason
Harrell, M.	Misc. Helper	8-24-20	Unsatisfactory
Harris, Wm.	M.M. Helper	8-24-20	Work secured elsewhere
Hayes, Arthur	Misc. Helper	9-9-20	Left—no reason
Heart, Emmitt	Sand Blast	D 9-26-21	not suited to our work
Holsey, Ed.	Helper	10-4-20	Left—no reason
Hunter, J.	Helper	9-15-20	Left—no reason

Ivory, M. L.	Corehelper	12-17-20	Business depression
Jones, Fred	Grinder	9-27-21	Not suited to work
Joseph, Chas.	Trucker	9-11-20	Worked one day—no notice
Jones, Leroy	Assembler	7-31-20	Leaving town
Keen, Chas.	Helper	8-13-20	Going South
Knighton, Cleave	Helper	7-12-20	Left—other position
Lawton, Carl W.	Helper	12-17-20	Laid off— business depression
Lee, Rupert	Helper	12-17-20	Laid off— business depression
Lee, John	Helper	12-17-20	Laid off— business depression
Lewis, Chester	Knockout man	9-13-20	Couldn't stand the dust
Lester, C.	Grinder	D 9-4-20	Not sufficiently active
Lewis, Jim T.	Knockout man	8-12-20	Leaving town
Lowe, Elbert	Helper	12-17-20	a/c business depression
Majors, Jim	Porter	8-31-21	ditto
Madison, H.	Furnace man	12-17-20	ditto
McDougall, L.	M. Helper	7-13-20	Left—no reason
McKinney, C.	M. Helper	8-16-20	Going South
Melrose, N.	Helper	10-4-20	To work in N.Y.
Myrick, J. S.	Mach. Oper.	9-9-20	Domestic troubles
Parrish, Edw.	Grinder	12-22-20	Going South
Perry, Fr.	Sand blast	12-17-20	Business depression
Powell, Thos.	Fdy. Helper	9-20-20	No reason
Roberson, Ora	Corehelper	11-2-20	Other position
Ruby, Harry	Trucker	8-14-20	going home
Sheppard, Mck.	Stock Helper	6-15-20	lack of work
Slappy, Wallace	Helper	8-7-20	dissatisfied
Sneed, Robert	Trucker	10-9-20	leaving town

Strong, Jos.	Knockout man	9-7-20	Going to Military School
Thorpe, H.	Corehelper	9-25-20	Another position
Thompson, F. O.	M. Helper	8-11-20	Left—no reason
Thornton, R.	Grinder	7-13-20	Left—no reason
Whitlow, Z.	Knockout man	12-17-20	Business depression
Wheeler, H.	Flask man	10-22-20	Work too hot
Wilson, Ulas	Knockout man	12-17-20	Business depression
Woods, Ulas	Helper	12-17-20	Business depression
Wright, Benj.	Painter	D 8-26-20	Did not want to work

SOURCE U.S. Department of Labor, Division of Negro Economics, Record Group no. 174 (National Archives, Washington, D.C.).

55. *Memorandum prepared by A. A. McLaughlin, general solicitor, for James C. Davis, director general of Railroads, U.S. Railroad Administration, 12 July 1921. Discusses the legal claims of black porters; emphasizes discrimination in assignments and wage rates in Alabama, Mississippi, and Virginia.*

United States Railroad Administration
James C. Davis
Director General of Railroads and Agent of the President
Washington

Memorandum for Director General: (through Ins. McLaughlin):
Replying to your attached memorandum of June 21st, 1921, I make the following report with regard to train porter suits:
General Order No. 27 increased the rates of pay of all railroad employees. It did not refer to classes; it simply listed the old rates and opposite each rate was placed the newly established rate. Therefore under General Order No. 27, every railroad employee, regardless of occupation or classification, was given an increase.
Article No. 6 to general Order No. 27, contains the following provision:

Article VI.—Colored firemen, trainmen, and Switchmen.
Effective June 1, 1918, colored men employed as firemen,

trainmen, and switchmen shall be paid the same rates of wages as are paid white men in the same capacities.

It was clearly the intent of this provision to prevent discrimination against colored employees; however, it is equally clear that a colored man would not be given the pay of a white man unless he performed the same class of duties performed by a white man. Nevertheless, controversies arose, as a result of which Supplement No. 12 to General Order No. 27 was issued under date of December 2nd, 1918, as follows:

Supplement No. 12 to General Order No. 27.
Washington, D.C., Dec. 2, 1918.

To carry out the intent of Article VI, of General Order No. 27, and retroactive to June 1, 1918, it is ordered:

1. Employees in a passenger train crew, except conductor, collector, and baggagemaster, qualified and regularly required to perform the following essential duties, will be designated as passenger brakemen or flagmen and paid accordingly:

   (a) Inspect cars and test signal and brake apparatus for the safety of train movement.

   (b) Use hand and lamp signals for the protection and movement of trains.

   (c) Open and close switches.

   (d) Couple and uncouple cars and engines and the hose and chain attachments thereof.

   (e) Compare watches when required by rule.

2. Where white brakemen are not employed, the compensation and overtime rule for colored brakemen shall be the same, for both passenger and freight service, as for the same positions on the minimum paid contiguous road.

3. This order shall not curtail the duties of employees heretofore classed as "train porters."

4. This order shall not infringe upon the seniority rights of white trainmen.

After the issuance of this Supplement, various colored train porters claimed that they were entitled to the designation of passenger brakemen or flagmen, and that they should be paid accordingly. Such claims were filed principally on the Southern roads—the Alabama & Vicksburg, the Vicksburg, Shreveport & Pacific, the Southern, the Atlantic Coast Line, the Richmond, Fredericksburg & Potomac and the Seaboard Air Line.

Many hundreds of claims have been filed by comparatively few lawyers. John M. Long of Richmond, represents a large number of porters on the Seaboard, and Joseph T. Sherier, (law partner of Jos. M. Cox, former Regional Counsel) represents twenty or more claims on the Southern, some of whom have filed actions in the Courts of the District of Columbia.

SOURCE *BWEGM,* Record Group 14, U.S. Railroad Administration, Reel 6, frame nos. 0030–0031.

56. *Robert M. McWade, U.S. Commissioner of Conciliation, to Wm. B. Wilson, Secretary of Labor, ca. 1918–19. Reports on the case of the African American Coal Trimmer Union, an affiliate of the Longshoremen's International Association; suggests union corruption and making of unreasonable demands in southern context.*

Esteemed Sir:—I have the honor to report in regard to the case of the Coal Trimmer Union, Colored, of the Longshoremen's International Association, that, so far as my instigations have gone, I am led to the conclusion that it had best be left in status quo, at least for several months to come.

This case has been passed upon by the Labor Adjustment Board, W. Z. Ripley, T. V. O'Connor, Lt. Commander Glenn Davis, Hans Jacobsen, and others, all of whom have approved and affirmed the verdict of the Labor Adjustment Boards, local and national. I have conferred on February 27, 1919, March 15, 1919, with Ike Holmes, Samuel Wright and Richard Butler, the Grievance Committee of this local union #45, which has "nearly 40 members," according to Ike Holmes's various statements. There's inside trouble in this colored body, affecting the alleged dishonesty of its officers, etc., which may have results at some of its subsequent meetings. There are, besides, two or three members who are eternally grouching and making trouble, refusing to be satisfied with any arrangements made for their benefit. They are now demanding "the same conditions and everything else that the white men get." This is the Southland, and such demands, especially in this section, would not at this time work out well, if we attempted to push them—for many obvious reasons. The whole matter can wait, and can be taken up at any time.

I am, Esteemed Sir . . .

SOURCE *BWEGM,* Record Group 280, U.S. Conciliation Service, Reel 1, frame no. 0183.

57. *Application of Harry Dean for purchase or allocation of vessels, J. B. Smull, vice president, to H. H. Ebey, district director, Emergency Fleet Corporation, San Francisco, 24 Oct. 1921. Officials discourage approval of African American* *application for charter of steamer for passengers and cargo service; argues that it would be difficult later to sell to whites any vessels "used in colored passenger traffic."*

Dear Sir: I enclose herewith copy of letter addressed to Senator Jones and received through Commissioner Lissner.

This letter is signed by one HARRY DEAN, who I understand is a colored man. I am enclosing also copy of my letter to him of October 15th, which was written before I knew that he was of the colored race. In this connection it is probably needless for me to state that it would be hardly expedient for us to place any passenger steamers in the hands of colored people to operate and I believe this applies with equal force to the advisability of giving them cargo steamers. They will probably want to combine both cargo and passenger traffic and as the matter has been taken up with Senator Jones, it is quite necessary that the matter receive our courteous consideration.

I might add that we had a similar inquiry from colored interests, on the Atlantic Coast for passenger steamers and it was considered by both Mr. Smull and Mr. Love at the time that it would be inadvisable to charter any steamers to these people as such steamers would get the name of having been used in colored passenger traffic and it would be difficult to place them in the regular passenger service thereafter.

This entire matter is passed on to you for handling.

S O U R C E *BWEGM,* Record Group 32, U.S. Shipping Board, Reel 21, frame no. 0626.

D. SOCIAL CONDITIONS, LAW, AND JUSTICE

58. *Letter from a migrant from Selma, Ala., to Chicago Defender, 19 May 1917. A seventeen-year-old female (an eighth grader at Knox Academy School) interrupts her education and looks for a job "on account of not having money enough" to continue her schooling.*

Dear Sir:

I am a reader of the Chicago Defender I think it is one of the Most Wonderful Paper of our race printed. Sirs I am writeing to see if You all will please get me a job. And Sir I can wash dishes, wash iron nursing work in groceries and dry good stores. Just any of these I can do. Sir, who so ever you get the job from please tell them to send me a ticket and I will pay them. When I get their as I have not got enough money to pay my way. I am a girl of 17 years old and in the 8 grade at Knox Academy

School. But on account of not having money enough I had to stop school. Sir I will thank you all with all my heart. May God Bless you All. Please answer in return mail.

source CSJMS.

59. *"I Keep My Children in School All the Time." Letter from a migrant from New Orleans to unnamed northern city, 17 May 1917. Expresses gratitude for aid in making forthcoming trip to the north possible; emphasizes keeping children in school and his wife out of the outside labor market.*

Dear Sir: I received your letter and was indeed glad to hear from you I am expecting to arrive in Chicago about the 15th of June as I want to get my wife and children place until I can send for them. I am going to place them with my father over in Paso Christian Miss and my expense will be very cheap. Of course I am very anxious to get work because I have been working and supporting my family for the last 15 years and my wife never had to work out yet and I keep my children in school all the time. I will wire you just before I arrive so you will expect me in the office. I will be very glad for any service [or] information that you will be able to give me as I am coming. I think I would like to work in Detroit Mich. I am not so

much on Chicago on account of my children. I am glad you can help me and place me in a job right away.

Yours truly. . . .

SOURCE CSJMS.

60. *"My Children I Wished to be Educate in a Different Community Than Here." Letter from a pharmacist and mailman, Augusta, Ga., to* Chicago Defender, *27 Apr. 1917. Accents college education and desire to educate children in system "where the school facilities are better and less prejudice shown and in fact where advantages are better for our people in all respect."*

Sir: Being a constant reader of your paper, I thought of no one better than you to write for information.

I'm desirous of leaving the south but before so doing I want to be sure of a job before pulling out. I'm a member of the race, a normal and college school graduate, a man of a family and can give reference. Confidentially this communication between you and me is to be kept a secret.

My children I wished to be educate in a different community than here. Where the school facilities are better and less prejudice shown and in fact where advantages are better for our people in all respect. At present I have a good position but I desire to leave the south. A good position even tho' its a laborer's job paying $4.50 or $5.00 a day will suit me till I can do better. Let it be a job there or any where else in the country, just so it is east or west. I'm quite sure you can put me in touch with some one. I'm a letter carrier now and am also a druggist by profession. Perhaps I may through your influence get a transfer to some eastern or western city.

Nevada or California as western states, I prefer, and I must say that I have nothing against Detroit, Mich.

I shall expect an early reply. Remember [k]eep this a secret please until I can perfect some arrangements.

Yours respectfully. . . .

SOURCE CSJMS.

The Omar Elementary School for African Americans in Logan County, West Virginia. Although southern blacks faced persistent inequality in the allocation of educational funds, African American elementary, junior high, and senior high schools expanded during the 1920s. Courtesy of Ohio State University.

61. *Letter from Fred D. McCracken, field agent, to James Ford, manager, U.S. Homes Registration Service, 10 July 1919. Discusses negative reactions to a U.S. Housing Corporation proposal for a black housing unit; many blacks disapproved of the proposal, arguing that it promoted residential segregation.*
To: Dr. James Ford, U.S. Housing Corporation, Department of Labor, Washington, D.C.
From: Fred D. McCracken, Field Agent, U.S.H.C., Dept. of Labor
Subject: Official investigation as to the situation concerning the plan for better housing for Negroes in Chicago, Ill., formulated by Mr. Chas. R. Bixby while Special Agent of the U.S. Housing Corporation.

I arrived in Chicago on Tuesday evening July 1st and immediately conferred with a number of Negroes who were familiar with the plan submitted by Mr. Bixby at a meeting called by him on June 20th at the Morning Star Baptist Church, colored. Among them were Negro real estate brokers. The opinion was divided as to the practicability of the scheme. Many of them were out spoken in their opinion that there was a "woodchuck in the wood pile" some where; some were of the opinion that the U.S. Government through the U.S. Housing Corporation were attempting to interfere as to their rights (the Negroes) to live in any section of block they might desire. They stated that the white men who are so vitally interested in the success of the Bixby plan were prominent real estate brokers on the South Side, prominent and influential members of the Hyde Park and Kenwood Improvement Associations and these Associations have gone on record and have made public statements that they propose to *"keep undesirables"* out of their neighborhoods, sections or blocks; and that these real estate brokers and these two associations are responsible for the bomb-war carried on in certain sections of the South Side against every Negro who has purchase[d] property in these sections.

I informed them all that I was here to speak with authority that the U.S. Department of Labor or the U.S. Housing Corporation was not a party or would be a party in any way, shape or form to any organization, plan or scheme that attempted in any way to interfere with the free movement of any person, group or type as to where they might desire to live, reside or buy. The U.S. Department of Labor or the U.S. Housing Corporation was only interested in remedying the critical condition as to housing in general and we all agreed that Chicago was sadly in need of better housing for the middle class of Negroes and that the plan of Mr. Bixby would remedy this evil to some extent and in no way as far as the U.S. government was interested attempted to prevent or discourage Negroes from living or buying in whatever neighborhood they might so desire.

Mr. Bixby pursuant to the telegram from you called me up by phone and I met him in the office of Mr. L. M. Smith, a prominent real estate broker, (white) on the south side and one claimed by the Negroes to be bitterly opposed to Negroes moving into certain blocks and who is also a prominent and influential member of the [line missing] could not be a party that interfered with the rights of individuals to live or buy wherever they might desire.

With Mr. Bixby I called on Mr. Wm. C. Linton, Editor of the Whip, a Negro newspaper recently started which carried a sensational story as to the Bixby meeting and the Bixby plan. (The clippings are herewith inclosed.) I reiterated by statement to Mr. Minton as to the position of the Department of Labor or The U.S. Housing Corporation and he was very glad to get the statement. Mr. Bixby then went over his plan and assured him, Minton, that it in no way attempted to segregate or prevent Negroes from living or buying in any blocks or neighborhood and that his scheme was the same as now in operation in other cities and that he thought that an injustice had been done by the articles contained in The Whip. Minton stated to Mr. Bixby that Negroes had no confidence in L. M. Smith or any others connected with the Hyde Park or Kenwood Associations or any of the white real estate operators; that they knew about the bombing of Negro homes on the South Side and might even be a party to it. Minton stated that he was glad to get Mr. Bixby's statement but would not commit himself as to the plan.

I then conferred with Forrester B. Washington, Supervisor of Negro Economics for the State of Illinois, of the Department of Labor. Mr. Washington stated that there were many Negroes of the opinion that there was something back of the OLIVE BRANCH of L. M. SMITH and he regretted that Mr. Bixby had not consulted him or members of his committee; he also stated that the Pastor of Olivet Baptist Church, where the U.S. Homes Registration Service is located, was not selected for the meeting of Mr. Bixby and that the Olivet Baptis[t] Church felt that it had been slighted and was feeling it keenly.

I then conferred with Mrs. Calloway, Manager of the U.S. Homes Registration Service at the Olivet Baptis[t] Church, and she stated that a Mr. Davis called on her and Dr. Williams, the Pastor, and stated that he wanted the church for the meeting called by Mr. Bixby. They readily gave their consent but to their surprise they received a letter the next day requesting them to attend the meeting at the Morning Star Baptist Church.

I then conferred with Mr. J. Bibb, Asst. Exec. Secy., Chicago branch National Association for the Advancement of Colored People and found him bitterly and viciously opposed to the Bixby scheme. He stated that Mr. Bixby had always trained with a crowd of white real estate operators strongly opposed to *Negroes living like folks* and that L. M. Smith and others interested were of the same type; that he had the record of Mr. Bixby and that his scheme contained dynamite, etc. I again reiterated my statement as to the position of the U.S. government. He stated that he was very glad to get that statement as he was of the opinion that THE WILSON ADMINIS- TRATION WAS BRINGING ITS SEGREGATION POLICIES TO CHICAGO.

SOURCE *BWEGM,* Record Group 3, U.S. Housing Corporation, Reel 24, frame nos. 0244–0245.

62. *"Preliminary Report of Situation at East St. Louis and National City," 22 June 1918. Conducted by supervisor of Community Work, Chicago Branch, and Community Organization Branch, Industrial Service Section, Ordnance Department. Detailed survey of housing and social conditions; emphasizes the large number of saloons—"a number of the worst hell-holes I have ever seen."*

1. The situation here is both complex and serious, due to the following general causes:
   a. The effects of the great race riot of July, 1917, when several whites and more than 130 negroes lost their lives.
   b. The poorest kind of housing—the result of the efforts of real estate men to realize the largest possible profits on small investments, with no thought of conditions inevitable from overcrowding, etc.
   c. Lack of proper sanitation due to the fact that a very large portion of the city is built on ground lower than the level of the river, hence a proper sewage system has not been provided and hundreds upon hundreds of buildings are without sewer connections.
   d. A miserable system of garbage collection resulting in absolutely foul alleys, especially sections occupied by the negroes, and foreignborn.
   e. Lack of storm water drainage which results in great ponds of water on vacant lots and even in streets, superinducing malarial conditions.
   f. Two hundred fifty saloons and hotels that are recognized merely as assignation houses of the worst type.
   g. Lack of fire equipment—this city of 90,000 being without a single piece of motor-driven apparatus; dependent upon horsedrawn engines for fire pressure, there being only about 40 lbs. pressure at the sedimentation basin. In 1914 the Underwriters suggested several important changes but nothing has been done as yet and the municipality pleads poverty as the excuse.

h.   Every industry in this city of many large industries is "foreign-owned" (even the leading stores being branches of St. Louis concerns) and the merchants and citizens generally openly charge that the big industries pay a very small tax.

i.   Whole blocks in National City are covered with horse-sale barns and other buildings of highly inflammable type, in which bulk and baled hay is stored by the carload. The moral hazard here is simply awful. Three of the plants in East St. Louis were recently damaged or destroyed by fires of an incendiary origin. All of this places the Government's interest in jeopardy.

j.   The YWCA is poorly housed and none too well supported but seems, however, to be doing fairly effective work. No attempt is made to reach the colored population. The YMCA is housed in two old buildings one formerly a hotel and is known as a railway YMCA although it is endeavoring to cover the whole field of YMCA work. The secretary advises me that they have 800 members about 400 of whom are railroad men. The various railroads contribute only about $160 a month to the support of the institution, a sum utterly inadequate considering the services rendered, for the railway men take so much of the room and the time of the staff that other very important work is neglected. The YMCA maintains an industrial secretary who has done a great work among the foreigners, reaching the adults through work among the children in playgrounds, garden clubs, etc., and this is highly spoken of by the managers of the principal industries. Just how the work is languishing for lack of funds, such big concerns as the Aluminum Ore Company refusing their support. This secretary is supervising about 2,000 junior and 350 adult gardens and has unlimited opportunities for constructive work if the proper financial support could be provided.

k.   National City has no saloons but immediately across the street in East St. Louis from the great plant of Nelson Morris and Company, there are a number of the worst *hell-holes* I have ever seen, as well as a number of so-called lunch-rooms, none of which would be allowed to exist for a moment in any other city—filthy, unsanitary, swarming with flies, operated by foreigners of various nationalities, patronized by whites and blacks, male and female, a menace which ought to be removed by some power.

l.   The plant of the East St. Louis Cotton Oil Co. (owned by Armour & Co.) is located at Brooklyn, adjoining National City. This village of several hundred negroes cannot be described to anyone who has never seen it. The buildings are all unpainted shacks with no sewerage, no walks, no gardens, no lawns—nothing but a number of indescribably filthy saloons which operate seven days in the week, regardless of the Illinois Law.

m. I was present at a meeting when it was stated that there is no place in the business section of East St. Louis where a negro, male or female, can buy a soda, ice-cream, candy, etc., with the result that the men patronize the saloons, and the women are compelled to trade in the dirty dumps which flourish in the negro section.

s o u r c e *BWEGM*, Record Group 1, War Labor Policies Board, Reel 19, frame nos. 0245–0246.

63. *Letter from Philip Hiss, chairman, Section on Housing, Advisory Commission of the Council of National Defense, to John A. Kelley, Columbus Chamber of Commerce, 22 Aug. 1917. Encourages building of housing for black workers and their families as investment against life-threatening diseases.*

Dear Mr. Kelley:

Thank you very much for your letter of August 20th.

You doubtless are familiar with the houses built in Cincinnati for colored people. Has your Chamber thought of forming a building company which would provide cheap, sanitary homes for the negroes thereby saving your city from many deaths and much disease which will otherwise surely penetrate into all classes of the population? Or, perhaps, the companies employing the labor would join in a plan to provide houses.

While building operations are generally about 20% higher now than three years ago, yet the prospects are that half of this, absorbed by labor, will not decrease immediately after the war, and that, therefore, a possible 10%, or even less, is all that is to be gained by postponement of building. Does it not seem sensible that a community should be willing to absorb part of this, because of improved sanitary conditions for the entire city, and that the companies would be willing to absorb the rest in order to insure more and better labor?

Columbus has the reputation of being a progressive city. Such a solving of the negro housing problem would undoubtedly add to that reputation. If we can be of any service in the way of general suggestions, or giving information of what other communities have done, please call on us.

The war will be won by sanitary housing of workers behind the lines quite as much as by good camp conditions at the front. If plans were made immediately, exterior walls could be erected before the cold weather and interiors finished soon after the first of the year, making use of builders during the "off season." If you suffer from a dearth of building labor, perhaps you could take over some of that employed on the Cantonment at Chillicothe.

We shall hope to hear from you further on this subject. We shall shortly be able to place before you several practical plans to meet different local conditions. These can be adapted by local architects, builders and real estate men.

Have wages increased materially in Columbus either in 1914 or this year? Have rents increased? Also, could you give us the names of the 15 or 16 companies you mention as executing war orders, either directly or indirectly, together with the commodity they are furnishing.

SOURCE *BWEGM,* Record Group 3, U.S. Housing Corporation, Reel 22, frame nos. 0528–0529.

64. *Columbus Chamber of Commerce to Section on Housing, Advisory Commission of the Council of National Defense, 20 Aug. 1917. Says housing in city is good, except for blacks. "This is our only housing problem, and, of course, it is a big one."*

Gentlemen: Yours of the 18th addressed to Mr. Gillette has come to our attention.

The industrial housing condition in Columbus is pretty good except the facilities for the negroes, of whom there are quite a number here. These negroes are settling in the cheaper neighborhoods, oftentimes to the great annoyance of the white people in the same vicinity. This is our only housing problem, and, of course, it is a big one.

There are some 15 or 16 local plants engaged in war work either directly or indirectly and the labor situation here is already becoming difficult, especially the common labor. Only a negro or a foreigner will work now-a-days in the foundries or difficult places of a factory, according to employers.

Trusting this is the information you want, and assuring you of our desire to co-operate, we are . . .

SOURCE *BWEGM,* Record Group 3, U.S. Housing Corporation, Reel 22, frame no. 0538.

65. *Letter from William C. Noland, Richmond, Va., to Philip Hiss, chairman, Section on Housing, Advisory Commission of the Council of National Defense, 25 Aug. 1917. Suggests overcrowding in black area of the city but concludes that "that race is gregarious by nature and I doubt if they consider themselves over-congested."*

Dear Sir:—Replying to your letter of the 18th. inst. I have to say as follows:—

Speaking generally, I believe that housing congestion does not yet exist here to the degree that would be considered congestion in the larger manufacturing cities in the north. I believe that such congestion as does exist here is found chiefly among the negroes, who constitute, I should say, about 25 or 30% of the city's population. However, that race is gregarious by nature and I doubt if they consider themselves over-congested. . . .

Hoping that the above covers your inquiries, and regretting that I could not reply sooner, I am,

Very truly yours,
/s/ Wm. C. Noland.

Dic./WCN.

SOURCE *BWEGM,* Record Group 3, U.S. Housing Corporation, Reel 22, frame no. 0551.

66. *Letters from C. Van Carey, Atlanta Real Estate Board, to J. H. Callaher and others, 28 Sept. 1918. Discusses the impact of black migration on vacancies in the city; concludes that "because of the traditions which affected their early training it is absolutely impossible to attempt to place white families in houses formerly occupied by negroes."*

Gentlemen; The undersigned Committee of the Atlanta Real Estate Board, which has undertaken to make a survey of the vacant house situation in Atlanta for benefit of the United States Housing Corporation, at your request, begs leave to report as follows:

The reports made to you by the postmen of Atlanta, through the Postmaster, were thoroughly analyzed by us, and our analysis was given to the Executive Secretary of the Atlanta Real Estate Board with instructions to compile a digest for us. A copy of his report is hereto attached.

We appointed a sub-committee consisting of Messrs. B. D. Watkins and A. B. Cates to examine the renting lists of the Agents in Atlanta. This work they did very carefully, showing as a result that we now have in this city forty-two houses of from seven to ten room capacity of which twelve are in good neighborhoods but of which only eight are in good condition.

The remaining thirty are not only in bad condition in but in addition are in business zones and not marketable to tenants requiring seven to ten room houses.

They report thirty-five-five and six-room houses of which nineteen are in good neighborhoods but of these only ten are in good condition, the remaining 16 being undesirable as residences for the average working man, as is indicated by the fact that they rent for from Five to Ten Dollars per month. They report a total of eighty-three and four room houses. They were unable to obtain complete reports upon the condition of these houses, but in order to be as accurate as possible, they have assumed that those not specifically stated to be bad are in good condition. Sixty then are in good condition and twenty are in bad condition. In apartments and flats containing these, four and five rooms each, there is a total of ten, all of which are in good condition. We wish to impress upon you that these are not Apartment houses, but are merely individual suites. Their survey showed that in Furnished Apartments and Furnished Houses there is a total of six, from five to twelve room capacity, all in good condition. Of two room houses they found a total of seven, four of which are in good condition and three in bad condition. They found six single rooms available as living quarters, all of which are in good condition.

To summarize they show a total of one hundred and eighty-six houses for rent in Atlanta, of which one hundred and four are in good condition. The digest of our Secretary on the analysis of the report by the mail carriers shows one hundred and six dwellings in good condition and a total of two hundred and twenty-five both good and bad. You will therefore observe that there is a difference and thirty-nine houses in the total reports of the postmen and our sub-committee, and a difference of two houses in the two reports on available dwellings. We arrive at the figure two-hundred and twenty-five for the postmen by listing the following:

Available dwellings	106
Uninhabitable	73
Boarding houses	27
Not marketable	19
TOTAL	225

This discrepancy is easily explained by the fact that a number of these houses are not listed with the Real Estate men, having been practically abandoned by their owners.

Our sub-committee ascertained the number of negro houses listed with the renting agents of Atlanta and found one of nine rooms, one of seven rooms, three of six rooms, seven of five rooms, twenty-one of four rooms, one hundred and thirty-seven of three rooms, one hundred and thirty-four of two rooms, and sixty-seven. This figure added to the one hundred and eighty-six vacancies, good and bad, listed with the Real Estate Agents, gives a total of five hundred and fifty-three vacant houses both white and colored in Atlanta. The report made by the postmen, which includes vacant buildings of all characters, including stores, shows a total of six hundred and sixty-five. Subtracting from six hundred and sixty-five the Renting Agent's total of five hundred and fifty-three, there is a remainder of one hundred and twelve, which is easily accounted for as being the stores and offices reported as vacant and for rent by the postmen.

These vacant stores deserve special mention. They are located in the three districts of Atlanta which correspond to the Bowery section of any city. They are small, largely in bad condition and have been made vacant principally by the fact that the business of the city has moved away from them, but to some extent by the fact that they were formerly occupied by cheap saloons before the days of prohibition.

With reference to your request to our Mr. Arnold to give you the availability of neighboring towns for residence purposes of Atlantans, please bear in mind that conditions here are somewhat different from the congested conditions of the North and East.

Sept. 27, 1918

Mr. H. H. Arnold, Chairman,
Mr. Benjamin D. Watkins,
Mr. M. C. Kiser,
Mr. A. B. Cates,
Mr. Geo. M. Brown,
Committee on Vacancies.
Gentlemen:

Complying with instructions given me last evening, following the lengthy session at which you analyzed a report on vacant property made by the Postmen of Atlanta, I beg leave to submit you a report of my digest.

It should be explained in the beginning that I have made no attempt to take into consideration vacant houses which are available for dwellings by *negroes*. This type of house is not under discussion, but if it were, I think it would be readily admitted that the somewhat large exodus of negroes to the North and East and to the Seaboard, which has been going on for the past eighteen months, has largely depleted our negro population and, as you gentlemen are well aware, has created a decided scarcity of common labor in this vicinity. Therefore, I admit the vacancies among the negro houses and have made no attempt to verify any report along this line. In this connection, however, I wish to direct your attention to the fact that because of the temperament of our people and because of the traditions which affected their early training it is absolutely impossible to attempt to place white families in houses formerly occupied by negroes, and any attempt along this line will be utterly futile and a waste of effort. Vacant negro houses, therefore, do not enter into the housing situation of Atlanta when we have under consideration the housing of white families.

I also wish to direct your attention to the fact that I have not listed as habitable houses those in the Ivy St. section, nor in certain portions of the Central Ave. section. Both of these sections are within the business zone. Many of the houses we know are being demolished, and those that remain have of such recent date contained occupants of so unsavory reputations that it would be impossible to induce respectable white tenants to take possession of them.

Permit me also to call your attention to the fact that the Postmen of Atlanta have done a most thorough piece of work in reporting to the Postmaster the vacant houses on their routes, these reports being the basis for my present report to you. The Postmen were very conscientious in their work, and reported as vacant all houses which had on them "For Rent" signs, and also they included. . . .

C. Van Carey
Atlanta Real Estate Board

SOURCE *BWEGM,* Record Group 3, U.S. Housing Corporation, Reel 22, frame nos. 0748–0749, 0753.

67. *"Better Community Organization." On War Camp Community Service training program at the Hampton Institute,* Atlanta Independent, *4 Jan. 1919 (full-page notice). Discusses war work among black women; includes training in establishment of organizations for black soldiers.*

Better Community Organization

Hampton, Va., January 20.—The War Camp Community Service is now holding its fourth school for the training of community organizers at Hampton Institute. Mrs. Eva White, of Washington, D.C., who is a member of the United States Commission on Living Conditions, is conducting this training work, which aims to prepare colored women to do constructive work along many lines, including the organization of colored soldiers, clubs, meeting the recreational needs of soldiers, establishing community standards on the lessons of thrift and morals, which have been brought home to the nation by the Great War, putting in definite foundations for the safeguarding of colored girls, the development of extension education, the organization of colored women into progressive mothers' clubs, which aim to develop independent responsibility for the care of young people, and the improvement of housing conditions.

The members of the War Camp Community Service Training School will cooperate with the United States Employment Service, the United States Housing Corporation, the United States Emergency Fleet corporation and other government agencies.

The speakers include James E. Rogers, of New York, director of the training schools, men's division, of the War Camp Community Service; President John M. Gandy, of the colored State Normal School at Petersburg; J. L. Einstein, who is in charge of War Camp Community work for colored people in Newport News; Miss Jane McCrady, of Boston, Special supervisor for War Camp Community Service in the south, and Mrs. Mary Church Terrell, of Washington, supervisor of the Service's colored work.

SOURCE *Atlanta Independent*, 16, no. 28 (4 Jan. 1919), p. 7.

68. *Interview by Mary Church Terrell, organizer, War Camp Community Services of Capt. Aikens, Executive Chief of Pensacola Camp. Reveals effort to overcome resistance to employment of black war workers in the south.*

Immediately after my interview with Mr. Merritt, I went to see Capt. Aikens. At first Capt. Aikens said positively and very forcibly "We don't want any Colored worker down here. I don't know what is to be gained by it." Then I tried to explain as well as I could in such an atmosphere what might be gained. When I had finished, Capt. Aikens said "Well I believe I ought to reserve my opinion on this question. That's a matter that should be taken up with the Board as a whole. We ought to act upon a question like that as a Body. It might be presented to me in an entirely different light from what it was before. I believe that in any work for any people which tends to uplift them is a good thing, I don't see how you could bring a Colored woman here to work among the Colored girls under the W.C.C.S. however. We did not raise the money for that purpose and I don't believe that the people would stand for it."

"I am not opposed to niggers, I would not live in a country where there are no niggers, but I want a nigger to stay in his place. There is as much difference between a white man and a nigger as there is between day and night." Conditions down here can never be changed!

As Capt. Aikens made that statement which brooked neither opposition nor difference of opinion, it seemed to me that I heard voices from the past. I heard the ancestors of Capt. Aikens telling both of my grandmothers that not only they themselves would always be slaves, but their daughters and granddaughters, until the end of time. And so, as the granddaughter of a slave grandmother and the daughter of a slave mother whom

Capt. Aikens was assuring that the conditions down here would never change, I was not disturbed by his prediction and I did not accept it as an axiom at all. I remained perfectly silent and did not argue the matter with the Capt. for trying to convert a Southern gentleman was not the mission on which I was sent.

"I have a black mammy in my home," said Capt. Aikens, "who has raised my daughter since she was one month old and she is nearly 16 years now. We consider her as a member of our family. We have a cook on one of our boats who has been working for us 20 years. Yes indeed I like niggers and c[a]n't get along without them. But to send a woman down here to work for the Colored girls under the W.C.C.S. will seriously affect its activities."

Then Capt. Aikens told about appointing a "nigger preacher" Borah by name. as Chm. of a Committee to raise money among Colored people during the United War Work drive. Although Borah had organized the churches," said the Capt., "he only raised $500.00 among the Colored people of the entire county. But several thousand dollars were contributed by Colored people by methods which I suggested. I asked an old darkey to give some money for the drive and he replied, 'Boss, I done give to that cause. I give my money to my preacher, but I believe I made a mistake.' " Capt. Aikens cited that incident as proof of the Colored man's lack of faith in members of his own race. "Darkeys have not any confidence in each other at all," he said. "They would not like for me to say that, but it is true. I can go out here right now and collect $10.00 to every one dollar a nigger can get from his own people. Niggers don't trust their own race, but they don't like to say they don't. Southern white people have the confidence of niggers. A nigger will trust a white man with everything he has got.

"When they were selling Liberty Bonds, I knew an old nigger who had saved some money. He had $500.00 and I told him to buy Liberty Bonds. So he went to the bank and drew that $500.00 out. 'What are going to do with this money' some-body asked him. 'I am going to buy Liberty bonds with it,' he replied. 'I don't know what that means, but Capt. Aikens done told me to buy Liberty bonds, and I know hit alright if he say so.' But they suspect fraud in everything that members of their race do.

"Booker T. Washington was the only man who knew how to train niggers, and he spoiled as many as he trained. It turns the niggers head to give him an education. He is not sufficiently brainy to receive it. Booker T. Washington's son came to see me not long ago to solicit a contribution for his school. He stood up right there while he was talking to me and took his hat off. That showed what that darkey was. He is a splendid nigger. I got a dandy letter from him not long ago thanking me for the contribution. In talking to me he showed he had some education, but he showed also that he knows his place.

"A nigger boy used to work for me, a good clean darkey. He told me he wanted an education. So he saved his money and went to a Nigger College in Tallahassee Florida, where he received his A.B. Degree. When he came back, he had some kind of an education, it is true, but the nigger was fairly bristling in him. He could not absorb it. Nothing makes him happier than to come to my house to do things for our family. Although he works down town all day long, he will come to our house at night, wash the dishes, scrub and wait on the table when we have company, and do anything else we want him to do. I had a dinner one night at which the Commander of the Naval Post out here was present." (Capt. Aikens mentioned that an officer was present at that dinner, and I think he said that Officer was the Commander of the Naval Post.) "So I called Jack in and said to the Officer, 'here is a good boy and I want you to do what you can for him. He can cook and clean well. In fact he can do anything. It is a shame to have a boy like him wasted in the trenches. If you want a good servant, you had better take Jack.' Not long ago I received a letter from Jack saying that he was a cook in the Navy."

When it was possible to interrupt the Captain without being impolite I asked him again whether he would object to having a Colored Woman sent down to work with the Colored girls of Pensacola. He replied that the W.C.C.S. had not accomplished much even with White girls and he doubted that it would be able to do anything at all for Colored girls, even though they undertook it.

s o u r c e Mary Church Terrell papers, War Camp Community Service, folder (2 of 2) 1918–19. Includes Mobile, Pensacola, Montgomery, Gulfport, Biloxi, Macon, Brunswick, Ga., Atlanta, Chattanooga, Memphis, Hattiesburg, Anniston, Ala. (Manuscript Division, Library of Congress).

69. *Mary Church Terrell, W.C.C.S., memo to Mr. Dickie and Dr. Fetter, "Report of conference with Mrs. Aime regarding need for work with Colored girls in New York City," ca. Mar. 1919. Offers evidence of racial barriers toward work with black women among northern white women: "Oh," said Mrs. Aime, very lightly and flippantly, "the world is not ready for democracy yet, Mrs. Terrell."*

I was sent by Mr. Farmer and Mr. Rivers to see Mrs. Haynes, who referred me to Mrs. Aime and to ask about having War Camp Community Service in New York City take up the work among colored women and colored girls. On Saturday morning, Feb. 1, I first saw Mr. Haynes who talked with me a very short while and then turned me over to Mrs. Aime if she would not start some work among colored women and girls because there was great need of it here in New York, where the colored population is between 100, and 125,000, and where I felt certain that work should be done for the women and girls of the colored as well as for those of other races.

She exclaimed: "Oh, Mrs. Terrell! I couldn't possibly do any work with negro women. I know nothing whatever about the negro mind or negro psychology and I would never know when a negro woman was telling me the truth."

I said: "Mrs. Aime, would you know when a woman of any other race were telling you the truth?"

She replied: "Oh, yes. I would know when an Irishwoman was telling me an untruth, but I know nothing whatever about negroes, positively."

I said: "Mrs. Aime, wouldn't you be willing to do something for the colored women and girls of New York City if you had the assistance of somebody who did know?"

She replied that if she worked with them at all she would have to have a woman who was a college graduate and who had had at least two years experience in social service work. I told her it would be possible to give her a college graduate, or a woman who had done social service work, but that the combination would not be easy to find.

"Well," she replied, "no matter what they know, or may have achieved, that fact is well-known that nobody is willing to receive colored girls, and it will be a long time before they are received into the sisterhood of American women."

I said: "For that reason it seems to me that something ought to be done for them. They have so many things to contend against that they need help more than any other girls in this country. Moreover, we have been fighting to make the world safe for democracy, and so long as girls representing one tenth of the population of the United States are undesirable and ignorant and immoral, the standard of the whole American nation will be dragged down unless something is done to prevent it."

"Oh," said Mrs. Aime, very lightly and flippantly, "the world is not ready for democracy yet, Mrs. Terrell."

Mrs. Aime went on to say that an artist friend of hers, who was a great artist, but who had had to do social service work to support his mother, had at one time conducted dances for colored girls in Pittsburgh. He had thus gained a great deal of knowledge about colored people, and the terrible things he had seen there she did not attempt to describe. She simply shuddered, leaving one to infer that they were too terrible to mention even between two women.

I told her that so long as colored women and colored girls were as bad as she seemed to think they were a menace to white men and white boys, and for that reason if for no other, something should be done for them.

She replied that she is a positive pessimist so far as negroes are concerned. Moreover, she continued, there is no possible assurance that this work will last longer than until the first of July, and even if I started work among colored women and girls it would take me two months to begin, and then it would scarcely be worth while to work only from April to July.

I then showed her a letter that had been written by a colored woman in New York making an appeal for the colored girls of New York City and urging their needs. She tossed the letter aside with great contempt, saying that it was not worth reading, that the writer was hopelessly inaccurate and she would pay no attention to the letter.

Mrs. Aime stated that Mr. Haynes had decided not to work with colored women and girls and she saw no reason for changing that decision. She said she did not know whether our machinery is suited to the needs of colored girls, to which I replied that if the machinery is suited to work among the girls of other races it will certainly be adequate for this purpose.

Mrs. Aime said that in the case of white girls she could get large groups, numbering sometimes as many as 500 girls. If I could prove, said she, that she could have access to as many colored girls as that it would be a consideration. I asked her how many colored girls, out of the 500 to whom she could have access, she would use in a group. She said she usually took about 80 for the first rally. She said it was easy to get great groups of white girls such as those that belong to the Friendly Society, Girl Scouts, the Protective League and several other organizations, whereas this was not possible with colored girls.

Mrs. Aime repeated that I must prove to her first, the need of the colored girls for the work W.C.C.S. is doing, and then I should have to show her the number of girls that could be reached. She suggested there were a good many colored people in DeWitt Clinton. She opened a map of New York City, divided off into sections on which there were names. One was marked DeWitt Clinton and another Manhattan Square and she said in these sections and West Harlem there were a great many colored girls, and that I should have to prove to her that they could be gotten together easily.

As I left Mrs. Aime I remarked again that since we have been fighting to make the world safe for democracy we certainly ought to do something for the colored girls of the United States, to which she replied that we were not ready for democracy yet.

If Mrs. Aime had been talking about Patagonians or Hottentots she could not have displayed more ignorance of their psychology and their mind than she did about the colored people of the United States.

As soon as I left Mrs. Aime I spoke with Mr. Stevens and urged him to let me see Mr. Haynes again. Mr. Stevens went into Mrs. Haynes' room and returned and said that Mr. Haynes was very busy, "must" I see him?

I told Mr. Stevens I wanted very much to see Mr. Haynes and that I would consume very little time.

Mr. Stevens then returned to Mr. Haynes and when he came back to me he asked: "Mrs. Terrell, do you insist upon seeing Mr. Haynes?"

I said: "Yes, Mr. Stevens, I think I do insist upon seeing Mr. Haynes and I will just consume a minute of his time." Then Mr. Stevens very graciously permitted me to enter and to see Mr. Haynes.

I did not take a seat and as I stood up I said: "Mr. Haynes, I have just seen Mrs. Aime who says she does not want to do any work for colored girls, because she knows nothing about negro psychology or the negro mind. I wish you would do what you can to soften Mrs. Aime's heart.

Mr. Haynes replied: "Mrs. Terrell, I think Mrs. Aime is very tired this morning and she is probably loath to start any new work now."

Then I said: "Good bye Mr. Haynes. Do all you can to soften Mrs. Aime's heart," and then the interview ended.

SOURCE Mary Church Terrell papers, War Camp Community Service, folder (2 of 2) 1918–19. Includes Mobile, Pensacola, Montgomery, Gulfport, Biloxi, Macon, Brunswick, Ga., Atlanta, Chattanooga, Memphis, Hattiesburg, Anniston, Ala. (Manuscript Division, Library of Congress).

70. *Letter from Macon, Ga., woman to friend in Chicago, ca. May 1917. Discusses the migration within the context of black family and community life, particularly the church.*

Dear Mary:—I just got in from B.Y.P.U. eat a little bite and got my writing together. Now May dear you must pardon me for not answering promp I no you will when I tell you the cause We had a soale stiring revival this year I mis you so much We baptised 14 and after the Revival had closed up come George B— confesing Crist so we baptized the first sunday in May and the third Sunday in May George were baptise May I cant tell you how I feel I wrote Ella J—A— Ella said she cried as far as she is from here so she no I cut up but I diden I am just as quite as I can be Sam H— joined to. Bos Jones Hattie J— boy Geo L— Mr. B— two boys Walice P— I don't know the others. Dear May I got a card from Mrs. Addie S— yesterday she is well an say washington D.C. is a pretty place but wages is not so good say it better forther on Cliford B— an his wife is back an give the North a bad name Old lady C— is in Cleavon an wonte to come home mighty bad so Cliford say. I gat a hering from Vick C— tell me to come on she living better than she ever did in her life Charlie J— is in Detroit he got there last weak Hattie J— lef Friday Oh I can call all has left here Leala J— is speaking of leaving soon There ware more people left last week then ever 2 hundred left at once the whites an colored people had a metting Thursday an Friday telling the people if they stay here they will treat them better an pay better. Huney they or hurted but they haven stop yet. The colored people say they or too late now George B— is on his head to go to Detroit Mrs. Anna W— is just like you left her she is urgin everybody to go on an she not getting ready May you dont no how I mis you I hate to pass your house Everybody is well as far as I no Will J— is on the gang for that same thing hapen about the eggs on Houston road. His wife tried to get him to leave here but he woulden Isiah j— is going to send for Hattie. In short Charlie S— wife quit him last weak he aint doin no better May it is lonesome here it fills my hart with sadiness to write to my friends that gone we dont no weather we will ever see one or nother any more or not My if I dont come to Chgo I will go to Detroit I dont think we will be so far apart an we will get chance to see each other agin I got a heap to tell you but I feel so sad in hart my definder diden come yesterday I dont no why it company to me to read it May I receive the paper you sent me an I see there or pleanty of work I can do I will let you no in my next lettr what I am goin to do but I cant get my mine settle to save my life. Love to Mr A—. May now is the time to leave here The weather is getting better I wont to live out from town I would not like to live rite in town My health woulden be good 75 blocks burned in Atlanta. they had fire department from Macon, Augusta, in Savanah—well all of the largest cities in Ga. to help put out that fire the whites believe the Gurmons drop that fire down Now may I hope we will meet agin so we can talk face to face just like I once have. I will write to Mrs. V— soon we hurd Mr L— is there I didn't tell the nabors, I was writing to you M. W— will write next weak to you

Now we no that we or to pray for each other by by

From

P.S. I will tell you this Ida gone out to see about a farm and wants me to take one but I feal like I make more up there then I will fooling with a farm May if I stay here I will go crazy I am told there is no meeting up there like we have here now May tell me about the houses you can write me on a pos card of some of the building. May tell me about the place. Lilian D— come here last night an tore my mind al to peaces I got your paper an note so I will keep up corespond with you.

SOURCE CSMJS.

71. *Letter from a woman migrant in Chicago to friend in Macon, Ga., ca. May–June 1917. Discusses black migration north within the context of black community and family life.*

My dear Sister—I was agreeably surprised to hear from you and to hear from home. I am well and thankful to say I am doing well. The weather and everything else was a surprise to me when I came. I got here in time to attend one of the greatest revivals in the history of my life—over 500 people joined the church. We had a Holy Ghost shower. You know I like to have run wild. It was snowing some nights and if you didn't hurry you could not get standing room. Please remember me kindly to any who ask of me. The people are rushing here by the thousands and I know if you come and rent a big house you can get all the roomers you want. You write me exactly when you are coming. I am not keeping house yet I am living with my brother and his wife. My son is in California but will be home soon. He spends his winter in California. I can get a nice place for you to stop until you can look around and see what you want. I am quite busy. I work in Swifts packing Co. in the sausage department. My daughter and I work for the same company—We get $1.50 a day and we pack so many sausages we dont have much time to play but it is a matter of a dollar with me and I feel that God made the path and I am walking therin.

Tell your husband work is plentiful here and he wont have to loaf if he wants to work. I know unless old man A— changed it was awful with his sould and G— also.

Well I am always glad to hear from my friends and if I can do anything to assist any of them to better their condition. please remember me to Mr. C— and his family I will write them all as soon as I can. Well I guess I have said about enough. I will be delighted to look into your face once more in life. Pray for me for I am heaven bound. I have made too many rounds to slip now. I know you will pray for prayer is the life of any sensible man or woman. Well goodbye from your sister in Christ

P.S. My brother moved the week after I came. When you fully decide to come write me and let me know what day you expect to leave and over what road and if I dont meet you I will have some one there to meet you and look after you. I will send you a paper as soon as one come along they send out extras two and three times a day.

SOURCE CSJMS.

72. *Affidavit of J. M. Anderson, staff correspondent,* Black Dispatch, *ca. Mar. 1918. On the removal of a black U.S. Army Lieutenant, Charles Trib-bett, from a train in Oklahoma for violation of Jim Crow laws.*

A F F I [D] A V I T. I, J. M. Anderson, staff correspondent of the BLACK DISPATCH, on the 1st day of March 1918, was on train 411 Frisco, having purchased a ticket from Oklahoma City, to Chickasha, Oklahoma.

When the train arrived at Chic[k]asha, the conductor, J. W. Barklow called the attention of the chief of police of Chic[k]asha, that there was a Negro on the Pullman who refused to ride in the separate coach, and he asked him to go down and see about it.

I followed the conductor and the chief of police to the entrance of the Pullman coach, I did not hear the conversation within the coach between Lieutenant Tribbett, and the cheif [sic] of police, however when they reached the door, I heard the cheif say: "its against the laws of the state of Oklahoma for you to ride in the coach you are now in."

Lieutenant Tribbett stood there for a few minutes, and then stated he had fully decided not to go into the separate coach, but that he was at the disposal of the cheif of police, and the cheif then placed his hands on Lieutenant Tribbett's arm, and without resistance, he walked down out of the coach, and was taken directly to the police station.

I met them there with a lawyer, when the cheif entered the police station, he said to attorney Fortune, well Bob I have a "bad egg" here.

After staying in the police station for about an hour, the cheif returned from a trip somewhere and said, that he found that he had no jurisdiction, that he had been instructed to turn the prisoner over the sheriff.

At the sherriff's office we were met by a crowd of folk, and the cheif said to the sheriff this fellow was riding in the Pullman and refused to get out. The conductor turned him over to me, the sheriff replied, I would have liked to have been conductor for about twenty minutes.

Lieut. Tribbett attempted to give his army title, when he was being docket, but the recorder said "Oh I dont want that stuff" Charles Tribbett is all that I need." One fellow in the crowd in a very loud voice stated that the conductor would have lost his job had he let that nigger continue to ride in the Pullman.

SOURCE *BWEGM,* Record Group 14, U.S. Railroad Administration, Reel 6, frame no. 0377.

73. *"General Unrest Among Negroes Feared in Macon." Ca. Oct. 1916. Report on special request, Police Department, Macon, Ga., to Department of Justice, for 40 magazine rifles from the Civil Service Commission to help prevent blacks from migrating north.*

—Fearing that the general unrest among the negroes of the city and the efforts that are being put forth on the part of the authorities to keep them from being transported from Macon to the north, may result in a riot which the city authorities will not be able to cope with, Chief of Police George S. Riley today recommended to the civil service commission that forty magazine rifles be purchased for the police department. At the present time the police only have their pistols and clubs.

Monday morning one thousand negroes congregated at the Southern railway depot expecting to leave for Michigan in a special train. The police dispersed them, but had difficulty in making several of them move on. Several arrests were made. It is said that a surliness now exists among a certain class of negroes and the police want to be able to cope with any situation that may arise.

SOURCE *BWEGM*, Record Group 60, Department of Justice, Reel 20, frame no. 0037.

74. *Letters from Walter White, assistant secretary, NAACP, to President Woodrow Wilson, 27 July 1920; and from White to Clyde B. Aitchison, chairman, Interstate Commerce Commission, 27 July 1920. On a Cleveland ticket agent who refused to sell a black man a prepaid ticket for his son to travel north from Birmingham, Ala.*

Sir: I am sending you enclosed herein a copy of a letter to Honorable Clyde B. Aitchison, Chairman of the Interstate Commerce Commission with reference to the refusal of a ticket agent at Cleveland, Ohio to sell to Mr. William H. Collier of that city a prepaid ticket which he wished to send to his son at Birmingham, Alabama.

The National Association for the Advancement of Colored People requests that you use your power to bring about the abrogation of this unjust and discriminatory practice on the part of the several railroads lines of the United States.

Sincerely yours,
/s/ Walter T. White
Assistant Secretary.

WW/EF

COPY July 27, 1920,
Mr. Clyde B. Aitchison, Chairman,
Interstate Commerce Commission
Warden Courts West
Washington, D.C.

Dear Sir:
We have been informed by the Cleveland Branch of the National Association for the Advancement of Colored People, that certain railroads

have revived the practice of refusing to sell prepaid tickets in Northern cities from Southern points.

In June 1919 we had a simular case when in Cleveland, Ohio, a ticket agent refused to sell to the Rev. H. C. Bailey, a colored minister, a ticket from Madison, Alabama, to Cleveland, Ohio, for the transportation of Rev. Bailey's daughter. We took the case up at that time with Mr. Walker D. Hines, Director General of railroads, since the government was then in charge of them.

On bringing this matter to the Director General's attention the order was immediately countermanded.

A short time ago Mr. William S. Collier, of 2487 E. 37th St., Cleveland, applied at a ticket office there for a prepaid ticket which he wished to send to his son in Birmingham, Alabama. Mr. Collier was informed by the ticket agent that they had not been selling this class of ticket from points south of the Ohio River for the past five months.

The National Association for the Advancement of Colored People, with its 341 branches, with a total membership of over 100,000 is presenting this case to the Interstate Commerce Committee asking that an immediate investigation be instituted into this specific case and that the unjust and discriminatory ruling be immediately countermanded. If there is no such ruling and the several railroads are arbitrarily practicing such rules we ask that the Interstate Commerce Committee take up this matter with the several lines and see that the practice is discontinued. Attempts have been made by these lines to justify such practices on the basis that this rule applies to white as well as to colored citizens. This however, is merely a subtifuge since experience has clearly demonstrated that the rule is for the purpose of checking migration of Negroes from the South.

I am sending a copy of this letter to President Wilson, for his information,

Yours truly,

ASST. SECY.

SOURCE *BWEGM,* Record Group 14, U.S. Railroad Administration, Reel 6, frame nos. 0408–0409.

75. *"Ku Klux Klan Organizers Busy in Georgia." Article in* Atlanta Independent, *1 Feb. 1919. On formation of a Klan unit in Columbus, Georgia; describes the organization as a "vile society."*

Columbus, Ga., Jan 17.—A society to be known as the Klu Klux Klan has been secretly organized in this city, and literature stating the purpose of the society is being distributed broadcast over the state. A charter has been granted for the operation of this organization by the State Department at

Atlanta, and workers of the Klan are busily establishing lodges throughout the smaller communities. The headquarters of the order are only exposed by the address given in the daily papers, which reads: "Address all communications to Ti-Bo-Him, Box 943, Columbus, Ga." Other than this address, nothing is known of the permanent quarters from which the vile society is formulating its plans.

Agents are Active

Agents of the organization are advised to "pick" the men who are to compose the society, the heads of the organization declaring that it is of great importance that those identified with the secrets be careful in disclosing the main object and purport of the organizations.

A pamphlet issued reads: "The spirit of the old Klu Klux Klan still lives and, while conditions are different, there exists those sacred principles to defend pure Americanism against Negro invasion; to forever maintain white supremacy; to shield the sanctity of the home and virtue of womanhood."

Other States Invaded

The spirit of the Klu Klux Klan is [e]stablishing itself throughout the entire Southland. At Nashville and Chattanooga, Tenn., the organization is being viewed with favor, and has collected together white citizens who have pledged themselves to support its principles and to adhere to its early traditions. In speaking of the operations of the Klu Klux Klan, a prominent white merchant of Columbus said: "Its noble work was, indeed, well done. The noblest heroes of history and the truest patriots of any nation were its members, who aided greatly in driving the Negroes from politics in this state. Our order can do even more than this."—Tampa Bulletin.

The above story of barbarity is so unbelievable and inconsistent with this age of free democracy that we do not vouch for its truthfulness. We are investigating its authenticity and whatever we find the truth to be we will give it to the public.   —Ed.

SOURCE CSJMS.

CHAPTER II

Recovery and Economic Expansion, 1922–1928

A. INTRODUCTION

Historical Context

During the 1920s, African Americans continued to shape their own experience within the larger context of urban economic, social, and political change. Between 1921 and 1922, market collapses in steel, iron, coal, cotton, and other raw materials curtailed the labor demands of the industrial sector and forced many black and white workers into the unemployment lines. In the major industrial centers of the nation, however, African Americans were the last hired and first fired. Their rate of unemployment was double, perhaps triple, that of white workers. Fortunately, by the close of 1922, the economy rebounded. Automotive, iron, steel, and electrical goods dramatically expanded to meet the growing demand for consumer products.

Under the impact of economic recovery, another 800,000 to one million African Americans left the south for northern and western cities, as rural blacks continued their movement into the urban south. By the late 1920s, over 43 percent of all blacks were living in cities of the north, south, and west. Black population movement was stimulated not only by the new labor demands of an expanding consumer-oriented urban economy, but also by the persistence of the segregationist system, new immigration restriction legislation, and the determined efforts of African Americans to gain economic and social justice. As during the war years, African Americans continued to play a key role in their own increasing transformation from a rural southern population to a new national urban one.

Although African Americans increasingly gained access to higher paid and better jobs than those offered by the rural sharecropping system, racial restrictions persisted. African Americans repeatedly complained of discrimination in employment, job assignments, pay, and treatment by white supervisors and white workers. In industry after industry—meat-packing, iron and steel, and automotive—blacks performed the most dis-agreeable tasks. In the auto industry, for example, employers hired blacks mainly in the foundry departments; few African Americans received jobs on the production line. The predominantly white labor movement also continued to exclude black workers from labor unions. Twenty-four na-tional labor unions, ten of them affiliates of the American Federation of Labor, barred blacks completely, while many others practiced more subtle forms of racial exclusion. Thus, throughout urban America, blacks worked on the bottom rung of the industrial ladder, receiving lower wages and facing greater industrial hazards than their white counterparts.

During the 1920s, the size and number of racially segregated urban neighborhoods also increased. The index of dissimilarity, a statistical device for measuring the extent of residential segregation by race, increased in all major cities, rising from nearly 67 to 85 percent in Chicago; 61 to 85 percent in Cleveland; and 64 to 78 percent in Boston. In New York, by the mid-1920s well over two-thirds of the city's black population lived in Harlem. The extent of residential segregation also increased in southern and western cities, although the percentages were lower.

Discriminatory real estate practices and the use of a variety of de facto measures continued to confine African Americans to certain sections of American cities. Throughout the 1920s, whites demonstrated a willingness to use violence to reinforce the color line in housing. When the brother of black physician Dr. Ossian Sweet bought a home in an all-white neighborhood in Detroit, a white mob gathered and stoned the building. Police made little effort to uphold the right of the Sweet family to occupy their home in a previously all-white community. When Dr. Sweet fired a gun into the mob, killing one of its members, however, he and several other persons, including his wife, were arrested for murder. The ensuing trial, though it resulted in acquittal, highlighted the very precarious place of blacks not only in the urban housing market but in the larger urban political economy.

Although African Americans continued to face stiff barriers to their progress in their new homes, they resisted the discriminatory racial attitudes and practices that they faced. Despite low wages, unequal and arduous work, the growth of the black urban proletariat established the economic and demographic foundation for the rise of new black institutions, civil rights, and political initiatives. Black workers provided a market for black business and professional people in such fields as law, medicine, dentistry, journalism, insurance, real estate, leisure, and cosmetics.

Defining themselves as "New Negroes," African Americans also launched new social movements, designed to end their subordinate place in American society. Under the impact of the Great Migration, black men and women strengthened the NAACP and escalated its campaign against

Black workers' homes were often located near coal tipples, factories, and railroad tracks, but during the economic recovery and expansion of the 1920s, some workers purchased automobiles and occupied single-family houses in good repair, as shown in this photograph from the southern West Virginia coal fields. Courtesy of Ohio State University.

racial inequality, which included lynchings, disfranchisement, and separate and unequal institutions and services for blacks and whites. During World War I, African Americans had "closed ranks," supported the war, and postponed their grievances in the interest of national defense, but in the war's aftermath they revived and extended their struggle against racial and class inequality. W. E. B. Du Bois, editor of the NAACP's *Crisis* magazine, captured the spirit of their fight. "We Soldiers of Democracy," he wrote, "return. . . . We return from fighting. We return fighting. Make way for Democracy. We saved it in France, and by the Great Jehovah, we will save it in the United States of America, or know the reason why."

During the period immediately after the war, the black quest for full citizenship rights was expressed in a variety of developments; the rise of the Harlem Renaissance, the resurgence of black power in state, local, and national politics, and a plethora of new social movements all reflected the growing political mobilization of African Americans in the wake of the Great Migration. Even as African Americans worked for racial unity and fuller access to the fruits of democracy, however, they often disagreed on the path to that goal. A. Philip Randolph, Milton P. Webster, and others in the Brotherhood of Sleeping Car Porters and Maids demanded full inclusion within the organized "house of labor" as part of a larger multiracial

working class. Although the union failed to gain AFL or employer recognition before the 1930s, it symbolized a growing class consciousness among black workers. Marcus Garvey, the Universal Negro Improvement Association, and the "Back to Africa Movement" also appealed to urban black workers, but they appealed to them as a "race" with distinct interests from whites, regardless of class background.

For their part, black women endured discrimination based on gender and race, within and beyond the black community. Yet, they defined their gender interests in largely racial terms and joined black men in a variety of social movements designed to improve the position of blacks in American society. Women like Ida B. Wells-Barnett, Mary Church Terrell, and others spearheaded the militant antilynching crusade and reinforced the NAACP's campaign for full citizenship and equal protection under the law. Others took an active lead in the black women's club movement, which figured prominently in the day-to-day affairs of the elite and the nonelite. These dimensions in African American life received widespread artistic and literary expression not only in the rise of the Harlem Renaissance, but also in the expansion of blues, gospel, and jazz as popular musical forms.

Although African Americans often struggled against the forces of Jim Crow all alone, they invariably gained the support of a small coterie of white allies. Social welfare, political, and civil rights organizations like the National Urban League, the NAACP, the Commission on Interracial Cooperation, and the Republican party, though weak, all represented varying degrees of black-white cooperation. The crusade against lynchings, disfranchisement, and racial discrimination in educational and social services gained substantial support from whites as well as blacks. Under the impact of the Great Depression and World War II, the interracial struggle for social justice would take on even greater significance.

Scholar and civil rights activist W. E. B. Du Bois (1868–1963) devoted his life to the cause of achieving equal rights for blacks. Du Bois help to set the militant tone of the New Negro in a Crisis *magazine editorial following the war: "We return. We return from fighting. We return fighting Make way for Democracy! We saved it in France, and by the Great Jehovah, we will save it in the U.S.A., or know the reason why!" Courtesy of the Schomberg Center for Research in Black Culture and the New York Public Library, Astor, Lenox and Tilden Foundations.*

Documents

The fate of black workers during the economic expansion of the mid-1920s is the subject of this section. Subsection IIB covers the experience of black men and women in a variety of industries: railroads, shipping, ore mines, steel mills, and commercial laundries, to name a few. These documents allow us to evaluate shifting patterns of racial discrimination in the work place. Some documents highlight the persistence, and even intensification, of racial discrimination and inequality, while others suggest the movement of black workers into the mainstream of the industrial economy. Documents in this section also suggest the process by which the expansion of the black industrial proletariat established the foundations for the growth of black urban communities, including a substantial infrastructure of black business and professional services. Equally important, the documents illuminate the ways that the expanding consumer-oriented economy, with its emphasis on mass marketing and retail chains, undercut the efforts of black business people and helped to precipitate the rise of a new cooperative movement within the African American business community.

While subsection IIB provides significant insight into the interrelationship between work and community, subsection IIC brings the black urban community, race relations, and politics into sharper focus. Specifically, these documents include a contemporary social survey of Toledo, Ohio's black community, the proselytizing work of a Catholic priest in St. Louis, Missouri's black community, the political activism of West Virginia's black population, and aspects of the NAACP's campaign for passage of a federal antilynching bill. Toledo offers a case study of the interrelationship between migration, work, residence, and institution building within a small black urban community. The selection from the priest Father William M. Markoe suggests that not only white Protestants and Jews but Catholics launched new interracial initiatives in the wake of the Great Mi-

---

Marcus Garvey (1887–1940), the founder of the Universal Negro Improvement Association, attracted millions of followers in the early 1920s with his fiery oratory and his calls for worldwide unity among blacks. When the League of Nations rejected Garvey's appeal to set up a colony in Africa, the UNIA established the Universal African Legion, an organization designed to drive European colonizers out of Africa. Garvey's paramilitary uniform symbolized his notions of self-determination, independence, and nationhood for African peoples. Courtesy of the Library of Congress.

gration. Finally, the West Virginia example shows how the resurgence of black political influence was not solely a northern phenomenon. Unlike blacks in most areas of the south, the document shows how West Virginia blacks retained the franchise and continued to vote and exercise political power during the segregationist era.

B. WORK AND LABOR RELATIONS

76. *"Application for Arrears of Pay, Etc., for Service in the Army, Navy, or Marine Corps"; and letter from C. J. Brown to Sidney F. Andrews, General Solicitor of Railroad Admininstration, 28 Aug. 1927. Black worker files for back pay for work on railroad during World War I.*

I, /s/ Chas. J. Brown, respectfully state that I am the identical person who served: RR Service.

This application is made to recover amounts believed to be due me from the United States as follows: back pay at Trainmans Rates minus the ½ paid Gen Order #27 Supplement #12 pg. #232. As some Employes did receive this Promised Equalized Wage for his service but with others Received less than ½ of it.

My post office address is: 1603 State St.
Nashville, Tenn.
Serial Number: C13959 War

/s/ Chas. Johnson Brown

If claimant is now serving in the Navy or the Marine Corps, the following certificate should be furnished by the Supply Officer or Paymaster:
U.S. ——————————————
Date ————————————

I HEREBY CERTIFY that I have not paid, and will not pay, any portion of the within claim.

/s/ Chas. J. Brown

Born six months before the end of slavery in 1865, Ida B. Wells-Barnett became a teacher, lecturer, journalist, and internationally known crusader against lynching. One historian has called her the "Lonely Warrior" because of her uncompromising stand on civil rights issues, which sometimes alienated her from other civil rights leaders. Courtesy of Carlson Publishing Co., New York.

Public Mass Meeting

— HELD BY —

Chicago Division

Brotherhood of Sleeping Car Porters

Sunday Afternoon, April 22,

3 P.M.

AT

Metropolitan Community ... Church ...

4100 SOUTH PARKWAY

A. PHILIP RANDOLPH

General Organizer,

will discuss every phase of the Strike Situation, and also the "So called offer to Settle with the Pullman Porters," so prominently played up by the Pittsburg Courier.

The success of the Brotherhood is of vital interest to all Negro workers. Learn more about it at this meeting.

Everybody Welcome   **Admission Free**

CHICAGO DIV. HEADQUARTERS

224 EAST PERSHING ROAD

M. P. WEBSTER, Organizer   GEO. W. CLARK, Sec.-Treas.

101

Mail this application, when completed, to Claims Division, General Accounting Office, Washington, D.C., and advise that office promptly of any change of address.

Dear sir in adition to my resant letter to you for reconciteration of my claim for compensation ariseing from serrvice rendered the goverment while operateing all R.R. under federal controal. please accept the readings of settlements which grew out of the same soarse and was filed in sense our s but received A settlement before as follows. U.S. PAYS RAILROAD 11.00 $ IN SETTLING OF CLAIMS.

Washington D.C. July 30.25

the united states railroad administration anounsted today it had reached A final settlement with a number of railroads growing out of 26 monts of federal controal director general davis paid the toledo stLouis and western;50.000.00 the following roads acepted to settle thare claims in full the T.P. i.400.000.00 Hocking vally 700.000.00 shortlines railroad received the following amounts the payments of these claims on final settlement is largly madeup of balance of compinsation due. these claims I am asking you for conciteration was filed before these was and iff this roar have made any settlement we have not received any and what we re asking is the blame be placerd on the right parties iff the goverment is due our settlement advise us and iff they have settled with the LOUISVILLE AND NASHVILLE RAILROADS FOR our service rendered them advise us and we will no ferther anoy you but at once call on the above road for an adjustment.

SOURCE *BWEGM,* Record Group 14, U.S. Railroad Administration, Reel 7, frame nos. 0018–0021.

77. *Letter from Walter S. Sailes, C. B. Joseph, and J. B. Dale, Norfolk, Va., to Admiral Laska, U.S. Seaman's Bureau, Washington, D.C., 20 Jan. 1922. Black seamen complain of unemployment despite available jobs and prior service during the war.*

Admiral Laska
U.S.S. Bureau
Washington D.C.

Brotherhood of Sleeping Car Porters flyer, 22 April 1928. Note the appeal for public support that the union made a central part of its work. Original at the Chicago Historical Society.

Hon. Gentleman Sir: We the undersign hereby desire to learn. from you. that if it is through your authority we the colored seamen of the various departments of this city is to be downttrodden and disregarded after our services as citizen has been rendered from time to time For quite a few weeks now there are lots of shipping from this port att there are men of the above name race who have served in their various lines and we are ignored. Of the stewards department of which we are distinctly speaking about there were men from the farms, firemen, sailors, and others who were place din the position of said department. and when non satisfactory result, is given, others are placed from time to time inlike manner. And we the colored who have been serving in such places and position, are left, unthought of we were driven out of the Sea Service Bureau office several times. by the managing gentlemen that we were occupying precious room. So please consider our case. as God ordained that every living being must live regard of race or colour.

Please respond if necessary.

S O U R C E *BWEGM,* Record Group 32, U.S. Shipping Board, Reel 21, frame no. 0757.

78. *Interview by Jeff Norrell of George Lemley, Midfield, Ala., 29 Oct. 1981. Recalls work on railroad engine pulling ore out of mines, the nature of black-white relations, and the organization of the Mine, Mill, and Smelters Union in the Birmingham, Ala., district.*

QUESTION: Rock tells me you were a railroad man, Mr. Lemley.

ANSWER: I was the stationary. That was where you run the engine pulling the ore out of the mine. I run the steam shovel, too.

QUESTION: Would you actually go down in the mine?

ANSWER: I'd go down and pull it out. There'd be a man down there to load that skip and I'd pull it out.

QUESTION: What mines did you work at?

ANSWER: I worked at four—Number Seven, Number Eight, Number Nine, and Number Ten.

QUESTION: Where were they located?

ANSWER: That's at Wenonah. Used to be Fossil.

QUESTION: Did you work for TCI?

ANSWER: Yes, sir.

QUESTION: When did you start to work?

ANSWER: 1923.

QUESTION: Did you work for them a long time?

ANSWER: Thirty-seven and a half years. I been retired twenty-two years.

QUESTION: Did you drive a train the whole time?

ANSWER: During slack times, the man that had the seniority over me, they'd run the engines and I'd work on the machinery.

QUESTION: Was that rough work?

ANSWER: No, sir.

QUESTION: Were most of the folks who dug out the ore black folks?

ANSWER: No. Black and white too.

QUESTION: How long was that underground railroad?

ANSWER: They had a main line that ran all the way from Ishkooda to Muscoda.

QUESTION: Was that different from the high line?

ANSWER: No, the High Line went over to Fairfield. It was built in 1924.

QUESTION: That was to carry ore?

ANSWER: Yeah. From Ishkooda and Wenonah and Muscoda. Muscoda used to be called Reeders. They changed to Wenonah from Fossil. Give them Indian names.

QUESTION: Why did they do that?

ANSWER: I don't know. When they changed the name, they had a big pageant.

QUESTION: Did the underground railroad have electric engines?

ANSWER: Yes, sir. I runned them motors about three or four year. It was just like a main line down there. We had lights to go by. We had side tracks to go on to pass one another. We had five motors going at one time.

QUESTION: What were ya'll carrying?

ANSWER: Carrying cars of ore! We'd take it to a rotary dump. We'd mash a button and it would turn them cars over. Then it would slide down to the main skip.

QUESTION: Is it still there?

ANSWER: Yeah.

QUESTION: Why did they put it underground?

ANSWER: They couldn't put it on top because the ore was underground. My father was the head blaster. The head blaster is responsible for all dynamiting that's done in the mines. They had an underground mule. At times it had two hundred mules in it.

QUESTION: Why did they have them underground?

ANSWER: That's where they worked. They took the mules down there and that's where they stayed. It would blind them to bring them out. If one got sick, they'd get a doctor to go down there to see about him. They wouldn't buy a mule if it didn't weight fourteen hundred pounds.

QUESTION: You said you had to quit school?

ANSWER: Yes, sir, in the second grade. I had bronchial asthma and I couldn't stay in school. The teacher got together with my mother and father. The fall of the year, I couldn't stay in school. I couldn't learn nothing. The principal knew the mine superintendent and he got him to give me a job.

QUESTION: Did any others of your family work in the ore mines?

ANSWER: All of us worked in the ore mines. My oldest brother, he never would go underground. He run the engine all the time. I went underground when the hard times come.

QUESTION: What would they do when they had an accident underground?

ANSWER: On my engine, I would ride thirty-five men at a time. I took them about two miles and then they would get on another motor. If a man got a leg broke or injured, it would take every bit of an hour to an hour and a half to get him out.

   If you were in that room and he was in that room and I was in that room, and you got killed, I wouldn't know it. They wouldn't tell you about it.

   A man got killed in the mine. I had to go down there the night after he got killed to pump the water out of the mine. The big shots from Birmingham were coming out and they didn't want the big shots to get their feet wet. I had to walk right in the bottom of that mine myself. I sat down on the rock that killed him by myself, right dead in the bottom of that mine, two miles underground.

QUESTION: Were the big shots coming to inspect how he got killed?

ANSWER: They were coming to look at it all, the rock and everything. You know how he got killed? An eight-pound hammer. He was trying to break up a rock and another rock sat down on him.

QUESTION: Did most accidents come from rocks falling on people?

ANSWER: Well, it used to be but they've gotten so tight on safety. They went to pin timbering.

   It wasn't nothing for a man to get killed in the mines. They didn't care nothing about you. The company rather a man get killed than a mule. If a mule got killed they had to buy one. If a man got killed, they could hire another one. That was the old saying. It wasn't really true.

QUESTION: Were you in a union?

ANSWER: Yes, sir. My daddy organized the first man on Red Mountain. The Mine, Mill, and Smelters Union. It was 1928, I believe. He was president of the local.

You didn't have no vacation. If you took off two days to go somewhere they'd fire you. Later we got vacation days, after we got the union. Then they used to work us ten hours a day. The union got it down to eight hours. They done good things. Of course, here in the last few years, like everything else, they've runned it into the ground.

Another thing, say he was foreman over me and you and you was his pet. And we're working only two or three days a week. He'd send me home and let you work regular. The union cut that out.

QUESTION: Were you shut down much?

ANSWER: Oh yeah. I was counted the regularest worker for thirty-seven and a half years. I never got hurt. Never hurt anybody. They mighty good to me. I thank them for the pension I get.

QUESTION: Did you feel like the company had done right by you?

ANSWER: They could have let me work on but I was going down. They know more about my condition than I did.

QUESTION: Even though you supported the union and thought it was a good thing, you don't have any hard feelings toward the company?

ANSWER: Why certainly not. I think it's one of the greatest companies in the world. We had some sorry bosses, but that's everywhere. I've got eight children. I sent them all through school. I got them from civil engineers to nurses to draftsmans.

QUESTION: Was there trouble between blacks and whites in the union?

ANSWER: You had some hotheaded blacks and some hotheaded whites. When the union went in, some blacks thought they would rule the company. Everything will go our way. Some blacks would say they should get a job because of their seniority. They may have been with the company longer, but they hadn't been on that job as long as the white man.

QUESTION: Did the company try to make trouble between the blacks and whites in the union?

ANSWER: No, sir. There's some hotheads in every group. In an organization you got to be able to give and take.

QUESTION: Were you out of work long during the Depression.

ANSWER: Sure, I was out of work. You couldn't go to that man and say "Mister, give me a potato or two for breakfast." He didn't have it.

My daddy formed a committee. They said they'd go out in the country and see if they could get anything to eat. My daddy went out for a week at a time. They'd bring in syrup and taters. My daddy was fair. He didn't give his children not nair drop more than he give the others.

QUESTION: Did you all live in Wenonah?

ANSWER: My daddy did. Of course, they got to marrying off.

QUESTION: Did your daddy live in a company house?

ANSWER: Yes, sir.

QUESTION: Were they good houses?

ANSWER: Oh, yes sir. When we first moved there from Raimund, they didn't have lights. We moved from Raimund to Magella, which was near Elmwood Cemetery. I was born at Valley View. My mother was Indian and Irish. Her hair was so long, I've seen her stand on it.

SOURCE Oral Interviews, Birmingham Collection, Department of Archives and Manuscripts (Birmingham Public Library).

79. *"Confidential Report on Negro Unemployment." Ca. 1928. Compiled from reports of local Negro Business Leagues by Albon L. Holsey, secretary, National Negro Business League, Tuskegee Institute. Covers Waterbury, Conn., Colp, Ill., Gary, Ind., and Philadelphia. Suggests that domestic service and common labor jobs offer more stability of employment than mass production positions.*

WATERBURY, CONNECTICUT: "I find that the Negro is relatively better employed than the white workers of the same class and skill. This applies more directly to the factory worker. It is peculiar to the Negro, however, to hold many positions of employment that are not affected by the very prosperous nor the very slack periods, but these positions offer him constant employment with no lost time. He far excels the foreigner in this class of work and is readily employed. For example, many of our factories employ Negro office janitors. The factory may get so slack that it will nearly close down, but the office is kept going; so the janitor finds his employment has not been affected by the slack times. He works as long as there is any one working and in many cases when no one is working he is continued as caretaker of the property and loses no time."

COLP, ILLINOIS: "Concerning the employment of colored people, their condition is very bad. I find that they are living under some unpleasant circumstances in southern Illinois. We are not permitted to work in the largest percentage of the mines in southern Illinois."

GARY, INDIANA: "Due to the fact that the steel mills, which are the chief source of employment through this region, are not running in full capacity at this particular time, it has caused much unrest among Negroes. We find, too, that this slump in business affects the Negro as a whole more so than it does any other one group of people."

PHILADELPHIA, PENNSYLVANIA: "Employment conditions in this territory have been unusually bad generally for the past eight or nine months. Since such large numbers of our men are employed in industrial work, the cessation of operation by several of our largest industries has worked a real hardship. In addition there has been noticed a general tendency to reduce wages to an unreasonable degree. Our local Association conducted a licensed employment service until November 1927, and we found this tendency daily growing more acute, particularly as affecting male labor. One of our largest churches is conducting what amounts to practically a soup kitchen daily, and the number of idle men upon the streets appears to increase each day. As against this, there is not any great unemployment among the women of our group, but wages have been sharply reduced." . . .

SOURCE *BWEGM*, Record Group 183, Bureau of Employment Security, Reel 14, frame no. 0920.

80. *Letter from Archibald Grimké et al., Brotherhood of Sleeping Car Porters, 24 Dec. 1927. Call for Negro Labor Conference, to be held at the John Wesley Church headquarters, New York.*

Dear Friend: What of the destiny of the Negro worker? What of his wage and work? What of his mind and spirit? Whither is he trending? What of his relations to the world of industry and to organized labor?

Do we know? Should we care? Can we afford to be indifferent, unconcerned and apathetic to the problems of the Negro worker? How is the Negro world of culture, education, profession and business related to the world of Negro labor?

Why not get together and seek cool and dispassionately, the light of fact and truth upon this question, big with promise or menace to Aframericans and white Americans?

To this end, permit us to invite you to attend the Negro Labor Conference which will be held Monday, January 9, from 2 to 6 P.M. in the auditorium of the YMCA, Twelfth Street Branch.

Notable addresses will be given. The agenda will be comprehensive. Prominent representatives of white labor and liberals will participate in the Conference. This will probably be the most epochal economic conference yet held by Negroes in the country, and we want the benefit of your judgment.

The Conference will begin Sunday afternoon Jan. 8th, 1928 at 2:30 to 6 P.M. with a big Mass Meeting at the John Wesley Church, 14th & Corcoran Streets, N.W., where we invite you also to send a representation.

Sincerely,

Archibald Grimké	Whitefield McKinlay
Neval H Thomas	F. Morris Murray
Robert J. Nelson	Mary Church Terrell
Those. Walker	Dr. M. O. Dumas
A. Philip Randolph	W. H. Des Verney
Director of Conference	Ass't. Gen'l Organizer

SOURCE *BWEGM*, Record Group 183, Bureau of Employment Security, Reel 16, frame no. 0178.

81. *Letter from Mary Anderson, director, Women's Bureau, to Lucy P. Garner, executive, Industrial Department, National Board, YWCA, 7 June 1927. Defends the Women's Bureau's decision to study black women in the laundry industry, where their numbers were large, rather than other industries.*

I have your letter of June 1st, in regard to an investigation of negro women in industry.

We are planning at this time to make a study of the women in laundries and inasmuch as negro women are employed in this industry more perhaps than in other industrial pursuits and also because we have never had a comprehensive study of women in laundries, this investigation ought to fit in with your plans.

The former study which we made was largely of negro women in the tobacco industry and we know that they are doing the same operations, namely, the re-handling of tobacco. We know that wages are low, working conditions poor, and that the white women are working in the factories where cigars and cigarettes are made. There is a clear division between the occupations of the white and colored women in this industry.

The lamp shade industry in Chicago, where the colored women are working, has as you know been surveyed by the University of Chicago. Where the colored women are working in the garment trade, where the union is strong, they belong to the union so that it seems to me that one of the largest groups of colored women will be found in the laundry industry.

I am trying also to figure out how it will be possible for us to employ a colored woman as we did before to do home visiting among the colored. If we could possibly do this, that is if our appropriation will permit us to employ an extra person, I wonder if Mrs. Penn would be available. We were so pleased with her before and she did such good, intelligent work. We would like very much to get her again. Although she is not on the Civil Service list, it would be possible for us to employ her from three to six months on a special piece of work.

I should like very much to have you submit the points that you would like to see covered in such a study.

SOURCE *BWEGM*, Record Group 86, Women's Bureau, Reel 16, frame nos. 0591–0592.

82. *Letters from Ethel Best, Women's Bureau, U.S. Department of Labor, to Mary Anderson, director, Women's Bureau, 29 Dec. 1927; and from Ethel Best to Anneta Dieckmann, industrial secretary, Young Women's Christian Association, 31 Dec. 1927. Explains opposition to a national YWCA proposal to study the experiences of black women in industry.*

12/29/27: A few days ago I had a letter from Miss Dieckmann enclosing one which she had just sent to you. Since then I have been trying to get into a proper frame of mind to answer it and I am enclosing my effort. If you think I have not succeeded will you dictate embodying somewhat my feelings on the subject, or I will write another if you wish. If however it is O.K. will you send it on to Miss D.

The outline she drew up for you seems to me just like the outline any one sitting in an office and not in close touch with things as they are might draw up. Of course we have quite a lot of facts that could be given in greater detail from our state studies on the Negro women but I am sure it is perfectly absurd to think they are coming into industry excepting very slightly and it would be like looking for the proverbial needle in a haystack to find them outside of laundries and restaurants. Her No. 111 "progress of Negro women in industry" would so far as I can judge from our experience have almost nothing under it and the Wage study "suggestions" under a, b, c, would each of them constitute a study in themselves—the same might also be said of her "Labor Turnover" and "Employment Policies and Attitudes."

This present laundry study will give them a great deal of information and judging from what we have so far gotten I should say the greatest trouble with the Negro woman progressing in industry was not prejudice (this is the north, not the south, I am speaking of) against her but she herself.

The complaint is that she is not as good a worker nor as steady and dependable as the white worker. How far that is true I do not know but without doubt her turnover in laundries is higher—whether due to her usually holding the lower paid and less skilled work or not I do not know until the material is tabulated by occupations.

I am also enclosing an Industrial Assembly Bulletin sent to me and you will see by that that she wants this material for a meeting next November. How do you suppose Miss D. thinks it would be possible to make a study and get it tabulated and even roughly in shape by that time? Miss Eldridge, the Negro woman worker for the Phyllis Wheatley Ass., I have talked with here and she made rather sweeping statements of the large number of Negro women in industry but she could only name a couple of plants—Cleveland Hardware and one garment plant where they were employed and of course laundries. The meat packing and glass industries and wood working plants have them in some cities but as a rule they are not on the same work as the white women. One more thing and then I will really stop. The Negro woman is I am quite sure not coming into industry in the south at least up to the present time. In Savannah when we were there women were employed in the Diamond March factory and one overall plant—which has since gone out of business. In Charleston they were in a bag factory and an asbestos plant. Outside of those two cities there employment was almost negligible in South Carolina and Georgia. But our state reports show all this.

Thank you for your nice letter with its names and advice as to whom to visit in the west. I am hoping that the work may go quite fast because in San Francisco we ought to be able to make our home visits through the Union groups and if you are willing I think we will try to get some of our visiting done at noon or directly after hours in the plants in Los Angeles. Miss Erickson said that when they were there some of the laundries were willing for them too interview girls in the plant and distances are so great that it would be a tremendous time saver if we could. Of course the holidays are delaying our work some here but we expect to finish about the middle of next week if we have any luck at all on our home visiting. It makes it bad of course that they work Saturday afternoon this week but we will go out around supper time and hope that they will not begin New Year's Eve celebrating until later.

We are advised against visiting in one section of the city here and as there are plenty of other places to go I think we will avoid it. They say it is not at all safe and certainly two should go and that takes too much time. We are finding exceptionally good guarding here and wages about the same as Detroit and also I think about the same proportion of white and colored workers. After this week will you please send our mail to General Delivery, Indianapolis and I will write Miss Larrabee about supplies.

I am enclosing a personal letter so will keep my New Year wishes for that.

12/31/27: My dear Miss Dieckmann: Your letter of the 20th with the enclosure of the copy of a letter sent to Miss Anderson was received a few days ago. I waited to answer it because I wanted a little time to think over your letter to Miss Anderson. But after all my opinions and reaction to that should be for Miss Anderson and I am pretty sure that in so far as the technical side of any study is concerned Miss Anderson and I are never far apart. As to the request that I should use my help in getting a study of Negro women in industry made by the Bureau, I must be quite honest and say that if Miss Anderson asks my advice I would advise against it at the present time.

From my experience throughout the country in the past nine years I should say that the number of Negro women in industry is comparatively very small and not increasing in anything but the laundry industry. As you know, we are at present making a study of that industry and I think that many interesting facts in regard to [N]egro women will appear when our facts are compiled. In the work histories which we are getting we very rarely find that the Negro workers have worked in any factory. Usually their previous experience has been in domestic service or in restaurants. In all our State studies we include factories where Negro women work and are in fact especially anxious to include them because of their rarity. It might be interesting to have your local Y. W. industrial secretaries check up this and see how many plants, exclusive of laundries and restaurants, they can find in their own communities which employ Negro women.

I am sorry that I am not more in sympathy with the study you want but it seems to me that there are so many more important things to be looked into,—many of them conditions which affect the Negro woman worker in laundries and restaurants,—that a study which affects such a very small and scattered group of women as the Negro women in industry.

SOURCE *BWEGM,* Record Group 86, Women's Bureau, Reel 16, frame nos. 0609–0610.

83. *Letter from Anneta Dieckmann, industrial secretary, YWCA, to Ethel Best, Women's Bureau, U.S. Department of Labor, 11 Jan. 1928. Defends the YWCA's proposal for a study of black women in industry, arguing that the "strategic importance of this group lies not in their numbers but in their position as pioneers."*

My dear Mrs. Best: Thank you for your letter of December 31 which reached me in the same mail as one from Miss Anderson. Miss Anderson says that the limited resources and personnel of the Bureau makes it impossible for the study of Negro women in industry to be undertaken at this time. We must regret the necessity for such a decision and do what we can in the long run to increase the resources of the Bureau. I am hoping that the report of the study of the laundry workers may be available before the National Interracial Conference whose dates have been tentatively set for November 18–21, for I think it will be a great pity if the Negro problem is considered by that conference without all the information possible on the status of Negro women workers.

I judge from your letter, however, that my previous letter did not make sufficiently clear the reasons for our request for such a study. We have checked up the employment of Negro women in industry in many communities again and again and I know that you are quite right in saying that the number so employed is comparatively small. I believe that you are also probably right in believing that the number is not increasing at present. Such employment is concentrated in certain centers and we hoped to have a study of the Women's Bureau on the industrial centers where Negro women are an important factor. Furthermore, our request is not dependent upon establishing the fact of increase but is rather aimed at a desire to discover how Negro women have fared after a decade of experience. The strategic importance of this group lies not in their numbers but in their position as pioneers. How much they have pioneered into positions of skill is one of the things which I think we need to know.

Have you any further information about your own schedule which would indicate if and when you can work with any of our girls on production records or records of lost time by way of Assembly preparation? Did you see Elizabeth Blum in Detroit and were you able to work out anything definite with her? An encouraging amount of experimentation in ways in which women workers may improve industry is going on, I think, among our industrial membership but very much more could be done if we were more ingenious in discovering the means at hand.

SOURCE *BWEGM*, Record Group 86, Women's Bureau, Reel 16, frame no. 0602.

84. *Claude A. Barnett, "We Win a Place in Industry." Opportunity, Mar. 1929. Analyzes the economic development of black Chicago during the era of the Great Migration, emphasizing the economic expansion of the mid-1920s.*

A decade has passed since the close of the great war, and the general migratory period which brought colored workers north in large numbers to invade fields of labor that were new to them. How nearly the colored laborer is holding his own in the general industrial realm, whether he has made good, whether there is an increasing demand for his labor, the extent to which he has been able to overcome the prejudice which naturally met him from competing whites, how employers regard him, the manner in which unemployment affects him and what the future seems to hold for him are questions which arise as one ponders the record of adventurers.

Chicago, the haven for the largest proportionate share of the influx of southern laborers, offers the most logical proving ground for such a group of inquiries as is contained in the foregoing paragraph.

The Negro population of Chicago was roughly estimated as 45,000 in 1910. It increased 275 per cent in almost direct response to the opportunities which were opened up for work at better wages than those which prevailed on the farms of the South. The pre-war population presented no noteworthy industrial aspects. In fifty years the number of colored citizens had gradually increased without any significant disturbance of their social or economic status.

Before the turn of the century, scions of the eastern line of colored caterers had come to this city and made a place for themselves which lasted for nearly a generation. Sixty per cent of the rest of the inhabitants were confined to jobs of the personal service variety. They were waiters, cooks, maids, porters, janitors. Some of the women were hairdressers and chiropodists, plying their trade among the rich white families.

The number of men and women employed in plants and factories before the war was negligible. The stockyards employed a few colored persons, mixed with Irish and Polish. In factories, however, it was exceptional to see a Negro except as a porter, and that was not the rule. There was a definite spirit of hostility exhibited by the lower class working man, it being unsafe for Negroes to venture alone into their residential districts. This antipathy was almost entirely traceable to their desire to keep the Negro from becoming a competitor for the jobs held by white men.

Most of Chicago's new laborers came from Georgia, Mississippi, and Alabama, off the plantations and cotton farms of states that were and are notorious for their small wages, the backwardness of their people, and the vicious character of their laws and treatment of colored people. They were eager to come and the industrialists were eager to get these men and women, but it would have been foolish on the part of any one to have expected these newcomers to fit immediately into the highly-organized and industrialized life of the north. Social problems immediately presented themselves. The turnover of the new Negro labor was high, but, when it was considered that once these farm hands were in northern cities they found greater opportunities for themselves than the labor agents of special interests had held out to them, their desire to get the best possible advantages explains somewhat the waste from turnover for which they were responsible.

There was an abundance of openings for skilled laborers, but these men and women from the fields were not qualified for the specialized tasks. Most of them were only competent to do the heavy, unskilled work. The industries employing large numbers of Negro workers were: slaughtering, packing of meat, and other food products; iron foundries and iron and steel products; laundries, needle trades; hotels, railroads, Pullman and dining car services, tanneries, taxicab upkeep and repair, and mail order houses.

But most important in an appraisal of the Negro in industry in Chicago is his position since it was realized that the best minds and agencies must apply themselves to the working out of an industrial program for the Negro. This program contemplated the retention of all the ground the Negro had gained with the thoroughly American objective of placing him wherever else it was possible. Two of the most effective agencies which undertook to deal with the problem were the Chicago Urban League and the Young Men's Christian Association. George R. Arthur, for some years executive secretary of the Y.M.C.A., co-operated directly and continuously with stock yards workers, placing men, discussing problems with the laborers and the company representatives, and suggesting factors that would tend to bring about an agreeable working status. The Illinois Free Employment Bureau under the direction of George W. Griffin, likewise performed creditable service.

The brunt of the task, however, has fallen upon the Urban League, under its two able secretaries, T. Arnold Hill and A. L. Foster. The League's special task has been to contact large employers of labor, seek openings for skilled and unskilled workers, and to help solve problems that might arise. Through the League's helpful influence the field for the Negro worker has been gradually expanded. As a result, Negroes have taken their places in the following industries in larger numbers than previously: First, laundries: Of fifteen large laundries employing 937 women there are 790 colored, a proportion which represents more than 84 per cent. Second, date, fig and nut factories: Negro women have a practical monopoly on this work—from six factories the statistics show a total of 635 colored and 48 white employed.

The steel industry has given increased opportunity. The Illinois Steel Work in 1910 had seven colored employees, 35 in 1916, 1,209 in 1919 which fell off to 338 during the after-the-war depression, but has since increased to 1,014 and a present average of 600. Other steel companies have given similar consideration, employing between 12 and 20 per cent colored help. The layoff of colored help has been in the same proportion as that of other employees.

Five years ago the By-Products Coke Company employed 13 per

cent Negroes, but today this percentage has been increased to 33⅓. The Beaver Products Company (roofing manufacturers) during a period of four years increased its Negro force from fifteen per cent common labor to 77 per cent, including skilled and semi-skilled employees.

The Urban League gives the following figures on the distribution of Negro workers in 1928:

Packing Houses	8,000
Steel Works and Foundries	3,800
Building Trades	6,000
Tanneries	1,200
Car Shops	1,000
Laundries (Approximately)	75%
Waiters and Cooks	3,200
Pullman Porters	2,800
Government Employees (Post Offices)	3,400
Red Caps	215
Musicians (Organized)	350
Musicians (Unorganized)	150
Police Department	124
Firemen	21
Corn Products Industry	1,000
Lamp Shade Factories	4,000
Date, Fig, and Nut Shelling	2,300
Overall and Apron Factories	1,000
Auto Accessories	850
Ladies Dresses and Men's Clothing	900
Commonwealth Edison Company	115
People's Gas Light and Coke Co.	75
Rapid Transit & Surface Lines—A few as janitors and porters.	
Bell Telephone Company—A few as janitors and porters.	

It will be noted that the second largest group in point of numbers is that employed in the building trades. In spite of advancement in these crafts, determined opposition has been offered by the labor unions. In some trades, such as bricklaying and plastering, the Negro is admitted somewhat freely to the unions, but in others—printers, plumbers, electricians, entrance is made very difficult for him, and some unions have established Jim Crow branches for Negroes.

Another indication of how the Negro is progressing industrially may be seen in the following list of what might be termed "unusual positions" held by Negroes with white concerns:

NAME	OCCUPATION	WHERE EMPLOYED
David Manson	Traffic Manager	Ohio Iron & Metal Company (retired)
Bertram Jamison	Engineer	Commonwealth Edison Co.
H. R. Lewis	Electrical Draftsman	Commonwealth Edison Co.
Jas. A. Meaghey	Junior Engineer	Board of Local Improvements
W. H. Sheridan	Junior Engineer	Board of Local Improvements
William Thornton	Junior Highway Engineer	State Highway Commission
Sam Cheever	Junior Highway Engineer	State Highway Commission
Oscar Randall	Civil Engineer	Sanitary Districts
Thomas Mayo	Chief Chemist	B. Heller Chemical Company
Richard Morgan	Chemist	B. Heller Chemical Company
W. A. Mollison	Chief Chemist	Imperial Belting Company
James Prince	Chemist	Argo Corn Products Company
E. M. Aiken	Chemist	American Maize Products Co.
Howard Shaw	Head Electrician	The Pullman Company
A. D. Watson	Electrical Engineer	The Pullman Company
James W. Camp	Bookkeeper	Johnson Hardware Company
Richard Jones	Assistant Manager	South Center Dept. Store
R. Lester Buffins	Architectural Draftsman	Charles S. Duke
Lemuel McDougal	Architectural Draftsman	Henry K. Holsman
Clifford Campbell	Architectural Draftsman	Board of Education
August Jennings	Meter Reader	Gas Company
Edward A. Jones	Meter Reader	Gas Company

It is the belief of the writer that while the number of Negroes found in these so-called "unusual positions" is increasing, the number of those engaged in domestic service is decreasing. This conclusion is drawn from analyses made of the classified advertising sections of the local daily papers, which show that while ninety per cent of the "situations wanted" as domestics is colored, ninety per cent of the positions offered is for whites. The general belief is that this condition is not due so much to prejudice as it is to the prevailing incompetence of the Negro domestic, as compared with the foreigner, and the unwillingness of colored domestics to accommodate themselves to the hours and habits required.

The Urban League has not only been busy placing Negroes in the larger white industrial establishments, but has conducted a thorough campaign in the colored districts to see that proprietors of white businesses give Negro boys and girls, and men and women, the opportunity to work which the patronage of Negroes deserved. A survey of seven white banks revealed a surprisingly large number of colored depositors but few colored employees. The Bankers State Bank and the Industrial State Bank each reported that more than 90 per cent of their depositors in the savings department were Negroes and about 25 per cent in the commercial department. While the Industrial Bank employs only one colored woman in its savings department and a colored janitor, the Bankers Bank employs only two Negroes in the capacity of chauffeur and janitor. The Franklin, Drexel State, and Kenwood National Banks each reported a large number of Negro depositors, yet in neither bank was a Negro employed in a position above that of janitor. In one bank a colored policeman was employed who has since been killed in line of duty. The Lincoln State Bank reported that it had 15,000 colored depositors and the Roosevelt State Bank admitted it had about one million dollars on deposit from Negroes. The former employs one colored woman in its savings department and two colored policemen. The Roosevelt Bank has a colored receiving clerk and a policeman.

About fifty drug stores were surveyed of those whose trade Negroes constitute from fifty to ninety-five per cent. While in almost every place a colored porter was employed, only 35 per cent of the stores employed full-time colored clerks and a few more than seven per cent had registered pharmacists who were colored. Walgreen Drug Company has recently opened one of its largest stores in the center of the Negro district with about twenty colored employees. The manager is white.

Twelve shoe stores, seven United Cigar Stores, and seven coal companies were visited. No shoe store had a full-time salesman, but in two cases the porter was allowed to wait on customers in the rush period. Three stores thought favorably of colored help and advised the investigator that consideration would be given at a later date. Colored trade was found to constitute from 75 to 95 per cent in these stores. The cigar stores had one colored manager. All other employees were white, except seven porters. Negro patronage was said to be eighty per cent for all the stores. In the seven coal companies the majority of those employed were colored, but these men were used as drivers and common laborers except for one salesman. Office forces were all white. In every case it was announced that the trade among whites was greater than among colored.

Inquiry at fourteen theatres revealed that there were 121 male and 37 female employees among whom 94 males and 32 females were colored. Six of the theatres, however, had forces entirely colored. Nine houses had colored cashiers. Other Negroes were employed as musicians, doormen, ushers, and operators.

Proprietors of eighty groceries, markets and fruit stores were interviewed. With but few exceptions the Negro patronage amounted to 90 per cent or more. In nearly 20 per cent of these stores delivery boys constituted the only colored part of the help, the rest of the work being done by members of the proprietor's family. In many other stores Negroes served as both clerks and porters. Fourteen markets employed butchers, all of whom were reported to be giving satisfactory service. There was a general opinion among these proprietors that since there was a considerable Negro trade, colored help should be used, white patrons often objecting to such clerks waiting on them and this was more evident in the meat markets than in the groceries.

There are employed two hundred clerks and other help in one hundred of the Greater Atlantic and Pacific Tea Stores. The National Tea Stores employ a manager in one store and several clerks in others. The Loblaw Groceries have indicated their willingness to employ Negroes in their stores in the colored district.

The Standard Oil Compnay has extended opportunities to the Negro as attendants and greasers in filling stations. This was a departure from custom brought about through H. N. Robinson of the industrial department of the Urban League after several months of effort. Six attendants and twenty-five greasers have been given employment.

The South Center Department Store, and the Silver Dollar Store, both established in 1928, have employed more than a forty per cent sales force of colored men and women. This has helped to destroy the belief that the two racial groups cannot work harmoniously together. The proprietors have openly expressed their satisfaction with the success of the plan.

As an evidence of the successful efforts of workers engaged in various fields, the following statements from employers are quoted:

Louis Kahn, proprietor of the South Center Department Store, writes: "I am pleased to state that the colored employees at the South Center Department Store are proving very satisfactory in their various capacities. They are steady in their attendance, diligent and anxious to make good. They are meeting all requirements expected."

John Paul, proprietor of the Myer-Paul Company: "We have at this time approximately thirty-five colored persons employed and the majority we acquired through the Urban League. We find them honest and a good percentage very efficient as a whole. We are very satisfied with them."

T. B. Clifford, manager of the sales department of the Standard Oil Company: "With reference to your request for information pertaining to the status of colored men employed by this company, please be advised that the attendants and greasers listed are still in our employ and are satisfactorily discharging their duties."

In some places Negroes have lost out because unemployment is widespread and has affected white and black alike. The Boston Department Store and the Stop and Shop Food Shops dismissed their colored employees with the explanation that white people wanted work, too. All the colored employees were given sterling recommendations as to their ability and character, with the added statement that they were being replaced because the policy of the stores was to employ white help.

A survey of the Negro in Industry in Chicago would be incomplete without some space given to the employment of Negroes by Negroes. A tabulation by W. H. Bolton shows the following Negro businesses in Chicago for 1927:

Artist	6	Dry Goods Stores	5
Bakeries	12	Electricians	9
Banks	2	Employment Agencies	16
Barber Shops	187	Express and Storage	51
Book Stores	4	Fish Markets	11
Bond & Investment Cos.	5	Florists	7
Brokers	5	Furnace Repairs	3
Cab Companies	9	Furniture Dealers	19
Churches	98	Garages	22
Chiropractors	23	Groceries	153
Cigar Stores	17	Haberdashers	3
Coal Companies	3	Hairdressing Parlors	103
Decorators	15	Hardware and Paint	3
Dentists	97	Insurance	11
Dressmakers	26	Inventors	3
Druggists	41	Jewelers	5
Laboratories	7	Optometrists	4
Ladies' Furnishings	8	Photographers	4
Laundries	6	Physicians	176

Lawyers	106	Plumbers	7
Locksmiths	3	Printers	20
Magazines	4	Real Estate Dealer	56
Manufacturers		Restaurants	98
Cigars	3	Service Stations	6
Ice Cream	3	Shoe Repairs	12
Hair Preparations	8	Shoe Stores	2
Medicinal Lights	1	Sign Painters	5
Sausage	2	Stone Cleaner	1
Toilet Preparations	6	Tailors	89
Mattress Makers	2	Transfer	15
Milk Distributor	1	Undertaker	28
Music Store	6	Variety Stores	15
Newspaper	6		

The above list is given to indicate the nature and extent of Negro enterprise. Most of these, including physicians, dentists, and so forth, employ one or more persons. It is not in agreement in all aspects with some other compilations, differing notably in regard to the number of physicians, which the Negro in Chicago gives as 241, but the figures above are adequate to give a reasonable picture of the Negro at work in his own pursuits in Chicago.

The colored insurance companies employ approximately 425 persons. The two banks have about 25 employees each. The newspapers give employment to sixty. The beauty parlors, drug stores, restaurants, groceries, hotels, real estate offices, physicians' and dentists' offices, and other such places all employ one or more persons. It has been conservatively estimated that 5,000 Negroes are employed either part time or full time in these different Negro establishments. Some of them, such as the *Chicago Defender*, the Binga State Bank and the Therapeutic Lamp Company of Paul E. Johnson, employ both white and colored help.

It can thus be seen from this survey that the Negro in Chicago has no cause for great pessimism so far as the immediate future of his industrial outlook is concerned. Since before the war, he has been making steady, normal progress. The maladjustment of the early post-war period has been straightened out and the industrial field for the Negro worker has been extended and secured in small and large white businesses in such a way as to more than offset any losses he may have suffered. In addition, the feeling between the races has improved and greater respect and appreciation for the Negro has been the result of his advancement.

Chicago today is on the verge of a big boom. Four years hence the city's leaders plan to hold another great world's fair that is expected to surpass anything the city has ever seen. Its promotion will involve the expenditure of many millions of dollars. Negroes now occupy a district in that section of the city which will benefit most from the fair. Not only are they going to benefit through increased property values, but they are in a position to get a fair share of the work preparing for the millions of visitors expected. Their place in the building trades will assure them of this. And even before the great fair there are indications that many other public improvements are on the way. Negro representatives in the state legislature, the city council and in other powerful political posts will fight to see that the Negro gets his part of this work which his taxes help to pay for.

All the time the Negro's leaders in Chicago are pushing, pushing, pushing. The Urban League, the Young Men's and Young Women's Christian Associations, the Illinois Free Employment Bureau, and other civic and social agencies have all contributed to help bring about a partial spirit of fair play in industrial relations. That, it is hoped, is going to be the spirit of the future of the Chicago Negro in industry in relation to his white brothers.

SOURCE Claude A. Barnett, "We Win a Place in Industry." *Opportunity*, 7, no. 3 (Mar. 1929): 82–86.

C. Expansion of Black Urban Communities

85. *Everett Johnson, "A Study of Negro Families in the Pinewood Avenue District of Toledo, Ohio."* Opportunity, *Aug. 1929. A contemporary social survey of black life in Toledo, Ohio; provides a case study of the expansion of northern black urban communities under the impact of the Great Migration.*

About a year ago, it was felt, by several social agencies in the city of Toledo, that some study should be made of the families in the city's major Negro district. This was necessary in order to have some basis upon which to deal intelligently with the Negro families of the entire city. Accordingly, the district which is noted on the accompanying map as the Pinewood Avenue District was designated as the district to be studied.

In order to have a clear background, it is necessary that one should know the general situation among Negroes in the city of Toledo. The city in itself is quite different from most other cities for several reasons: first, because on a whole its Negro population is quite below the proportion found in other cities of similar size. Secondly, rather than one heavily concentrated Negro residential section, it has eight, which are scattered over the various parts of the city. The reason for this may possibly be that these eight residential sections are all found either in the midst of or bordering on the industrial centers of the city, and the people in those districts are usually employed by the concerns adjacent to their homes.

A direct example of that is shown in the district noted as the Hill Avenue District and the Crystal District, both of which are adjacent to the Round Houses and shops of the New York Central Railroad, at which most of these Negroes are employed. Also, we find in the Stickney Avenue District, which is about the second largest Negro district, that the majority of Negroes are employed by the Willys Overland Company, the nearest industry to that district. [Note: Map of city deleted here.]

So it is with the other districts, with the greatest possible exception being the district studied, which is the primary residential district, and represents, as far as employment is concerned, the homes of the Negro middle class, and shows a more heterogeneous grouping than the other districts. This district, although not the oldest district in the city of Toledo, as far as the history of the entire city is concerned, is the district which borders directly upon the downtown business section, and the employees of this district are primarily drawn from this group. From all indications, it appears that sooner or later this district will contain most all of the Negro population of the city of Toledo.

It has been noted in the last few years the trend of the movement of

the population from other districts, with the possible exception of the Stickney Avenue District, with this district stretching northward and westward from its former confines. Geographically, it is approximately the center of the city, and any great increase would have to be made primarily to the west, as the east and south limits run into the business section, and the northern limits run into the most select winter residential sections of the city, leaving only the westward limit as a possibility for any further overflow.

Toledo shows a close similarity to other northern cities, perhaps not from the standpoint of segregation or discrimination, but from a standpoint of the Negro population itself. There is decidedly a strong line between the old families of Toledo and the newcomers, with the old families representing a hopeless minority. There is the feeling, which is prevalent, that the length of time in the city is the measure of fitness for leadership and that the judgment of the mass rests in the hands of this minority. This sentiment is disappearing gradually, as the influx from the other places begins to make its influence felt.

Population

The district studied in the survey, known as the Pinewood Avenue District, is bounded by the following streets: Washington, Eric, Dorr, Ewing, and the Creek. Out of a total of 548 families studied, it was found that 461 were whole families, and 87, or 16 percent, were broken. This percentage is high, as compared with the average population of the city. In the same families, we find a total of 741 children, or 1.3 per cent child per family. This is low for the general population.

In order to verify more thoroughly these figures, we have turned first to the survey made in October 1923 by Mr. Forrester B. Washington, and we find in his figures for the same district that the average Negro family had two children. From the Board of Education, we find that there are

---

Clarence L. Johnson and his wife, Cleopatra, established their tailoring business in 1921. They had come to Milwaukee in 1920 from Beloit, Wisconsin, where Clarence worked in a foundry at the Fairbanks-Morse Corporation. The Johnsons were graduates of Tuskegee Institute, where they majored in tailoring. Courtesy of the Milwaukee Black Heritage Project, University of Wisconsin-Milwaukee.

approximately 1700 Negro students in the public schools. We have endeavored to ascertain the actual population by the comparison of figures, and by estimates given by the Chamber of Commerce, the Toledo Public Library, the Social Service Federation and the Frederick Douglass Community Association, which was founded by the late Albertus Brown, who himself came to Toledo to practice law, and who sensed the necessity for adequate facilities for the social and recreational needs of the people. Comparing all the figures submitted, we feel safe in assuming that there are approximately 14,000 Negroes in the city of Toledo, an increase of 40 per cent over the figures of 1923. Using the estimate of 305,000 as the entire population of Toledo, we find the Negro comprises about 4.5 percent of the population. Upon investigation of the different churches and various industrial concerns, we find that 40 per cent of the total Negro population are single men, and 20 percent children, with about 8 per cent single women. This may help to answer many of the problems which are present in the district.

Migration

Figures show that the length of time spent in the city of Toledo by the average Negro is about nine years. The figure includes the native born, as well as the recent migrant. It is interesting to note that 84 per cent of the Negroes of Toledo are migrants, and of this number, 33.4 per cent were from so-called East South Central States—Kentucky, Tennessee, Alabama and Mississippi; the second largest group, or 26.3 per cent, were born in the East North Central States—Ohio, Michigan, Illinois and Indiana; the third largest group, or 16.6 per cent were born in the South Atlantic States—Virginia, North Carolina, South Carolina, Georgia and Florida; the fourth largest group, 9.2 per cent were born in the West South Central States—Arkansas, Louisiana, Texas and Oklahoma. The other states of the United States and Canada furnished the remainder, or about 14.5 per cent.

Since the survey of 1923, one finds that the largest increase has come from the second group—Ohio, Michigan, Illinois and Indiana. This only corroborates the well-known opinion that Toledo has not received the direct migration, but has been the indirect place of residence. Toledo has not been a lure in the same sense as the other larger northern cities, and many of the migrants, who have gone to the other cities first, have ultimately come to Toledo to stay. It has been found that southern Ohio, that part of Ohio south of Columbus, has been the direct stopping place of most of the migrants, with Michigan next, and Indiana, third. This fact should be considered as a matter of utmost importance to the employers of Toledo, because it means a more contented and stabilized Negro laborer, and a Negro citizenry who will have greater civic interest, because they have come to Toledo to make their homes.

Housing

It is a significant fact that the average number of rooms per Negro family is four. Most of the families, about 80 per cent, live in the cottage type, or, what we have called, the single residence. We note a decided movement in certain districts of Toledo toward the building of the tenement house. Another source of interest to the city of Toledo would be to know that 30 percent of the Negro families own, or are buying, their homes. This is a much larger proportion of homes owners than is found in Detroit or Chicago.

Condition of Property

Regarding the matter of lighting, we find that most of the homes occupied by the Negro are lighted by electricity. We find, however, that there are a large number lighted by gas, and a surprisingly large number that are still in a primitive, backwood stage, of using lamplight.

Sanitary Conditions

We find that in the houses that are lighted by the lamps, that there are not toilet facilities at all, except outside. These conditions exist in one block in the district studied, and it would be a very easy matter for both situations, light and toilet, to be remedied. In the same locality, there is not decent walking space, and that this pathway could not be dignified by being called a street, nevertheless, we find a real estate firm is now building a tenement house thereon, which rather than improving the neighborhood, will only serve to detract from it.

The Negro Himself

About 8 per cent of the adult Negroes studied in the survey were reported as college graduates, and we find that the average Negro in this district has completed the seventh grade. This is about average for the country, and is certainly a sign of progress along educational lines.

Religious Life

Within the district studied there are four Baptist churches, three churches are connected with the regular denominations, and one each of the following denominations: Methodist Episcopal, Colored Methodist Episcopal, African Methodist Episcopal Zion, Presbyterian and Episcopalian. Of the twelve church buildings, four are of brick construction, and the others are small, inadequate frame buildings, including, two of the store-front type. The valuation of these buildings is about $175,000. To this should be added about $25,000 as the value of the parsonages owned by the five larger churches in this district, bringing the total valuation to $200,000 or more. This is a commendable showing, when it is remembered that most of these buildings have been acquired within the last ten years. Five of the pastors of these churches are college men, and three are graduates of reputable theological seminaries.

One of the findings of the Washington survey was that over 66 per cent of the Negro population were not members of any church. The percentage of membership is about the same today. Concurrent with this apparent failure on the part of the churches to increase substantially their membership in the past five years is the rapid increase of those commercial institutions which serve as breeding places for vice and crime.

While the district is not now overchurched, we find that the danger of overchurching is imminent, and should be strongly discouraged. Instead of establishing more churches, the larger and stronger churches should inaugurate forms of extension work in the districts of the newcomers. A more internal type of work also could be done, including home visitation, social and recreational activities among the young, evening classes in singing, auxiliary elementary eductaional, public speaking, etc.

Other than the churchers, the Pinewood Avenue District is almost wholly devoid of helpful social and welfare agencies. The growth of the city, the rapid multiplication of unwholsome agencies and the increasing of the leisure time of the Negro youth make it imperative that there should be new and additional social and religious agencies. It should be noted that an expansion campaign of the Y.M.C.A. is just now getting under way, and that the plans call for a branch of the "Y" in the Pinewood Avenue District. A similar institution for girls and women, either by establishing a Y.W.C.A., or by greatly expanding the program of the Colored Working Girls Home, is also a vital necessity.

Leisure Time

There were 11 pool and billiard rooms studied, all of which were licensed, all charging the same fee of 5 cents per game, and all running from 7:00 to 12:00 midnight. In most of these, we find they are not by their appearance any too attractive, and their standards are certainly not what they should be. Gambling appeared to be one of the recreational activities of nearly all of these pool rooms. Although in only about one-third of them do we find liquor served openly, yet in all, with the exception of one, there is always the pocket bootlegger, who is ready to furnish and deliver liquor to those who wish it. In all except two the presence of minors was noted: boys decidedly under the age of eighteen, which is contrary to a City Ordinance. In one, it was found that women frequent the place and play cards.

Industrial Status

Today there are about 6,000 Negroes gainfully employed in the business establishments of this city. The larger groups are found in the automobile factories, foundries and construction companies. There has been a steady increase since this initial entry into the industries in the number that have come into the skilled class. There are now of the employed Negro males about 20 per cent in the skilled class, and about the same percentage in the semi-skilled. This percentage on a whole is not as large as the percentage which is found in a number of the other northern industrial centers.

We find few unusual positions occupied by Negroes, such as Master Electrician in a department store, and superintendent of a building. In the last few years, Toledo has seen a great increase in the employment of women in industry. Unfortunately, the Negro woman faces a stronger barrier of prejudice in these factories than the man, and we find as a result that the majority of women employed are either domestic servants, or maids, stock girls and elevator girls in the department stores. In the last year, Toledo suffered a distinct loss in the closing of one of its leading factories which has been employing a large percentage of Negro laborers, but those who were in the skilled trades were readily located in other factories, and scarcity of employment at the present day exists for Negroes only in the unskilled class.

S O U R C E Everett Johnson, "A Study of Negro Families in the Pinewood Avenue District of Toledo, Ohio." *Opportunity*, 7, no. 8 (Aug. 1929).

86. *Albon L. Holsey, "The C.M.A. Stores Face the Chains."* Opportunity, *July 1929. Describes the cooperative efforts of black businessmen in Montgomery* *and other southern cities to face the competition of white-owned commercial chains.*

On August 10, 1928, a dozen Negro grocers in Montgomery, Alabama met and organized the Colored Merchants' Association and agreed to operate their stores as C.M.A. Stores. H. C. Ball was elected president and David F. Lowe, Jr., secretary.

The idea of this cooperative merchandizing effort initiated with A. C. Brown, who for more than twenty years has been a successful grocer in Montgomery. Sharing alike Mr. Brown's enthusiasm was Mr. David F. Lowe (since deceased), one of the pioneer merchants of Montgomery. The Association was organized in Mr. Lowe's store. At the present time there are fourteen stores in the organization and each member reports from twenty to sixty per cent increases in gross volume as a result of the new plan of operation.

The Association meets every Tuesday night at a member store at which time their purchasing needs are combined and on the day following, the wholesale grocers in Montgomery are asked to quote prices on the large quantity orders. Originally, Mr. Ball, the president, did all of the buying. Later a buying committee was formed with Mr. Ball as chairman. The members of the committee are assigned the task of securing bids on certain related commodities such as meat and lard, butter and eggs, flour and fee stuffs, sugar and rice. Since Mr. Ball serves as buyer without salary, the committee plan was adopted, at his suggestion, to spread the details and thus relieve him of some of the burdens which the increasing business necessitated.

Another function of the Association is to sell the merchandise as rapidly as possible so that the quick turn-over may lead to larger profits and more stable operating conditions. Consequently, they pool their advertising appropriations, and once each week in a ten-inch, three-column advertisement announce their specials and bargains in the *Montgomery Advertiser* and *Montgomery Journal*—daily newspapers in Montgomery. In addition to the advertising in the daily papers, a reproduction of the newspaper copy is distributed as hand bills to all the colored homes in the vicinity of each store. At least a half dozen staple products such as lard, sugar, bacon, etc., are featured each week at special prices, while other bargains such as flour, canned goods, etc., are listed as second specials.

Mr. A. C. Brown, in commenting on the history of the organization, said, "In the face of the stiffest competition which we have ever known, we decided that such an organization was the only method by which we could preserve our business."

The Colored Merchants' Association in Montgomery affiliates with the Local Negro Buisness League in Montgomery and Mr. Morris Smith, president of the Montgomery, League, invited the Secretary of the National League to visit Montgomery and see something of the work which the C.M.A. Stores were doing. Consequently a meeting was arranged in November, 1928, and the Secretary of the National League met the Colored Merchants' Association as a group and later visited their stores.

The Montgomery plan was laid before Dr. R. R. Moton, President of the National Negro Business League, and he immediately decided that the League should undertake to spread the idea of the C.M.A. Stores to other cities. The Secretary of the League was, therefore, duly authorized to work out plans for extending this cooperative merchandising idea into other communities. About the same time a request came from Mr. W. S. Scales, president of the Local Business League in Winston-Salem, North Carolina, for a representative from the National League to come and help to stimulate interest in the League's work. Winston-Salem was then selected as the next city to undertake to organize a Colored Merchants' Association.

It is necessary to briefly retrace our steps in order to fully understand the details of the Winston-Salem project. Several years ago the writer was invited by Mrs. A. D. Zuber, who was then the teacher of Home Economics at Tuskegee Institute, to deliver a series of talks to the students of her classes. These talks covered in a general way the subject of Better Buying and the Economic Value of Advertising. Following the talks, a demonstration of nationally advertised merchandise was arranged under the direction of the Tuskegee Home Economics Department. The value and importance of these talks may be judged by a letter which we have recieved from one of the young women who was a member of that class and who has since graduated, and become a home manager:

> Since I have married, more and more I realized the significance of your talks. Most of the things I buy have been standard advertised merchandize, but once in a while I let the desire for a bargain get the better of my good judgment and I buy an unadvertised product, which invariably proves unsatisfactory. So I have about convinced myself that such buying is just an expensive experiement.

In February, 1929, a conference of the Executives of the Grocery Industry was called by the United States Department of Commerce. This conference was held in Louisville because previously Louisville had been selected for a survey of the retail and wholesale grocery business to determine what wastes in the business could be eliminated; and correspondingly, how profits in that buisness might be increased and stabilized. The

Secretary of the National League was invited to attend this conference. While there, he met Dr. Carl Dipman, editor of the Progressive Grocer. Dr. Dipman was a conference speaker and had set up in Louisville a model grocery store; a store twenty-seven by forty feet, which is so arranged that it can handle an annual gross buisness of from $75,000 to $100,000 with an average stock of $3,000.

The Montgomery Association, the tie-up with national advertisers and the model grocery store were the three major ideas combined in the "Winston-Salem Experiment" as we called it in the beginning. We arrived in Winston-Salem on the 15th of April and immediately there was called a meeting of the retail grocers of Winston-Salem to whom the plan of organization of the Association was presented. Naturally, there was some reluctance at first, but one or two men, such as A. L. Hanes, attended the first meeting and stuck from the very beginning throughout the entire intensive endeavor.

By April 22nd, a few of the grocers had agreed to form the Association and pledged to begin operation as C.M.A. Stores on Saturday, May 4th. Much hard work was ahead in order that everything might be ready for the opening date under the new plan. Customer interest had to be stimulated and the model store set up.

Through the courtesy of Dr. S. G. Atkins, President of the Winston-Salem Teachers' College, arrangements were made for the home economics students of the College and the home economics students from the high school which is nearby to hear a series of five lectures on Better Buying, beginning Monday, April 22nd. Through the courtesy of Mrs. J. L. Maxwell, Executive Secretary, these lectures were repeated in the evening at the Y.W.C.A. for the benefit of the housewives of the city. As a climax to the week's lectures, the demonstration of nationally advertised merchandise was held in the auditorium of the Teachers' College on Saturday, April 27th. Forty-six national advertisers cooperated by supplying educational literature and a generous supply of delicious foods. The Home Economics teachers of the College and high school formed an assisting committee to help with the demonstration. The committee members were as follows: Miss Harriet E. Harris, Teachers' College, Chairman; Miss Camilla R. Stinson, Teachers' College; Miss Pinkie E. Thrift, Teachers' College; Miss Glee Willoughby, High School; Miss Alberta Baynard, High School.

Twenty-four women students were assigned to the various tables and booths, and the following refreshments were served free to the guests: Armour's Star Ham sandwiches made with Lowe Brothers bread, Lady Anne Coffee (Vaughn Coffee Mills) with pure cream and Crystal Domino Sugar, Pillsbury's Hot Cakes with Airline Honey and Karo Syrup, hot biscuits (Obelisk) with Nucoa, Welch's Grape Juice Punch with Nabisco Wafers, Best Foods Mayonnaise with Sunshine Crackers, etc.

The hot cakes and biscuits were cooked for each guest on a Hotpoint Electric Range which was loaned through the courtesy of the southern Public Utilities Company of Winston-Salem. A local furniture store set up a model four-room house in the auditorium with every modern convenience. More than four hundred persons were served and three thousand pieces of literature were distributed.

By this time Winston-Salem was beginning to ask questions and it was apparent that some very excellent results were going to be realized.

The next step in our program was to remodel one of the grocery stores according to the plans and specifications which we brought with us from Louisville. The store of Mr. James A. Ellington, 723 East Seventh Street, was selected and we began work remodeling his store on Monday night, April 29th. By working at night we were able to get the store remodeled and a fresh stock of goods placed on his shelves by midnight Friday, May 3rd.

Another step in the process of store improvement was the installation of a uniform system of record-keeping in the colored stores. The system was based upon the findings of the Louisville survey. In order to get the job started a meeting was held with the upper classes boys of the high school. This was done through the courtesy of the principal, Mr. J. A. Carter. We explained to the boys, first, what we were attempting to do in Winston-Salem; also we told them of the system of record-keeping which we had worked out and stated that it was necessary to take inventories of the colored stores at once. We emphasized that we had no funds with which to pay them for their service, but that this would give them an opportunity to learn at first hand some fundamental principles of retail business. We asked for ten boys to volunteer, and twenty-three responded. These boys were placed under the general supervision of John Hope, Jr., of Morehouse College, Atlanta, who was voluntarily assisting in the Winston-Salem campaign. He organized the boys and supervised the first inventory which was taken in the Ellington store.

On Saturday, May, 4th, the C.M.A. Stores of Winston-Salem were thrown open to the public. The afternoon before, the announcement appeared in the daily papers as a paid-for advertisement. All that day there was a steady stream of colored patrons entering the colored stores, and at the end of the first day's business, the records of the stores showed from thirty to one hundred fifty per cent increased business.

Winston-Salem was at last awake and everyone was talking. The housewives were taking a new interest in the colored stores, and the store keepers themselves were amazed at the results.

As a climax to the campaign, Dr. R. R. Moton, President of the National League, addressed the Winston-Salem citizens on Monday evening, May 6th. On the same platform with Dr. Moton was Dr. Gordon James, Director of the Domestic Commerce Division of the United States Department of Commerce. The people turned out in large numbers for they were thoroughly convinced by this time that the principle of cooperation in Negro business had been demonstrated. The messages of Dr. James and Dr. Moton brought added interest to the effort. The heads of the commercial departments of Hampton Institute and Bluefield Institute brought some of their advanced students to Winston-Salem for the meeting on May 6th and to inspect the model store. Other visitors included Mr. P. B. Young, Editor of the Norfolk *Journal and Guide,* and Messrs. H. C. Ball and F. M. Lowe, representing the C.M.A. Stores in Montgomery, Alabama.

The Business League's campaign in Winston-Salem ended May 6th. At that time there were twenty-four members of the Colored Merchants' Association. Since then, eleven more have joined. The Officers of the Winston-Salem Association are: J. H. Lowe, President; J. H. Harrison, Vice-President; R. E. Walker, Treasurer; W. S. Scales, Association Buyer, C. A. Irvin, Secretary.

From the very beginning of the campaign, the daily papers of Winston-Salem gave unstinted support to our efforts, and the advertising of the Negro grocery stores in these papers was a new point of contact between the races.

Some of the other benefits may be enumerated as follows:

(a)   The increased business of the colored stores will necessitate the employment of several new clerks.

(b)   Some of the high school boys who volunteered to help with the inventories of the grocery stores will be hired as clerks in these stores.

(c)   The more rapid stock turnovers mean greater and quicker profits for the colored grocers.

(d)   The C.M.A. Stores are paying cash for their goods and securing larger discounts.

(e)   The C.M.A. Stores are selling mostly for cash on their big days, Friday and Saturday. Eventually their business will be all cash in selling and buying.

(f)   The advertised merchandise which was displayed and sampled during the demonstration moved very rapidly from the shelves of the C.M.A. Stores. This has caused national advertisers to ask some serious questions concerning the buying power of Negroes.

(g) Along with better buying there has come to the C.M.A. Stores better selling because of reduced costs of operation.

(h) The model store demonstrated maximum convenience and maximum attractiveness.

In promoting the better merchandising plan in Winston-Salem, the National Negro Business League had the active interest and support of such organizations as the United States Department of Commerce, the Association of National Advertisers, the Associated Negro Press, the Commission on Inter-racial Cooperation, the National Association of Retail Grocers, and the National Urban League.

Dr. Carl Dipman, Editor of the *Progressive Grocer* wired: "Hearty congratulations on your model store and the great work you are doing. Am sure your efforts will prove a great constructive force not only for Winston-Salem but will be felt throughout the country."

Mr. M. L. Toumle, Secretary of the National Wholesale Grocers' Association wrote: "Such efforts as you are making to bring about more intelligent and better methods of cooperation between wholesalers and retailers are fundamentally sound."

The Norfolk Journal and Guide said: "If it could be possible to carry the plan (Winston-Salem campaign) to other cities in rapid succession, Negro business would undergo a real rehabilitation."

The Winston-Salem campaign has provided it "can be done" and the idea is destined to spread into other communities. Plans for the future include a uniform color scheme for the C.M.A. Stores, an emblem or trademark for the stores, and expert Negro buyers for local associations— thus opening an entirely new field for the young men of our race.

ANNOUNCING

THE C.M.A. STORES

(Colored Merchants Association)

An Organization of Progressive Local Grocers

Under our new organization plans, the member stores will be attractive and convenient. Cooperative buying will enable each store to maintain a uniform, standard service and to sell

Quality Merchandise at Lowest Prices

Cash Specials for Saturday May 4th

Lard (fine quality) per pound 12½c	Sugar, 2 pounds for 11c
Flour (excellent quality) 12 pounds for 48c	Rice, 4 pounds for 25c
Octagon soap, 6 bars	Tomatoes (No. 2 full pack)

for 25c

California Yellow Cling
Peaches (Large size—best
quality) 24c

2 cans for 25c

Lowe Bros. Blue Ribbon
Bread, loaf 9c

These and many other bargains will be offered at our opening sale Saturday,

May 4th—Bargain Tables in Each Store
Visit Ellington's—the Demonstration Store
723 East Seventh Street
Same Prices at Each Store—Orders Delivered—
Telephone Orders Will Receive the Same Prompt and Courteous Attention
"There is a C.M.A. Store in Your Neighborhood"

W. T. Christian
Ridge Ave. and 9th St.
Phone 1345

F. A. Carrigan
4th and Linden Sts.
Phone 1639-J

James A. Ellington
723 East 7th Street
Phone 1223-W

Dan Anderson
1100 N. Trade St.

Marcus Graham
1001 Vargrave St.
Phone 9200

J. C. Christian
2301 N. Cherry St.
Phone 9283

Royal Puryear
716 East 2nd St.
Phone 1359

Charles Robinson
Salem

Samuel Farmer
410 East 7th St.

Aaron Davis
1439 East 11th St.
Phone 4029-J

Hairston Grocery Co.
1200 Cleveland Ave.
Phone 1547

T. H. Hooper
700 Patterson Ave.

L. C. Kerns
1292 Shuttle St.
Phone 3410

Sam Dismuke
12 N. Main St.

K. D. Craig
Salem

Curtis Graham
Glenn Ave./Gale

A. L. Hanes
18 Park Avenue
Phone 9255

R. E. Walker
2130 Waughtown
Phone 4315-J

F. S. Simmons
1230 Centerville
Phone 2493-W

James Craig
Clements Road

W. F. Wilson
200 East 7th St.

Bakeries
Lowe Brothers, 936 N. Trade Street
Phone 2456
David Stevens, 314 East 4th Street

Advertisement appearing in *Winston-Salem Journal* of May 4th, 1929.

SOURCE Albon L. Holsey, "The C.M.A. Stores Face the Chains." *Opportunity,* 7, no. 7 (July 1929): 210–13.

87. *Father William M. Markoe, S.J., "Recollections of My Experiences in the Field of Race Relations (1900–1925)." Reveals aspects of race relations, particularly white Catholic–Black relations, in St. Paul, Minn., and St. Louis, Mo.; opens with statements comparing work among blacks and Native Americans.*

1922

While with the Indians I kept writing and publishing articles in behalf of the Negro. In 1922 I wrote a brief history of the Catholic mission work among American Negroes. This was copyrighted by the Continental Press, Inc. in 1923, and published by the Bodley Press, Inc., Boston, as a part of the work entitled, "Builders of the Nation." This was a work of several volumes composed of contributions from many authors covering a wide range of subjects.

In working with the Sioux I found it difficult to achieve a meeting of minds between myself and the Indians. This was in spite of the fact that from childhood I had a kind of romantic admiration for the American Indian. This lack of rapport was due chiefly I believe to a partial language barrier, the skepticism of the Indian concerning white people in general, and the complete difference in cultural background. I experienced none of these handicaps in establishing a meeting of minds between myself and Negroes. I was practically never conscious of belonging to another race and, on the contrary, habitually felt that I was one of them. This became more and more true as I sympathized with their grievances and fought to alleviate them.

During my second and last year with the Indians I began to compile a classified scientific file on the Negro and the subject of race relations. My method followed the Dewey library system. In time my file contained thousands of notes, clippings, and references. I was now subscribing to a number of Negro newspapers and magazines. I was reading Negro authors and collecting books written by them and others on the question of race relations.

1923

In the summer of 1923 I arrived in St. Louis to study Theology at St. Louis University. I had not been to St. Louis since I passed through the city enroute from Florissant to Spokane in 1918. On that occasion I called at the Visitation convent to say good-bye to my younger sister, now Sister Mary Joseph, and to my older sister who had also joined the Visitation Community and taken the name of Sister Anne Marie. Also I said farewell for the last time to my aunt, Mother Evangelista. She died in the presence of my brother, John Markoe, S.J., while I was in Spokane.

In joining the Jesuit Community at the University I was reunited to some old compatriots who had worked with me among the Negroes in both the Florissant and Spokane areas. Chief among these was Mr. Austin Bork and Mr. Charles Owens. The latter had been a boon companion and helper at Mt. St. Michaels. He had come to St. Louis the year before I arrived. He seemed only to be waiting for me to come and join him. His first words after greeting me were: "Bill, there are so many tens of thousands of Negroes living at the door of this University that they seem to be hanging out of the windows of the hundreds of tenements by their eye brows." This remark was apropos in light of the fact that heretofore he and I had had to walk for miles searching for Negroes. Another great helper who had often joined with me in such a search in the Spokane area, and who was one of the most zealous and brilliant men I ever knew, was Mr. Joseph Ledit, S.J. But, alas, he was too brilliant! He had been sent to Europe to study theology. I was not to see him again for some years.

It did not take long to get to work. Like Abraham and Lot, I told Mr. Bork I would go east of Grand Boulevard and he could go west. While Mr. Bork with Mr. Edward Maher surveyed the whole western area from Grand to Taylor Avenue, and from Washington Boulevard as far north as St. Louis Avenue, Mr. Owens and I explored from Grand to the River and from Washington to Cass Avenue. We met hundreds and before long became acquainted with thousands of Negroes. Never had we met more delightful or friendly people. In our excursions we met not only those living on the street or avenue in the front, but we also covered all the alleys and met those living in the rear. For the first time I discovered residential alleys. In taking addresses by street and number we would also always have to note "front" or "rear." As in previous experiences we found the people to have most attractive and interesting personalities, a remarkable degree of culture and refinement, to possess a wonderful sense of humor, and to be most friendly. They were also the soul of hospitality. We never lacked something to eat!

The poorer Negroes lived east of Grand Avenue. Many of them had come only recently from the South. The first world war with the resulting need for labor in the North had started this migration. West of Grand Avenue was where, for the most part, the better to do, higher class, more educated people lived. When I had been a lay student at St. Louis University in 1912 no Negroes to my knowledge lived west of Grand Avenue. Grand Avenue was the dividing line between the whites and the so-called black belt. Now the dividing line had receded as far as Taylor Avenue, and in spots even further west.

Our first efforts were directed toward getting acquainted with as many people as possible and in familiarizing ourselves with neighborhoods. Connecting the front of a street with the rear there were passages called "gangways." These were a great convenience as it saved one going all the way to the corner to get to the rear. Before long we were acquainted with just about every gangway between Grand Avenue and the River on all the streets. The tenements swarmed with families. Each family would have from one to three rooms. The buildings ranged from three to six stories in height. We climbed hundreds of rickety stairs knocking on every door on every floor to meet the people. The living facilities were abominable and woefully sub-standard. Every tenement seemed to be in complete disrepair and suffering from neglect. Of course, the Negroes were only tenants and could barely scrape together the exorbitant rents they had to pay let alone keep in repair the landlords' buildings.

After becoming acquainted with thousands of Negroes we would continue to call on them repeatedly, taking block by block, to become better known. We especially gained the devoted affection of the children who would not wait for us to arrive but would watch for us and sally forth to meet us. It was largely through them, and our kindness to them, that we won the confidence and the hearts of the parents. In this visitation work, we brought up the subject of religion only gradually. Maybe we would simply leave some holy pictures which were highly appreciated. We soon began to discover that approximately half of all these people were affiliated with no church and had never been baptized. It is a mistake to think that all Negroes are either Baptists or Methodists, or are some kind of Pentecostals or are even Christian in any sense, other than naturally having Christian sentiments in their hearts. And as heretofore we found that these people never knew that they could be Catholics. They thought the Catholic Church was a white man's church. This illusion of theirs spoke volumes concerning our neglect of the Negro. Here they were living in a great metropolitan, largely Catholic, community, many of them for generations, and they did not even know that they could be Catholics, much less had they ever been invited to become such! Why did we deliberately pursue the Indian to save his soul, and at the same time inconsistently and deliberately by-pass the thousands and thousands of religiously inclined Negroes at our door steps?

Having gained the friendship and confidence of thousands of people through hundreds of visitations throughout the whole area east of Grand Avenue our next move was to plan mission centers for those who manifested interest in the Catholic faith. We naturally set our sights on an old Jesuit church in the middle of the field we had been cultivating. This was St. Joseph's Church at the corner of Eleventh and Biddle Streets whose pastor was Father Ferdinand D. Moeller, S.J. His was an old German parish from which most of the German parishioners had moved away with the influx of thousands of Negroes. St. Joseph's Church was second in size only to the new Cathedral on Lindell Boulevard. Practically all of the parish's old geographic area was now inhabited by Negroes. A few German families remained and others who had left returned for Mass on Sundays because of sentimental attachment to the old church. Also a parish school, much diminished in size, was still functioning for white children only.

This was the situation when we called on Father Moeller, the pastor, to ask for permission to assemble Negroes in his church to instruct them in the faith. Finally he hesitatingly told us we could use a small chapel at the rear of the vast church with a separate entrance on Eleventh Street. So here we began to catechize our first St. Louis Colored converts. Our catechumens consisted of both adults and children. To instruct them we had to enlist the help of more Scholastics, and soon we were forced to solicit the help of students from the city's Catholic colleges.

Everything was functioning peacefully and successfully as the holy season of Christmas approached. We naturally began to plan a Christmas party with all the trimmings for our flock. The pupils at the Visitation Academy donated several hundred stockings, every one loaded with candy and nuts, with a toy attached. We also begged a barrel of fine apples, and a tree which we nicely decorated, and finally one of the Scholastics volunteered to play the role of Santa Claus. Invitations were issued to all and sundry Negroes in the whole area in the form of dodgers that we had printed for the purpose. All was ready for the great feast of Christmas and the party. All had been prepared with the pastor's approval.

Then bang! The ax fell! I received a phone call from Father Moeller saying he wanted to see me. This was about two days before Christmas. Our party was planned for Christmas afternoon. I hastened to the St. Joseph rectory and was told by Father Moeller that several of his white parishioners were objecting to our work in his parish for the Negroes and were vehemently objecting to our planned Christmas party to be held at the rear of the church in the basement. Consequently, he was forced to tell us to cancel the Christmas party and to cease all our activities for Negroes in his parish!

Now we were really on a spot. The party was ready, the guests were invited, but there was no place to hold it. Then the happy thought came to me to seek refuge with Monsignor Timothy Dempsey, the friend of the poor and underprivileged, and pastor of the nearby St. Patrick's Church on Sixth and Biddle Streets. We called on Monsignor Dempsey and explained our plight. "Sure," he said, "Bring them all to St. Patrick's. You can have your party in our school hall, and you can conduct your mission in our church. Sure, if we cannot make good Catholics out of them, we will make good Democrats." That was the end of our mission at St. Joseph's and the beginning of our mission at St. Patrick's Parish. We were turned away by our own Jesuit parish. We were embraced by a diocesan priest's parish.

But how did we avoid giving scandal to our people? We organized about a dozen Scholastics, and on the day of the Christmas party we stationed a couple of them at the St. Joseph's hall and as the hundreds of people began to come they explained to them that the hall was too small (literally true) and then they directed each new arrival to another Scholastic on the corner of Eleventh and Biddle who passed them on to another Scholastic down the street, and so on to another, until all of our guests were safely in the large St. Patrick's parish hall where a wonderful party was enjoyed by all. To this day these Negroes do not know that they were ejected from St. Joseph's Parish by the narrow minded prejudice of a few parishioners and what we thought was the weakness of their pastor, an old man who wished to avoid trouble and have peace at any price. The work continued at St. Patrick's and we began to have converts baptized, children and adults, and received into the Church. . . .

In conducting our catechetical centers at St. Joseph's and St. Patrick's Churches we began to be intrigued by a large, silent, tomb-like church on the corner of Nineteenth and Lucas Streets which we usually passed as we walked deeper into the ghetto to make our visitations to Negro families. We never saw anyone go into or come out of this church. Next to it stood a brick residence that appeared to be a rectory. Finally our curiosity got the best of us. So one day with my Scholastic companion I boldly rang the bell at the front door of the residence. A congenial woman opened the door and we asked her if a priest lived in the house. She invited us in and introduced herself as Miss Mary Adrian, the priest's sister and housekeeper. Soon we were seated and having a pleasant visit with Father Adrian, one of four priest brothers in the archdiocese.

We asked Father Adrian if his church was still functioning. He answered that it was but not for long, because the Baptists were negotiating to buy it. He told us he had already sold the school to the Langdon furniture Company as a warehouse. He, himself, was going to retire to St. Mary's Infirmary on Papin Street where he would act as resident chaplain. He said there was nothing more to be done in the parish as the people had all moved away. His was an old German parish and he told us only three men remained. The name of the parish was St. Nicholas.

I began reflecting on the situation he described. Within his parish limits thousands of people were living. On a hot evening some would sit on his church steps. I had personally visited most of these people in their

poor tenement homes. About half of them were unbaptized. In their midst
stood the large beautiful old St. Nicholas Church. There stood a substantial comfortable rectory. Alas, the school and the nuns were gone! What
did Father Adrian mean when he said the people were all gone? Are not
Negroes people? Wasn't the church and school and rectory built to save
souls? Didn't the thousands of people, wonderful men, women, adoles-
cents, and children still in the parish have souls? Is a good shepherd responsible only for the sheep in the fold and not for those wondering and
straying outside it? Didn't Christ die for all? Wasn't His Church meant for
all?

Finally I made bold to ask Father Adrian if he would object to our
using his church to instruct Negroes in the faith. He answered that he had
no objection at all. He was retiring before long and we could do what we
liked in his church. He even said we were welcome to use his baptistry in
which one of our priests could baptize converts we might make with the
grace of God. This conference with Father Adrian took place on a Friday.
We immediately sallied forth to invite the many Negroes to his parish to
come to the church the following Sunday afternoon for catechism and
Benediction. We continued scouring the neighborhood on Saturday. On
Sunday afternoon we had one hundred and sixty Colored people, adults
and children, in the church, all non-Catholics, learning the fundamentals
of the Catholic faith.

Within nine months after coming to St. Louis in 1923 we had over
two hundred converts baptized. Their names were all duly entered in the
various parish baptismal registers and in a private register that we Scholastics kept at St. Louis University. Later we ever had individual photographs
made of all the children we had baptized. We continued carrying on our
centers east and west of Grand Avenue. By now many nuns and lay cate-
chists, Colored and white, were enlisted in the work. A Catholic young
woman Colored teacher at the Banneker Public School, Miss Barbara
Hudlin, personally led many of her pupils to the St. Nicholas Center.

1924

. . . Having our St. Nicholas experience behind us we felt like veterans and
boldly called on Father Rogers, the pastor at St. Malachy's. He received
us graciously. We asked him about the state of affairs in his parish. He
informed us that there were only twelve men left in his parish, that they
all lived on Clark Avenue west of Grand Avenue, and that they attended
the Jesuit St. Francis Xavier Church on Grand and Lindell Boulevards,
commonly called the College Church, being on the campus of St. Louis

University. His school was long since closed. The Sisters had sold their once flourishing academy across the street. He supported himself and what was left of the parish by having a large bingo party every Sunday afternoon in his church hall. This was patronized by sentimental old timers who came back to their old church to help keep it afloat. A few would also return on occasion to assist at Mass on Sunday.

We then told Father Rogers of our achievements at St. Nicholas of which he had heard rumors. We asked him if it wouldn't be possible to achieve the same results in his church and school. He answered that we possibly could, but that he had been appointed to take care of the remnants of St. Malachy's, the handful of remaining white parishioners. He was not responsible for the Colored people in his parish. However, he said, if his remaining parishioners had no objection to our using their church and school for a missionary enterprise such as we had inaugurated at St. Nicholas, he would have no personal objection. So he said he would call a meeting of the twelve men left who attended the College Church and present our proposal to them for their approval. We were to hear from him after this meeting. Finally after two weeks he phoned and asked me to come and see him. When we arrived he gently informed us that his men had met and had unanimously passed a resolution to the effect that rather than have the "niggers" use the St. Malachy's plant they would prefer to see it turned into a pickle factory.

Baffled, we returned to the University walking through the tens of thousands of Negroes who had engulfed the whole of St. Malachy parish area. There the Colored population was even more densely concentrated than in St. Nicholas Parish. When I next saw the Archbishop I appealed to him over the heads of the prejudiced St. Malachy's people, but in vain! So St. Malachy's School was allowed to crumble to ruins, while the whole plant deteriorated, until sixteen years later when the Archbishop begged the Jesuits to take over the church. By then it was nearly too late!

SOURCE Papers of Father William M. Markoe, S.J., Archives Division (Marquette University Library, Milwaukee, Wisconsin).

88. *Letter from Fremont L. Pugsley, lawyer, Henniker, N.H., to NAACP, 8 Dec. 1922. Describes defeat of the Dyer Anti-Lynching bill in the Senate; suggests that southern senators who opposed the bill should be impeached for violation of their oaths of office.*

Dear Sir: I would call your attention to LAWLESSNESS IN HIGH PLACES. If I am correctly informed, the Dyer Anti-lynching bill has been defeated in the United States senate by the action of a minority group of senators, mostly southern, and without any manifest intention on their part to aid in the enactment of any legislation whatever on this subject. They seem rather to be opposed to the enactment of any legislation by Congress against lynching. Such opposition amounts to a refusal to give effect to the very important provisions of the federal constitution.

Article 5 of Amendments to the Constitution of the United States declares: "No person shall be deprived of life, liberty or property without due process of law."

Article 14 of the same says: "All persons born or naturalized in the United States, and subject to the jurisdiction thereof, are citizens of the United States and of the state wherein they reside. No state shall make or enforce any law which shall abridge the privileges or immunities of citizens of the United States; nor shall any state deprive any person of life, liberty or property without due process of law, nor deny to any person within its jurisdiction the equal protection of the laws."

Article 6 of the Constitution says: "The senators and representatives before mentioned, and the members of the several state legislatures and all executive and judicial officers, both of the United States and of the several states, shall be bound by oath or affirmation to support this constitution."

Now a lynching, as usually performed, is the most violent manner possible for depriving a person of life without due process of law. It is therefore a most flagrant defiance and violation of the constitution of the United States. This offense is by no means rare. There have been an average of one hundred and seven lynchings annually in our country for the last thirty years, and between eighty-nine and ninety per cent of these have occurred in fourteen of our most southerly states. The percentage of persons punished by state authorities for taking part in lynchings I have not at hand, but it appears to be very small. Of course, none have been punished by federal authority, for lack of law in support of the federal constitution; yet the persons lynched were, in nearly all cases, citizens of the United States as well as of the states wherein they were lynched. It is evident that those states wherein most of the lynchings take place assume little or no responsibility for enforcing either their own laws or the constitution of the United States, though their officials are bound by their oaths or affirmations to do so.

In view of the foregoing law and facts, how can a representative or a senator in Congress consistently refuse to enact law, in support of the constitution, to punish lynching? The chief function of Congress is to enact laws for the purpose of supporting and enforcing the constitution. Every representative and every senator has made oath to do this very thing. Nevertheless, when law is required to protect the lives of citizens of the United States, according to provisions of the constitution, a sufficient number of senators, a minority of them, in spite of their oaths to support the constitution, have, by the disreputable method of filibuster, prevented the enactment of any such law!

Is not such action a plain violation of their oaths? Does it not practically amount to perjury? Is it not sufficient ground for their impeachment and removal from office? It seems to me that it is unless they shall repent forthwith and aid in the passing of the necessary law.

s o u r c e Theodore Kornwiebel, ed., *Federal Surveillance of Afro-Americans, 1917–1925* (Frederick, Md.: University Publications of America, 1985) (hereinafter cited as *FSAA*), Record Group 60, Department of Justice, Reel 14, frame nos. 0448–0449.

89. *Report of resolution, Rhode Island State Sunday School Association: Promoting Religious Education in Rhode Island, 17 Oct. 1922. Supports the passage of the Dyer Anti-Lynching bill; decries the existence of organizations that favor violence over due process of law.*

Dear Mr. President: The following resolution was passed at the Forty-Second Annual Convention of the Rhode Island State Sunday School Association held in Providence, October 12, 1922:—

> Resolved:—That this State Sunday School Convention issue protest against the evil known as lynching, and against the existence of all anti-social and unpatriotic organizations whether secret or open, which favor violence as against the due process of law;
> And be it further Resolved:—That we send to the President of the United States and to our representatives in Congress, respectful requests that the Dyer Anti-Lynching Bill may be passed during the next session of Congress.

In harmony with this resolution and speaking for the Association, may I respectfully urge you to use all the influences at your command to secure the passage of this bill, which will do a great deal to remove a shameful blot from our country.

s o u r c e *FSAA*, Record Group 60, Department of Justice, Reel 14, frame no. 0471.

90. *Letter from Ara Lee Settle, Section 6, Armstrong Technical School, Washington, D.C., to President Warren G. Harding, 18 June 1922. Letter of 15-year-old student calling for support of Dyer Anti-Lynching bill; reminds the president of blacks' service to the nation during the recent war.*

Dear Sir: I am taking the liberty of intruding this letter upon you, because I feel that the issues involved are as important as any questions that have ever been pressed upon you. It is to urge your support of the Dyer Bill.

Mr. President, lynching has been committed in the south for many years, but when the last presidential election took place, practically every colored boy and girl in America was for Warren G. Harding as president. Why did we want you? The answer was: He is a Republican and will stop that terrible crime—lynching. You were elected, but now and then there could be heard of a few lynchings. Mr. President, why do they lynch the Negro? Has not he done his full share or bit in the making of this new land? When America was fighting for independence, was not Crispus Attucks, a [N]egro, the first man killed? There are many others that could be named, but time and space will not permit me. When the trumpet was blown for civil strife, did not the Negro give his life as well as the Anglo-Saxon? During the world war, Negro boys also sacrificed their lives as well, and as bravely as the white man, that democracy might rule the earth. This reminds me of our glorious song "My Country 'tis of Thee, Sweet land of Liberty." Mr. President, you are aware of the fact that we have not our full liberty but still we sing the song by faith in the future.

I admit that there are some lawless Negroes in America, as well as whites, capable of committing horrible crimes. All people are not as good as others, but, Mr. President, what good does lynching do? One man may be lynched for a crime of which another has committed. It does not tend to make a nation better, it only brings race prejudice and hatred. What good or use is the law, if the lynchers are going to put the law in their own hands. Mr. President, imagine yourself about to be lynched for something of which you know nothing about. Men sieze you from some place of refuge, carry you to the heart of the town, place a rope around you and burn you, while men, women and children are jeering amidst all your pain and agony. It is enough to make one ashamed not to use his full influence against this horrible crime.

A bill has been introduced in Congress by Representative Dyer (a Republican) to prevent lynching, or make it a criminal offense. Mr. President, it is incumbent upon you, the chief executive of all Americans to urge the passage of this bill. If lynching is permitted in the south, finally it will spread to the north, doing nothing but kindling the flames of racial and personal hatred, and sowing the seeds of internal strife. There are some courageous and conscientious senators who are in favor of the passage of the bill, but, Mr. President, we are looking to you to see it through. If this country had more men such as Mr. Dyer it would be "Sweet land of Liberty."

One might say, push the bill away until a more opportune time presents itself when they would be more able to debate on it. But as a well known man said, "Today is the only real day promised" Why not do that today and hurl lynching into a bottomless pit to remain forever? Mr. President, we are looking and pleading to you.

During the war the colored people were very patriotic, they bought Liberty Bonds, War Saving Stamps, Thrift Stamps, and meatless, sugarless, wheatless days, also they crocheted, knitted and embroideried for the boys over there while they were fighting for "dear old America," but mind you some of the same Colored boys have since returned to America and have been lynched in a way that has been heretofore explained.

When lynching has been expurged, then we may all sing from our hearts with a true meaning:

> My country 'tis of thee,
> Sweet land of Liberty,
> Of thee I Sing.
> Land where my fathers died,
> Land of the Pilgrims pride,
> Frome every mountain side,
> Let Freedom ring.

Once more, Mr. Harding, we are looking to you, to you, to you.

SOURCE *FSAA,* Record Group 60, Department of Justice, Reel 14, frame nos. 0485–0486.

91. *Letter from F. Cyrus, Corsicana, Texas, to President Warren G. Harding, 15 May 1922. Encloses newsclipping about three blacks recently lynched; advocates support for the Dyer Anti-lynching bill.*

Hon. Warren G. Harding, President of the United States America: Supreme Executive of its Administrative affairs and Defender of its Constitution wherein it reads, in art. V. No person shall be held to answer for a capital or otherwise Infamous crime unless on a presentment—or Indictment—of a Grandjury—where as this article has been grossly violated in the County of Freestone Town of Kirven State of Texas By Burning a live 3 colerod men and hanging one By an Infuriated mob. had they been given a trial by Jury they Could have Proved their Innocence it Could Easily been Proven two white men committed the crime

I am also sending you the news paper account of the affair. For Humanity sake and justice to an oppressed a Composite part of this Federal nation the Afro Americans urge the Present Congress to pass the Dyer anti lynching Bill. Congress should pass a bill to disfranchise *every man who Participates in Lynching*

I am a Poor Colerod American with no protection for my life and Property. I give my name But do not desire it be used altho a letter from you in answer to this would be gratifying and kept strictly

SOURCE *FSAA,* Record Group 60, Department of Justice, Reel 14, frame nos. 0535–0536.

92. *Pamphlet, "Lest We Forget: The Old Story." Ca. 1923. Publication of the West Virginia Colored Bureau, Republican State Headquarters. Shows how blacks continued to remain active in electoral politics in the Mountain State at a time when blacks elsewhere faced the increasing impact of disfranchisement.*

Lest We Forget

The Old Story

The Republican Party was organized as a protest against Negro slavery and, under the leadership of the first Republican President, Abraham Lincoln, slavery was abolished. In Republican Congresses under the leadership of great Republican statemen the great war amendments to the Federal Constitution were adopted—the 13th prohibiting slavery and involuntary servitude; the 14th guaranteeing the protection of the freedmen in the enjoyment of life, liberty and property; the 15th giving the freedmen the right to vote.

The Democratic Party opposed the liberation of slaves and its leaders fought the great war amendments to the bitter end and, in States in which the party was in absolute control, nullified them as far as they could.

Every Republican President has given Negroes a share in the conduct of the government under which we live by appointing representative members of the race to high positions over the protest of the Democratic leaders.

Every Democratic President has refused to appoint Negroes to important positions and has permitted those employed or seeking employment under the civil service to be humiliated and discriminated against.

The Democratic Party is controlled and dominated by the 114 Democratic members of the United States Congress who are sure to be elected from the Bourbon South which has disfranchised and jim crowed the Negroes—which denies them equal educational advantages, holds them in peonage and lynches them and opposes laws to prevent lynching.

No Democratic President, however fair he may be, can give the Negro a square deal because to be elected he must depend upon the 114 electoral votes from the Southern States which remain Democratic because the Democratic Party has robbed the Negroes of those States of their ballots.

No Democratic Congress can pass legislation in the interest of Negroes because 114 Democratic Congressmen and Senators from those same Southern States will not permit it.

What About West Virginia?

The real progress of the Negroes of West Virginia began when the Republican Party came into power in the State.

For 40 years the Republican Party has frustrated attempts of the Democratic Party to have disfranchisement and jim crow car laws enacted in West Virginia.

Republican Legislatures have made more liberal appropriations for the Negro educational institutions than the Democratic Legislatures.

The Republican Party was responsible for the greatest industrial development of West Virginia has provided employment in the mines and other industries for thousands of Negroes, thus giving them the opportunity to leave the South with its oppression and to come to this land of opportunity.

Tangible Evidence of a "Square Deal"

During the past five years, Republican Legislatures have enacted the following laws urged by Negroes:

1. Establishment of Insane Asylum;
2. Establishment of Deaf and Blind School;
3. Establishment of Boys' Industrial School;
4. Establishment of Girls' Industrial Home;
5. Creation of Bureau of Negro Welfare and Statistics;
6. Passage of law prohibiting the showing of such plays and pictures as "The Birth of a Nation";
7. Passage of the strongest Anti-Lynching Law ever placed upon the statute books.

During the same time, Republican Legislatures have appropriated more than TWO MILLION DOLLARS for the support of Negro educational and eleemosynary institutions.

Under the present Republican State Administration, Negroes hold 37 positions (heads and employees in State institutions excepted.)

In counties and municipalities under Republican control, Negroes hold 67 elective and appointive positions.

There are four Negro members of the Republican State Executive Committee, one of whom is a woman, and 27 Negro members of the Republican County Executive Committees, 12 of whom are women.

There is not a single Negro holding a public office of any kind, either elective or appointive, in a county or city whose officials are members of the Democratic Party and no Negro is a member of any Democratic Committee.

In Republican Counties, there are more and better elementary and high schools for Negroes, they are more liberally supported, and terms are longer and the teachers are better paid than those in counties controlled by the Democratic Party.

The last Democratic Governor not only did not appoint Negroes as State Librarian and Assistant State Librarian, positions Negroes had held for 16 years under Republican Governors, but out of the 14 janitors appointed by Governor Cornwell only one was a Negro. The Democratic Party does not even permit us to wash spittoons at the State's expense, when it is in power.

What the Platforms Say

THE REPUBLICAN STATE CONVENTION held at Huntington in August, in its platform, said the following:

The Colored Citizen

The Republican Party in West Virginia has given to the citizens of the Negro race opportunities that have been denied them wherever the Democratic party is in the ascendancy. It has provided for the Negro political and economical equality and has protected him from racial prejudice. West Virginia is the only State south of the Mason and Dixon line where the Negro population has shown an increase in the last decade. Facilities for the education of colored citizens have enabled them to educate their children and the percent of illiteracy in this State among Negroes is lower than in any other State south of Pennsylvania. Appreciative of his freedom from racial prejudice and of his opportunities to make an honest living unmolested, and to educate his children, the Negro has come to West Virginia and found a place in the economic and civic life of the State.

Anti-Lynching Law

We call attention to the splendid anti-lynching law passed by the Republican Legislature of 1921, and heartily commend the Republican State Senate of the 1923 session for its prompt and effective killing of the bill to annul this law, which was introduced into and enthusiastically passed by the Democratic House of the same Legislature.

THE DEMOCRATIC STATE CONVENTION, in its platform adopted at Huntington in August, said nothing about the Negro, but pledged itself to abolish bureaus and curtail appropriations and every sane Negro knows from experience that when the Democratic Party begins cutting out departments, institutions and offices and cutting down expenses, the first and most severe cuts are the things, places and money for Negroes.

THE SOCIALIST AND FARMER-LABOR PARTIES on whose tickets LaFollette and Wheeler are running in this state said nothing about the Negro, but he may look for the worse if, by voting this ticket, Negroes aid the Democratic Party to elect its candidates. . . .

Lest We Forget

Negroes should see that they are registered and urge every other man and woman of your race to do the same, go to the polls early and vote the Republican ticket straight, as the only sure means of keeping the enemies of the political, educational and industrial progress of the Race out of office.

Lest we forget and, in forgetting, repent under the heel of the oppressor when memory is aroused too late,

VOTE THE REPUBLICAN TICKET

(Issued by the Colored Bureau, Republican State Headquarters.)

SOURCE Thaddeus E. Harris Papers, Miscellany, 1922–1933 (Manuscript Division, Jerkins Library, Duke University).

93. *Robert F. Leftridge, Philadelphia, Republican Presidential Campaign,*
"To the Colored Republican Voters of West Virginia: Published in the Interest
of the Candidacy of the Hon. Herbert Hoover for President." May 1928. Recog-
nizes the significance of the black vote in the Mountain State and appeals for
support.

To The
Colored Republican Voters
Of West Virginia

Published in the Interest of
the Candidacy of the

HON. HERBERT HOOVER
FOR PRESIDENT

Primaries to be held

TUESDAY, MAY 29th, 1928

It has been truly said by a great American, that a man is not fit to hold
high public office, or to do good work in our American democracy, unless
he is able to have genuine fellow feeling for, understanding of, and sympathy with his fellow Americans, whatever their creed, or their birthplace,
the section in which they live, or the work which they do, provided they
possess the only kind of Americanism that counts, the Americanism of the
spirit.

I believe that men in public office should have a keen and lively sense
of their obligation in civic matters, of their duty to help forward great
causes, and to strive for the betterment of conditions that are unjust to
their fellows, the men and women less fortunate in life. America was
founded in the belief that it is possible for men and women of diverse
habits, faiths, and breeds, to live together in understanding, peace and
friendship: So far as they could the founders of this great Republic wrote
tolerance into the Constitution.

As a group of people identified with a race who are in the minority,
and who since emancipation have been denied the right of responsibility
and successfully usurped of the natural and unalienable rights of mankind,
we should ever be zealous, and more than careful in our scrutiny of candidates presenting themselves for our franchise consideration. Particularly is
this so, if the candidate aspires to the highest office within the power of
the nation of bestow.

Opportunity is now at hand to exert your influence and lend your
aid in behalf of one, who when occasion presented, has ever championed
our cause. During the last national disaster in the Mississippi Valley, this

man in his program of relief administration, performed without regard to color, race, or creed. Only the relief of suffering humanity was uppermost in his mind. Periodically, it seems to be the natural order of things, for a man of outstanding capabilities to rise up in public life (a veritable Moses, a Lincoln, a Roosevelt), with a great compassionate understanding of the needs of all of the people. When you support Hoover, you support yourself.

When the leaders of capital, labor and industry, unanimously endorse the candidacy of a man; when pulpit, press and leaders of national thought espouse his cause, it behooves our group to give him serious consideration. Certainly no candidate since the immortal Roosevelt has held forth such prospect for a brighter day for us. His record proves it, and certainly no candidate since Mr. Roosevelt is more deserving of your wholehearted support.

BY ROBT. F. LEFTRIDGE.
Philadelphia, Pa.

SOURCE *BWEGM,* Record Group 183, Bureau of Employment Security, Reel 15, frame no. 0053.

94. *"Kelly Miller Says." Issued by the Committee of Forty-Eight, Philadelphia, ca. May 1928. The Howard University dean criticized the Republican party for courting the votes of the white south and failing to denounce the Ku Klux Klan.*

KELLY MILLER
Says:

Race, Religion and Rum

Mr. Norman Thomas, the Socialist candidate for the presidency, has said that Race, Religion and Rum will constitute the chief issues of the campaign. The genuine advocates of prohibition regret this UNHOLY alliance. Race intolerance and religious bigotry are obvious vices while TEMPERANCE is universally extolled as a virtue. The propagandists of race hatred and religious bigotry are insidiously stealing the livery of heaven in which to serve the Devil. The evil genius of these evil issues is embodied in the Ku Klux Klan. The basic clause in the creed of this order is that a one hundred per cent American must be ALL WHITE and all PROTESTANT. The Negro American meets the full measure of the SECOND REQUIREMENT but cannot possibly qualify under the FIRST. His only salvation, therefore, is to change the definition since he can never answer to its terms.

Strange transpositions take place in political history. The Ku Klux Klan of the older day was pledged to the undoing of the works of the

Republican party. In turn the Grand Old Party was committed to its utter destruction. This constituted its boasted achievement in the days of Reconstruction. It was thought that the dragon of unAmericanism was hatred which was not wholly extirpiated [sic]. Just as the original Ku Klux Klan arose after the Civil War for the express purpose of keeping the Negro in his putative place; so its rejuvenescence after the World War had precisely the same objective. But in addition to its main feature it took on the collateral purpose of properly subordinating NON-PROTESTANTS and FOREIGNERS. This extension of the brackets so as to include the Catholic and the Jew lightened the pressure upon the Negro. Indeed it was soon found that a rejuvenescence of the nefarious order was not necessary to handle the Negro. As the basis of operation shifted from South to North, religious bigotry has received the chief stress of emphasis. Very little has been said or done concerning the brother in black. But nevertheless the basic principle remains, THE NEGRO RACE IS HELD IN DEEPEST DESPITE.

Ku Klux Klan Anti-Negro

The Klan is anti-Negro, and the Negro who allows himself to ignore or overlook this basic fact is what Solomon or any other wise man would call A FOOL. As the movement has shifted from North to South, its political allegiance has turned from the DEMOCRATIC to the REPUBLICAN party. The triumph of tolerance over bigotry in Madison Square Garden four years ago DROVE THE KLAN out of the DEMOCRATIC PARTY, whence it sought hospitality in the part of its former enemies and destroyers. Here it was given asylum, if not welcome. John W. Davis and Robert L. Lafollette, candidates of the Democratic and Progressive parties for the presidency, both denounced the order by name in scathing and unmistakable terms, while President and candidate Coolidge observed the SILENCE of the SPHINX. When General Dawes sought to give the Klan his playful endorsement, Mr. Coolidge forthwith put a padlock on the lips of his running mate. According to his political cunning, he cautioned neither avowal nor disavowal, but votes. The Klan now controls the REPUBLICAN party in INDIANA, with ONE GOVERNOR in the PENITENTIARY and another out. In other mid-western States the Wizards of Wickedness are so influential within the fold of the Grand Old Party that the leaders and rulers dare not utter one condemnatory word.

Smith Outspoken, Hoover Silent, on Klan

Governor Smith in his Oklahoma address, boldly as is his wont, DENOUNCED THE KU KLUX KLAN IN TERMS AS CLEAR AND UNMISTAKABLE AS

THE SMITH LANGUAGE USUALLY IS. But not one condemnatory word has escaped the prudent lips of President Coolidge, candidate Hoover, Manager Work, or any other ruler in the ranks of Republicandom. The hoped for reinforcement in the South comes from the Ku Klux ranks. The LILY WHITES are but another name for the KLANSMEN, translated into political terms.

The Republican party becomes the acquiescent beneficiary of the evil machinations of the most insidious order that has ever been permitted to raise its head in America. The question naturally arises, "What will Mr. Hoover do when he succeeds to the presidency with such a heavy handicap of accepted assistance?" Can he meet the JUST DEMANDS OF THE NEGRO AND SATISFY THE KU KLUX KLAN AT THE SAME TIME? Their claims are antithetic. Candor compels frank admiration of Secretary Work who can work his black wheel horses and lily white steeds in the same harness. Prof. John R. Hawkins and Senator Simmons, who by waving the red shirt of white supremacy drove the Negro Republican out of North Carolina are now pulling for the same candidate, though Senator Simmons has not expressed repentance nor Mr. Hawkins a change of heart. Surely politics makes strange bedfellows. Can this fellowship survive the election? We must rely upon the political genius of Mr. Hoover to harmonize the inharmonious. If the Negro's Republicanism can stand the strain of this campaign, IT WILL CERTAINLY ENDURE FOREVER! Bigotry is hard to beat. You may as well go reason with the wolf why he has made the ewe bleat for the lamb as try to argue with RACE HATRED and RELIGIOUS BIGOTRY. There is nothing to do with this wave of hysteria but let it wear itself out. Like all other fanatical movements, it has its own length. The Billy Sunday psychology is short lived. The lynching of Negroes, the persecution of the Catholics, the same fanaticism of bigot are not transient phases of the disordered spirit. The wave is now in the ascendant. It will hardly subside before election.

SOURCE *BWEGM,* Record Group 183, Bureau of Employment Security, Reel 15, frame no. 0034.

CHAPTER III

THE GREAT DEPRESSION, 1929–1939

A. INTRODUCTION

Historical Context

The Great Depression brought mass suffering to the country as a whole. Unemployment rose to an estimated 25 percent of the labor force, national income dropped by nearly 50 percent, and nearly 20 million Americans turned to public and private relief agencies for help. Still, African Americans suffered far more than their white counterparts and got what they frequently called a "raw deal" rather than a "new deal" from their government.

Cotton prices dropped from nearly 20 cents per pound during the 1920s to less than 6 cents by early 1933. At the same time, the increasing use of mechanical devices, including experimentation with mechanical cotton pickers, reduced the number of workers needed for plowing, hoeing, weeding, and harvesting. The number of black sharecroppers dropped from over 390,000 during the late 1920s to under 300,000 as the depression took hold and spread during the early 1930s. Making matters worse, public and private relief efforts were virtually nonexistent in the rural south, forcing black farm families to continue their movement into the nation's urban centers. During the depression years, the percentage of blacks living in cities rose from about 44 percent in 1930 to nearly 50 percent by 1940.

Although blacks continued their rural-to-urban migration during the 1930s, urban blacks fared little better than their rural counterparts. By 1932, for example, black urban unemployment had reached well over 50 percent, more than twice the national rate. In northern and southern cities, black workers faced special difficulties trying to keep their jobs. Many unemployed white workers competed for the so-called Negro jobs, including street cleaning, garbage collection, and domestic service. In the urban south, white workers rallied around such slogans as "No Jobs for Niggers Until Every White Man Has a Job." Violence and intimidation increased as white workers campaigned to remove blacks from their jobs. By 1933, nearly a dozen black firemen had lost their lives as unionized white workers and the railroad brotherhoods, coveting their jobs on southern railroads, launched their violent attacks. After declining during the 1920s, the number of lynchings also increased.

In northern cities, hard times forced many black women to participate in the notorious "slave market." Black women congregated on the sidewalks of major cities, where white women drove up in their automobiles seeking domestic help. Employers paid the women as little as $5.00 weekly for full-time work. Even so, employers, including some working-class white women, frequently paid the women at an even lower rate than

that agreed upon. As one contemporary study noted, "Fortunate, indeed, is she who gets the full hourly rate promised."

African Americans got little aid from their government during the early years of the Great Depression. Indeed, Republican President Herbert Hoover neglected the needs of all the nation's poor and destitute citizens during the final years of his administration. Hoover believed that federal aid to corporations would stimulate production, create jobs, increase consumer spending, "trickle down" to the rest of the economy, and lift people out of the depression. Unfortunately, such policies as well as the first years of the New Deal provided little help to poor blacks.

Still, despite their dissatisfaction with the Hoover administration, African Americans rallied to the banner "who but Hoover" in the presidential contest of 1932. The Republican party still loomed large as the party of emancipation, and African Americans would only slowly turn toward the Democratic party. From the vantage point of African Americans, Franklin Delano Roosevelt's record as an advocate of civil rights was little better than Hoover's. Moreover, during its national convention, the Democratic party had defeated an NAACP proposal for a civil rights plank that called for an end to racial discrimination.

During the early years of his administration, F.D.R. failed to build confidence among black voters. He opposed efforts to pass a federal anti-lynching law and refused to meet with civil rights leaders at the White House, arguing that he needed southern white support to implement his New Deal social programs. Thus, African Americans faced an uphill battle to gain benefits from the New Deal programs—the National Recovery Administration (NRA), the Agricultural Adjustment Administration (AAA), the Works Progress (later Projects) Administration (WPA), the Federal Emergency Relief Administration (FERA), and the Civilian Conservation Corps (CCC), to name only a few.

African Americans bitterly complained that such agencies discriminated against them. New Deal programs provided for unequal benefit levels for black and white recipients, particularly in the south, where state and local officials sanctioned separate and unequal pay scales for blacks and whites. Southern officials frequently remarked that African Americans re-

Unemployed blacks line up outside the State Employment Service in Memphis, Tennessee, in 1938. During the depression black relief recipients received far less aid than did their white counterparts. Courtesy of the Library of Congress.

quired far less as a livelihood than did their white counterparts. By exempting common laborers, agricultural workers, and domestic service employees from minimum wage and participatory provisions, the NRA and the new social security programs eliminated nearly 60 percent of African American workers and their families from benefits.

By the mid-1930s, a variety of forces helped to transform the relationship between African Americans and the New Deal. The Communist party, Socialist party, and the fledgling Congress of Industrial Organizations all facilitated the emergence of new interracial alliances and fresh intellectual, cultural, and legal perspectives on race. Yet it was the growing political influence of the black urban community itself that played the key role in prodding F.D.R. toward a more helpful focus on the needs of blacks.

As the black urban population continued to expand, African Americans could claim a definitive balance of power in close elections. In over 15 states, particularly the large industrial states of Pennsylvania, Ohio, Michigan, New York, Illinois, and Indiana, their votes grew increasingly important. As early as 1932, the editor of the black weekly *Pittsburgh Courier* had encouraged blacks to support the Democratic party: "My friends, go turn Lincoln's picture to the wall. That debt has been paid in full." Four years later black voters played a crucial role in returning F.D.R. to the White House.

By 1939, African Americans had gradually increased their share of New Deal housing, relief, and work programs. As a result of government

relief and work projects, African American income from federal sources nearly equaled their wages from employment in agriculture and domestic service. F.D.R. employed a growing number of African Americans, the "Black Cabinet," in key government agencies like the Department of Interior, the Department of Labor, and the Office of the Attorney General.

Despite shifting conceptions of race and the New Deal's growing response to the needs of blacks, on the eve of World War II poverty, unemployment, and racial discrimination continued to convulse the African American community. Even the most egalitarian of New Deal programs failed to reverse the entrenched pattern of racial inequality in American institutions. In fact, federal policy joined an ongoing set of historical forces—discriminatory real estate agents, restrictive covenants, and white neighborhood opposition—in the rise and expansion of racially segregated urban communities, by sanctioning racial segregation in the urban housing market. For its part the WPA established regulations ending racial discrimination in its programs, but southern whites continued to evade the rules and made it more difficult for blacks than whites to gain adequate public works jobs and relief.

Finally, despite the vigorous interracial activities of the Communist party and the CIO, disproportionate numbers of blacks continued to depend on public service and relief programs. Before the nation turned sharply toward defense production, many whites had returned to better jobs in the private and public sectors.

Thus, from the onset of the Great Depression through the 1930s, African Americans had to wage a strong offensive against the barriers of racial and class inequality. Through the vigorous defense of their own rights, however, African Americans helped to usher in a new set of social relations in American society. The New Deal order, which sanctioned federal efforts to relieve hunger, homelessness, disease, and other social ills, owed much to the activism of African Americans during the Great Depression.

President Franklin D. Roosevelt responded to the growing importance of the black vote in national elections by appointing increasing numbers of blacks to federal posts. Member of the "Black Cabinet," as these appointees came to be called, gather for a photograph in 1938. Courtesy of the Library of Congress.

Documents

This section covers the impact of the depression on the lives of urban and rural blacks, their encounters with New Deal social welfare programs, and their responses to hard times. Subsection IIIB offers special reports on the problems of African Americans in diverse settings and sectors of the economy, the impact of New Deal programs, and the troubled and often violent state of race relations in American society. This section includes a detailed report of the gruesome lynching of Claude Neal in Marianna, Florida, and the intensification of the campaign for a federal antilynching law.

Subsection IIIC provides life histories of black men and women, farmers and industrial workers, and educated members of the black middle class, namely, teachers. These documents suggest not only the myriad ways that southern blacks adapted to hard times, but the differential impact of the depression on individuals, families, and their communities. Gardening, mutual assistance, domestic service, intermittent labor in heavy industries, and growing support of the New Deal and the Democratic party all receive attention in these documents. Some of them discuss the depression against the backdrop of earlier times, including the dreams and memories of the

adults whose parents and grandparents had been slaves. Thus, these selections enable us to assess aspects of socioeconomic and cultural continuity, as well as change, in the lives of African Americans during the industrial age.

B. OLD DEAL/NEW DEAL

95. *"National Conference on the Problems of the Negro and Negro Youth." Report, National Youth Administration, Division of Negro Affairs, Jan. 1937. Analyzes the impact of the depression and a broad range of New Deal programs on African Americans; concludes with a call for greater federal control to combat racial discrimination at the local and state levels.*

Recommendations on Increased Opportunity for Employment and Economic Security

The stark reality of the present employment situation in the United States as it affects Negroes calls for a blunt recital of the disabilities under which they labor. Their social and economic existence is tragically at stake. Despite the tremendous efforts of the Governmental agencies during the past three or four years to rescue the country from the destroying effects of the depression, the mass Negro population of the United States still, at this time, January, 1937, is living on the lowest levels of existence, with attendant hunger and misery.

It is a matter of common knowledge that the Negro has not shared equitably in all the services the Government offers its citizens. We are mindful of the fact that during the past four years many benefits have come to him that before that time he did not have. But there still remain numerous instances of racial difference and inequality from which he suffers. While presenting specifically recommendations for action touching the Negro, we are not unmindful of the condition which faces the country,

Black men and women at work on a Mississippi plantation in 1940. The efforts by administrators of New Deal agencies in Washington to end racial discrimination in government programs were largely ignored by local southern administrators. Courtesy of the Library of Congress.

calling for the continuance of the policies and practices which have been in effect for the past four years.

We urge that in emergency relief and work programs care be exercised to secure Federal control and supervision of these programs in all their phases as opposed to the decentralization through reference to states and localities. We further urge that in all administration of these programs specific steps be made to eliminate racial discrimination. And finally, it is our urgent belief that not less than nine hundred million dollars ($900,000,000) must be appropriated for Federal emergency relief work for the period up to June 30, 1937 if the basic needs of the needy and indigent American population are to be met.

Unemployment

Unemployment is the greatest menace in modern society to workers black and white. According to general economic opinion many millions of job-

less workers as a result of the general increase in the population and constant technological progress, will continue to imperil the nation.

The principle of the shorter work week is sound in view of modern machinery and rationalization which increase the rate of production and resultantly displace workers in industry. The shorter work week is fundamental to the Negro group, who, as marginal workers, being the last hired and the first fired, will benefit from increased employment provided by legislation for a thirty hour week.

This conference, therefore, herewith recommends that the thirty hour week be adopted by the Congress as a national work week of the country, without any reduction in wages, as the basic remedy for unemployment.

Collective Bargaining

It is a recognized fact that the employers of the nation enjoy the right of organization, as corporations, trusts, holding companies, manufacturing associations and chambers of commerce, for the purpose of advancing their economic interests. Therefore, this conference endorses the principle of the Wagner Labor Disputes Bill as sound, which grants the workers the right of bona fide collective bargaining, through trade union organization and the selection and designation of representatives of their own choosing, without intimidation or coercion, to safeguard their economic rights, as being in the interest of the security of the workers' and the public's good. This conference advises and insists that no union which excludes Negro workers from membership shall enjoy the benefits of this Bill.

This conference, however, is aware of, and condemns discrimination that are practiced upon Negro workers by some of the trade union organizations through the color bar in their constitutions and rituals and other subtle forms of excluding Negro workers and, herewith, recommends that the National Labor Relations Board, take the necessary action calculated to protest the interests of Negro workers in certain classes of work from

As the number of blacks living in major cities increased during the 1930s, black political and community organizations encouraged the newcomers to register to vote. Here, blacks line up to register in Atlanta. Courtesy of the Atlanta Historical Society.

discrimination by trade unions, since it definitely and harmfully effects Negro workers' opportunities for work and wages.

Regulation of Labor Standards

We commend the trend in government, by legislation and administrative ruling, for regulation of labor standards in public works, in work done on government contracts, and in private industry, to the end that decent living standards may be maintained for all workers in America. We believe that in all such regulation the Federal Government has the responsibility to avoid differentials in standards based on regions, or on other bases which directly or indirectly militate against Negro workers. We believe that such regulation should define discrimination against Negro workers as an unfair practice, which the Government should prohibit.

$1,500 Minimum Wage for Federal and District Employees

We recommend and strongly urge the enactment into law at this session of Congress or as soon thereafter as possible, the following:

1. Minimum basic wage of $1,500.00 for all United States and District Government employees in Washington and in the field services.
2. Automatic promotions under the United States classified and apportioned civil service,—temporary and emergency agencies, as well as the normal or regular divisions of the government.
3. A 5-day, 30 hour work week,
4. Optional 30-year retirement, and
5. A Civil Service Appeal Board, at least one of whom shall be a Negro.

Use of Federal Funds

When Federal funds are used either through grants or loans for projects, state or local, which deny benefits to individuals because of race, that use contravenes the Federal Constitution. But more than this, the practice further retards economic improvement of the Negro. It is our consensus that in such programs as low cost housing, resettlement communities, TVA projects and similar enterprises in which the Negro has suffered from discriminatory policies, the various Federal bureaus have the responsibility to prevent any denial of benefits in any project.

Farm Tenants and Agricultural Workers

The problem of farm tenancy is an acute one for the Negro people, inasmuch as nearly half of the Negro population is agricultural—and three-

---

A smiling couple moves into their new home in a government-sponsored housing project in Newport News, Virginia, in 1937. Such government assistance played a key part in the shift of black voters from the Republican to the Democratic party. Courtesy of the Library of Virginia.

---

fourths of these are tenants. Today there are 700,000 Negro tenant families in the south alone. Tenancy for this class has been and remains a device for continuing the production of the commercial crop of cotton as developed under the institution of slavery. The social and economic limitations of this status are as fixed as they are unfortunate. Living standards for those tenants are the lowest of any groups of workers in America,—mortality, illiteracy and general social disorganization the greatest. Moreover tenancy is increasing at a rapid rate involving white as well as Negro producers.

We therefore, recommend immediate federal action to remedy a fundamental agricultural problem and a serious situation for a large part of the Negro population.

Specifically, we recommend:

(a)   The enactment of legislation making possible large scale government purchase of land for resale or lease on long terms to tenants or cooperatives composed of tenants and small farm owners who desire to attain the status of ownership; and direct assistance, supervision and protection for these tenants in getting established on the land.

With regard to the legislation suggested above we earnestly urge the following safeguards to protect Negro tenants:

(1)   That the size of the farm allotted to tenants, the amount of direct assistance given tenants in feed, stock, implements, and improvement loans be such as to give reasonable assurance that the tenant or tenants in cooperatives can earn sufficient income to maintain a decent living standard and pay off the loan.

(2)   That selection of tenant families shall be on basis of need, with no discrimination on account of race, creed, color, political or union affiliation.

(3)   That, in keeping with American traditions, the administration of such agencies as are created by this legislation be so devised as to prohibit racial discrimination.

(4)   That qualified Negro personnel be included in the administrative staff appointed to carry out the purposes of such legislation.

(b)   The extension of government production loans to the end of reducing excessive burden of credit costs to small producers and to take the place of essential production and subsistence loans not hitherto available to these small producers except through extremely exploiting credit merchants.

(c)   The enactment of legislation providing minimum wages for farm workers, protection in their right to collective bargaining, and, their inclusion into social security laws.

(d)   The extension of the provision of government grants to land grant agricultural institutions.

(e)   Encouragement of states to revise landlord-tenant contracts to the end of providing greater security and recognition of tenants' rights in law; and requiring that these contracts be made in writing.

(f)   That, in such federal programs as the Soil Conservation Act the tenants receive directly their share in the parity payments.

(g)   We urge that the interests of Negro tenant farmers be safeguarded as to equitable and fair participation in the present Farm Tenant Security program now being carried out by the Resettlement Administration.

Domestic Workers

The problem of Negro domestic workers in the United States, affecting as it does 85 percent of all Negro women workers, is one which demands immediate action by the federal government. Their wages, hours and standards of living, even lower than those for white workers, in both rural and urban communities offer a challenge to American ideals of social legislation.

Immediately, we believe it to be necessary for Congress to enact legislation, establishing minimum standards for these workers, protecting them with adequate social security and workmen's compensation legislation and guaranteeing to them the right to organize and bargain collectively. We believe further that the United States Employment Service, and Federal relief agencies should establish policies to prevent assignment to domestic jobs below certain decent wage and labor standards, and to provide adequate relief to such domestic workers as cannot secure jobs at wages sufficient to provide a decent standard of living.

Railway Workers

It is an established policy on the part of the twenty-one standard railroad unions to exclude Negro workers on the railroad from membership. These unions control agreements affecting rates of pay and rules governing the general working conditions. Agreements entered into by the unions and railroads in this particular have resulted in limited Negro employment in the transportation industry.

This conference therefore recommends that the National Mediation Board and other agencies charged with responsibility, take cognizance of this unjust condition and set up the necessary procedure to correct it.

Professional and Technical Workers

Negro technical men have been denied opportunity for employment such as will give them wide experience, and it is recommended that Negroes, qualified as technical, professional, secretarial and clerical workers, such as project managers, engineers, accountants, architects, physicians, lawyers, dentists, U.S. Reserve Officers and the like, be given employment.

Negro Nurses

We call especial attention to Negro nurses. There are four Federal nursing services:

1. U.S. Public Health Service
2. U.S. Veterans Bureau
3. The Army Nursing Service
4. The Navy Nursing Service

The only one of these services which admits Negroes is the U.S. Veterans Bureau. This is confined to service at the Tuskegee Veterans Facility. None of the other services admits them, although nurses have passed the Civil Service examinations.

We recommend that these limitations be removed from Negro nurses. We further recommend that the U.S. Government do this as an example to city and state services which now discriminate against Negro nurses.

United States Employment Service

We recommend that the Federal office of the United States Employment Service include qualified Negroes on all formulative and administrative national, state and local committees and enforce an equitable distribution of administrative and supervisory positions in national, state and local offices, apportioning the personnel on the basis of the population percentage of Negroes.

We further recommend that the United States Employment Service program emphasize the opening of new employment opportunities for Negroes, the apprenticeship training of Negro youth and the elimination of segregation in all phases of its services.

Social Security

While we approve the principle of the Social Security Act, we recognize the fact that it should be broadened so as to include workers and services that are not now embraced. We recommend that the security and protection of domestic, agricultural and professional workers, constituting approximately sixty-five percent of all Negroes employed, be provided for by appropriate legislation.

We endorse the sentiment for increased allowances and for Federal supervision.

Preference for Federal as Against State Control of Projects

This conference wishes to go on record as favoring federal as against state control of projects. The Negro is not averse to federal supervision and the experience of the past convinces us that there will be more equitable safeguards of participation in these projects if there is federal guidance and control. Where projects must be turned over to the state committees for management, it is recommended that the plans for such projects have definite clauses against discrimination before they become the property of state authorities.

Protection of Negro Labor on Government Contracts

1. Discrimination against skilled and unskilled Negroes should be prohibited on federal projects. This can be done by extending such technique as developed by the Housing Division of PWA with the cooperation of the Department of Labor in dealing with various projects.

We recommend the clauses protecting skilled labor introduced in the contracts for various projects under the departments mentioned, and urge that the principle be extended to all government projects.

2. We feel that this direct method of fighting discrimination should be extended immediately to all "force accounts projects" and all other projects where the federal government is a direct party to the contract. We recognize, however, that this is a temporary procedure only, and therefore recommend that Negro skilled laborers as well as those of other races be employed solely on the basis of their efficiency.

Civil Service

We affirm our belief in the principle of Civil Service as an appropriate instrument for selecting employees for the federal government. We call attention to the abuses and practices which have interfered with the orderly employment of Negroes. Possibly this explains the virtual exclusion of Negroes from the administrative staffs of the several departments and agencies of the federal government as well as the professions, secretarial, and clerical branches. The use of photographs on application blanks and the routine of selecting one of the three ranking persons certified for appointment have all too frequently meant the exclusion of Negroes from governmental employment, and the reduction of Negro employees connected with the postal service.

We recommend that the person ranking highest on a given civil service examination be appointed, and that the use of photographs, and that the present practice which permits the selection of one of the three highest ranking persons instead of the highest ranking person be prohibited. We recommend also that a member of the Negro race be appointed to the Civil Service Commission.

Participation in Administrative Functions

So important is it to have the needs of Negroes presented and interpreted in the formulation and exercise of administrative policies it is recommended that efficient and capable Negroes be employed on the boards and administrative and supervisory staffs of every department of the Federal Government, and in every locality of the country in which a federal program is launched and operated for the improvement of life and conditions among the people.

Cooperatives and Credit Unions

Since the Farm Credit Administration is a cooperative organization and each farmer borrower is a stockholder of the organization from which he borrows and is expected to attend annual meetings and participate in the election of officers of the organization, this committee recommends that the Farm Credit Administration make a special effort to have Negro borrowers informed of their rights as stockholders and encourage them to participate freely in the stockholders meetings.

The committee recommends further that provision be made to inform eligible groups of the advantages of various types of cooperative services and credit unions under the Farm Credit Administration and other federal agencies.

Apprenticeship Training

This conference approves in principle the organization, the administration, and the objectives of the Federal Program of Apprentice Training.

In view of the special needs of Negro youth for the facilities intended to be provided by the Apprentice Training Program, we recommend the following:

(1)   That a well qualified Negro be appointed to membership on the Federal Committee on Apprentice Training.
(2)   That a well qualified Negro be appointed to membership on each State Committee on Apprentice Training.
(3)   That State Advisory Committees on Apprentice Training include in their membership a fair proportion of qualified Negroes. . . .

Recommendations on Security of Life and Equal Protection Under the Law

Basic to any consideration of the status of the Negro in American life and of relations between white and Negro Americans are two considerations: lynching and denial of the right to vote, such denial being on the basis of race, in certain states of the United States, this being done in violation of the Federal Constitution. It is self-evident that there can be no physical or other security for any American, white or Negro, save that the laws of the

Federal Government be enforced in every section of the country without regard to race or color.

Lynching

We therefore strongly urge the passage by the first session of the 75th Congress without delay of a strong federal anti-lynching law. The imposition of civil liability upon the political subdivision of the state which permits lynching within its jurisdiction is an essential feature of any such law. No American dare deny that there are certain states which either cannot or will not prevent lynchings or punish lynchers, and that it is therefore obligatory upon the National Congress to enact legislation to this end.

Disfranchisement

It is the considered judgment of this conference that the full and free use of the ballot, now denied to Negroes in the states where three-fourths of the Negro population lives, is essential to the effective expression of the wishes of the Negro people and the enforcement of their just demands. This basic need can be guaranteed in large measure by the Federal Government through legislation regulating the election of Senators and Representatives in Congress. Such legislation should prohibit both the name and party symbol of any political party or other organization which denies to any qualified voter full participation in the choice of its candidates for office and the name of any candidate of any such party from appearing on any official ballot to be used in an election for Senator or Representative in Congress or Presidential Elector.

New Federal Corrupt Practices Act Recommended

We urge that the President recommend to the Congress the enactment of a new Corrupt Practices Act, in which it shall be declared that a primary selection of candidates to be elected to Federal Office shall be an integral part of a general election.

Civil Rights Act for the District of Columbia

The city of Washington, as capital of the nation, should be an example for the entire United States in freedom from discrimination against any citizen or group of citizens in any public place on account of race, creed or color. Yet as a matter of fact, discrimination in public places in the District of Columbia, including Federal buildings and places under immediate Federal control, is as vicious and extreme as in any section of the United States. For this reason this conference urges that there be presented to Congress and speedily passed a bill assuring to all persons the right to equal accommodation, without discrimination or segregation, in all places of public accommodation within the District of Columbia.

Amendment to Wagner-Connery National Labor Relations Act

We urge an amendment to the Wagner-Connery National Labor Relations Act to bar any labor union from being declared the spokesman for the workers in any given industry if that labor union denies membership in it to any otherwise eligible person on account of race, creed or color.

Discrimination and Segregation by Interstate Carriers

It is strongly recommended that the Interstate Commerce Act be amended to provide that no interstate carrier shall segregate or in any way discriminate against any interstate passager on account of race, creed or color.

Civil Liberties

We endorse the work of the LaFollette Senate Committee now investigating denials of civil liberties, and urge additional appropriations and the employment of Negroes for the continuance of the investigation.

Discrimination in Employment on Federal Finance Acts

We urge upon the Congress the enactment of legislation requiring the inclusion in all contracts for construction financed in whole or in part by the Federal Government a standard clause prohibiting discrimination in employment on account of race, creed or color.

Police Brutality in the District of Columbia

We are in the midst of a nationwide campaign against lawlessness. Lawlessness of police in Washington, the nation's capital, startlingly demonstrated by the reliably reported killing of more than 40 Negroes by the police during the last ten years, cannot be tolerated by Federal authority if the Federal Government is going to lead a crusade against lawlessness in the country at large. For this reason this conference urges that the Congress investigate police brutality in the District of Columbia.

Equal Protection of the Law

We urge that all Federal law enforcement agencies be employed to the limit of their jurisdiction to secure for Negroes the benefits of due process and the equal protection of the law.

Capitalization of the Word "Negro"

We urge that the authority of the Federal Government be employed to require the capitalization of the word *Negro* in all official documents and all publications issuing from the Government printing office.

Armed Forces

We urge that the President of the United States as Commander-in-Chief of the Army and Navy issue such orders as may be necessary to restore the 9th and 10th Calvary, and 24th Infantry to combat status and give Negroes proportionate representation in all branches of the Army; that enlistment in every arm and division of the armed forces on land, sea and air be opened to Negroes on the same terms and conditions as to any other citizens of the United States, and the promotions in both the enlisted and officer personnel be made without discrimination as race and color.

National Conference on the Problems of the Negro and Negro Youth

Who's Who at the Conference

Panel #1

Abbott, Robert S.	Editor, Chicago Defender	Chicago, Ill.
Arthur, George R.	Secretary, Y.M.C.A.	Chicago, Ill.

Atwell, E. T.	Nat'l Recreation Assoc.	New York City
Austin, Rev. J. C.	Nat'l Baptist Assoc.	Chicago, Ill.
Bousfield, Dr. M. O.	Medical Advisor, Julius Rosewald Fund	Chicago, Ill.
Brown, Charlotte H.	President, Palmer Memorial Institute	Sedalia, N.C.
Browning, Chas. P.	Asst. State Director NYA of Illinois	Chicago, Ill.
Bullock, Ralph W.	Asst. State Director NYA of Georgia	Atlanta, Ga.
Burch, Mrs. W. C.	President, Nat'l Asso. Teachers in Colored Schools	Washington, D.C.
Burroughs, Nannie H.	Executive Secretary, Home Missionary Society for the Baptist Church	Washington, D.C.
Clark, Felton G.	Dean, Southern University	Baton Rouge, La.
Davis, John W.	President, West Virginia State College	Institute, W.Va.
Daniel, V. E.	President, Asso. of Colleges and Secondary Schools of Southern States	Marshall, Texas
Dickerson, Addie W.	International Council of Women of the Darker Races	Philadelphia, Pa.
Fauset, Crystal Byrd	WPA Supervisor	Philadelphia, Pa.
Florence C. W.	President, Lincoln Univ.	Jefferson City, Mo.
Hale, Wm, J.	President, Tenn. A&M College	Nashville, Tenn.
Hamilton, Julia West	Nat'l Asso. of Colored Women	Washington, D.C.
Hill, T. Arnold	Director of Industrial Relations, Nat'l Urban League	New York City
Houston, Chas. H.	Attorney, N.A.A.C.P.	New York City
Hunter, Jane E.	Chairman, Nat'l Phyllis Wheatley Organizations	Cleveland, Ohio
Johnson, Chas. S.	Dept. of Social Science Fisk University	Nashville, Tenn.

Jones, David D.	President, Bennett College	Greensboro, N.C.
Jones, Bishop R. E.	M.E. Church	Columbus, Ohio
Lee, J. R. E.	President, Florida A&M College	Tallahassee, Fla.
Murphy, George, B.	Editor, Afro-American	Baltimore, Md.
Patterson, F. D.	President, Tuskegee Inst.	Tuskegee, Ala.
Perkins, D. W.	Nat'l Lawyers Asso.	Jacksonville, Fla.
Potter, M. D.	Editor, Tampa Bulletin	Tampa, Fla.
Randolph, A. Philip	President, Brotherhood of Sleeping Car Porters	New York City
Ransom, Bishop R. C.	A.M.E. Church	Wilberforce, Ohio
Savory, P. M. H.	Publisher, Amsterdam News	New York City
Slowe, Dean Lucy D.	Exec. Secretary Nat'l Council of Negro Women	Washington, D.C.
Smith, William A.	Asst. State Director NYA of New Jersey	Newark, N.J.
Spaulding, C. C.	Nat'l Business League	Durham, N.C.
Staupers, Mabel K.	Nat'l Graduate Nurses Asso.	New York City
Thomas, Jesse O.	Manager, Negro Exhibition Texas Centennial Exp.	Dallas, Texas
Terrell, Mary Church	Nat'l Assoc. Colored Women	Washington, D.C.
Vann, Robert L.	Editor, Pittsburgh Courier	Pittsburgh, Pa.
Walls, W. J.	Bishop A.M.E. Zion Church	Chicago, Ill.
Washington, Forrester B.	President, Atlanta School of Social Work	Atlanta, Ga.
Watson, J. B.	President, Arkansas A.M.&N. College	Pine Bluff, Ark.
White, Lorenzo	Hampton, Institute	Hampton, Va.
White, Walter	Executive Secretary N.A.A.C.P.	New York City
Whittaker, M. F.	President, Asso. of Land Grant College Presidents	Orangeburg, S.C.

Wilkinson, Garnet C.	Asst. Supt. of Public Schools in the District	Washington, D.C.
Wilson, J. Finley	Grand Exalted Ruler I.B.P.O.E.	Washington, D.C.

Panel #2

Allen, Gerald	Recreation Supervisor Public Schools	Baltimore, Md.
Carter, Jeanette	Rep. of Chicago Defender	Washington, D.C.
Chase, Valerie	Prin. Terrell Jr. High School	Washington, D.C.
Daniels, Mrs. Constance	Rep. of Afro-American	Washington, D.C.
Davis, John F.	Executive Secretary Nat'l Negro Congress	Washington, D.C.
Ferebee, Dr. Dorothy	Youth Health Committee	Washington, D.C.
Ferguson, Dutton	Rep. Amsterdam News	Washington, D.C.
Fountain, W. A.	President, Morris Brown University	Atlanta, Ga.
Grary, G. N. T.	President, Postal Alliance	Washington, D.C.
Green, Cyrus	Nat'l Urban League	Tampa, Fla.
Gregg, G. A.	President, Shorter College	N. Little Rock, Ark.
Hale, Wm. J., Jr.	Extension Work	Taft, Okla.
Hamilton, Col. W. A.	Commander, 428 Infantry	Washington, D.C.
Hamilton, T. B.	Tax Commissioner for City of Pittsburgh	Pittsburgh, Pa.
Hawkins, John R.	Financial Secretary A.M.E. Church	Washington, D.C.
Holmes, D. O. W.	Dean, Graduate School Howard University	Washington, D.C.
Hope, Mrs. John	Nat'l Council of Negro Women	Atlanta, Ga.
Houston, W. L.	President, Washington Bar Association	Washington, D.C.
Hueston, W. C.	Educational Director, I.B.P.O.E.	Washington, D.C.

Hughes, Mrs. Lucy M.	Worthy Superior, Household of Ruth	Cameron, Texas
Hughes, W. A. C.	Supervisor of Missions M.E. Church	Philadelphia, Pa.
Imes, G. Lake	Adviser, CCC Camps	Washington, D.C.
Jernagin, Rev. W. H.	Nat'l Sunday School & BYPU Conference of the Baptist Church	Washington, D.C.
Johnson, Major C. C.	Secretary, YMCA	Washington, D.C.
Johnson, Mordecai	President, Howard Univ.	Washington, D.C.
Long, Dr. Howard	Asst. Supt. Public Schools	Washington, D.C.
Love, Edgar A.	Dist. Supt. M.E. Church	Washington, D.C.
LuValle, J. A. G.	Editor, Washington Tribune	Washington, D.C.
Mehlinger, Louis	Department of Justice	Washington, D.C.
McCoy, Rev. L. M.	President, Rust College	Holly Springs, Miss.
McGuire, Mrs. Virginia	Advisor, Girls Camps	Washington, D.C.
Mizelle, Ralph	Attorney	New York City
Rhodes, Mrs. Geraldine	Civic Worker	Washington, D.C.
Rogers, G. D.	Nat'l Insurance Asso.	Washington, D.C.
Scott, Emmett J.	Secretary, Howard Univ.	Washington, D.C.
Spaulding, Jane E.	Nat'l Council of Negro Women	West Virginia
Taliaferro, Clara Smyth	Social Workers Organizations	Washington, D.C.
Thompson, Prof. Chas.	Editor, Journal Negro Education	Washington, D.C.
Washington, Blanche	Howard Law School	Washington, D.C.
Wilkerson, Prof. D. A.	Howard University Teachers Union	Washington, D.C.
Williams, Rev. R. M.	Asbury M.E. Church	Washington, D.C.

Consultants

Atkins, James A.	Division of Education, WPA
Brown, Edgar G.	Emergency Conservation Work
Brown, Dr. R. C.	U.S. Public Health Service

Caliver, Ambrose	Office of Education, Dept. of the Interior
Cohron, George E.	U.S. Employment Service
Evans, Joseph H. B.	Resettlement Administration
Hall, Charles E.	Department of Commerce
Hastie, Wm. H.	Department of Interior
Horne, Frank S.	National Youth Association
Hunt, Harry A.	Farm Credit Administration
Jones, Dewey R.	Department of Interior
Jones, Eugene Kinckle	Adviser, Negro Affairs, Dept. of Commerce
Lawson, Edward	Publicity (WPA and ANP)
Lewis, Vinita	Children's Bureau, Dept. of Labor
Oxley, Lawrence A.	Chief, Div. of Negro Labor, Dept. of Labor
Smith, Alfred Edgar	Administrative Assistant, WPA
Thompkins, Wm. J.	Recorder of Deeds
Trigg, H. L.	Office of Education, Dept. of Interior
Weaver, Robert C.	Adviser, Negro Affairs, Dept. of Interior
Weisiger, J. A.	Department of Labor
Whitten, J. W.	Works Progress Administration

SOURCE National Youth Administration (NYA), Division of Negro Affairs, Reel 3, frame no. 0001, in John B. Kirby, ed., *New Deal Agencies and Black America* (Frederick, Md.: University Publications of America, 1984) (hereinafter cited as *NDABA*).

96. *"Report on Negro Labor of the Inter-departmental Group." Report, National Urban League to National Youth Administration, Division of Negro Affairs, 18 Apr. 1934. Discusses the displacement of black workers with the advent of minimum wage standards, the discriminatory policies of labor unions, and the harmful effects of New Deal legislation on black workers.*

Effect of N.R.A. Codes upon Negroes

The National Urban League requested all their district organizations to send in reports of complaint of discrimination against Negroes under Code. From the northern cities the reports were not as disturbing as those received from the southern cities where very serious situations were indicated. These are best summarized as follows:

(1) Displacement of Negro workers has been accentuated by the operation of the N.R.A. and the kinds of occupations open to Negroes are narrowing.

(2) Violations of wage and hour agreements were being made.

(3)   Intimidation of the Negroes for economic reasons has increased.

At the same time it must be recognized that the majority of complaints along these lines as contained, for example, in the report of complaints of violations of the N.R.A. received by the Atlanta Urban League, came from the employees in small concerns and engaged in service occupations.

(a)   Slight additional evidence that small concerns have been the chief offenders in this regard is contained in the fact that while in Ohio and Massachusetts small concerns showed the largest increases in wages per worker, according to the P.R.A. survey in North Carolina, small concerns showed the smallest increases.

It is correct to say that the larger concerns which have complied with code provisions sharply increasing the Negroes' wages have suffered some competitive disadvantage. But the evidence indicates that even these concerns which have complied with code provisions have not eliminated or significantly reduced the racial differential.

The appended table, computed from figures on wages in ten representative southern concerns compiled by the Southern State Industrial Council, indicates that in these concerns the spread in wages between Negroes and white workers in identical occupations has not been significantly decreased as compared with past years, although the spread has been reduced 40% as compared with the first half of 1933, when hard-pressed manufacturers presumably sharply increased the spread as a method of reducing costs.

The report of the Joint Committee on National Recovery on Negro workers under the N.R.A. presents evidence that many provisions in the codes have been, in effect, discriminatory against black workers. It lists three major devices which have had that effect. The first is the occupational differential. "Proponents of Codes exempt from maximum hours provisions and minimum wage scales those occupations in which Negro workers are chiefly to be found." (Example: Outside crews and cleaners in cotton textiles; of 13,000 Negroes in Industry, 10,000 come with this category.) The second is the geographical differential. "Certain Industries employ large number of Negroes as unskilled labor in the South but not elsewhere." (Example: Lumber. Negro labor 60% in the South but only 37% in all United States.) The third is the "grandfather clause" appearing in 18 approved codes and providing minimum scales for identical classes of labor based on wages received July 15, 1929, obviously perpetuating colored and white differential.

If the indicated fact that completely complying companies have not reduced the racial differential except as compared with the first half of 1933 is combined with the strong evidences of discrimination against Negroes, both under code provisions and in spite of code provisions, two observations can be made:

(1)   Individual complying companies and industries with the less discriminatory provisions have suffered a competitive disadvantage.

(2)   The immediate effect of the N.R.A. decreasing the spread between the wages of white and colored labor has been nullified to an undetermined extent by discriminations against Negroes. If the comparison is made between the last half of 1933 and any recent year, the spread in total income—as distinct from wage rates—between southern white labor as a whole and southern Negro labor as a whole has been increased.

Two courses have been suggested to eliminate these conditions:

(1)   Increase the North-South differential spread for the industries which have suffered more due to their more favorable treatment to Negro labor, and

(2)   Eliminate and counteract those Code provisions which have discriminated against Negroes.

Summary of Reports of Ten Southern Concerns Compiled by Southern Industrial Conference

	Average wage white workers	Average spread white less colored	Percent spread
1st ½ 1930	$27.25	$2.32	8.5
2nd ½ 1930	26.64	2.26	8.5
1st ½ 1931	26.38	2.23	8.5
2nd ½ 1931	25.77	2.67	10.4
1st ½ 1932	23.80	2.00	8.8
2nd ½ 1932	22.02	1.44	6.5
1st ½ 1933	21.28	2.62	12.3
2nd ½ 1933	27.83	2.15	7.7

Based on wage reports from ten southern manufacturers for identical classes of labor. This table, while giving a general picture, cannot be regarded as statistically accurate owing to the smallness of the sample.

Negro and Trade Unions

Although it is impossible to judge accurately the number of Negro trade union members, it is safe to say that there were in 1930 no more than about 50,000 colored members of national unions. The majority of these were connected in four organizations: The hod carriers' union, The United Mine Workers, the longshoremen's union, and the Pullman Porters' union. These colored union members represented about 3.3% of the 1,497,273 Negroes engaged in transportation, extraction of minerals and manufacturing in 1930. In the case of all American wage-earners, white and colored, outside of agricultural industries, the degree of unionization was something over twenty percent. Although a part of this difference in the degree of organization is accounted for by the disproportionately large number of Negro semi-skilled and unskilled workers (in 1930, 46.6% of the total Negro non-agriculture workers were unskilled and semi-skilled but only 5.4% of them skilled; while twenty-nine percent of the native-born non-agriculture white workers were semi-skilled and unskilled and 17.4% skilled), this great difference in union strength is due chiefly to another set of influences.

The attitude of American labor unions towards Negro workers has been the chief cause of this proportionately small Negro activity. Throughout the history of the American labor movement there has been a disinclination on the part of these organizations to extend full and equal membership to Negro workers. Thus, even as late as today there are some twenty-six unions whose constitutions or rituals limit membership to white men. Ten of these unions are affiliated with the American Federation of Labor. This statement, however, does not send the whole picture because the most flagrant cases of discrimination against colored workers have occurred in organizations which have no written clauses pertaining to Negroes. The very nature of the American Federation of Labor leaves much of the authority in matters of membership and participation in the hands of local unions. Thus, the absence of references to race in constitutional provisions is relatively unimportant.

An example of this situation and the possible results which develop from it is presented by the present status of Negro artisans in St. Louis, Missouri, where in 1930 there were more than 600 skilled Negro mechanics in the building trades. The Urban League of that city attempted for several years to obtain recognition and work for Negro building mechanics. The following is a summary of the League's experience:

> In 1920 an attempt was made by a prominent Negro contractor in St. Louis to organize a class for Negro bricklayers at one of

the colored high schools. At the time this attempt was made, objections were raised by white union officials and statements were published to the effect that Negroes were not permitted to become members of the building trades unions. The fact that this class was established at that time indicated a desire on the part of Negroes to better qualify themselves as craftsmen and to meet the requirements of union membership. The opposition on the part of the union officials indicates what attitude the Negro mechanic has had to overcome here in St. Louis. In other words, over a period of time we have had ample proof of the fact that the Negro is not wanted in the building trades unions in this city irrespective of his training or qualifications. To further emphasize this fact, numerous instances can be recalled of buildings erected and financed by Negro capital on which it was impossible for a Negro mechanic to obtain work because the contractors were obliged to hire union labor. Two notable buildings costing several hundred thousands of dollars to construct, and on which Negroes were not able to obtain work except as laborers, are Poro College Building and Peoples Finance Building.

Although there are a considerable number of well qualified, experienced Negro mechanics in St. Louis, the highest recognition which has been obtainable has been that of laborer. There is a local of Negro hod-carriers and building laborers in St. Louis which is recognized by the building trades organizations. Skilled mechanics, even in instances where they have already hold membership in the International Unions and possessing International cards from locals in other cities showing them to be in standing, have failed to get the proper consideration to which they were entitled as members of the International Unions. Consequently, through their inability to obtain work, large numbers of these men have lapsed in their obligations to the International Unions.

During the past year the League has also sought an opportunity for Negro mechanics in the colored schools. We have been cooperating with a group of men who have been interested in this matter for some time. We have had two hearings before the Building Committee of the Board of Education in which these claims of the colored mechanics were put forth. At the second hearing, officials of the labor unions were invited to participate by the Building Committee. Work was solicited from the Board of Education on the theory that inasmuch as there is a duel system of education, Negro workers should be entitled to at least some of the work in the colored schools. Inasmuch as the Board of Education practices an open shop policy, the colored mechanics feel that they are entitled to consideration irrespective of their non-affiliation with any labor organizations. The Building Committee of the Board of Education however saw fit to take into consideration the attitude of the labor unions and as yet no work has been obtainable although the Board of Education has sent communications to the League indicating that it was sympathetic with the claims of the Negro mechanic. In a recent interview with the Building Commissioner, the Industrial Secretary was told frankly that no Negro mechanics could be given work unless they were members of the unions.

The League knows actually of at least twelve Negro mechanics who have made personal or written applications to the building trades unions. At least six men have applied to the Board of Education for work as mechanics. Four men have made application to the Secretary of the bricklayers' local. There are at least fifty excellent Negro bricklayers, practically all of whom at some time or other have held International cards with locals in other cities. There are between 75 and 100 good Negro plasterers in St. Louis several of whom are small contractors. There are a number of Negro painters. The League in recent months has been responsible for the organization of a group of eighteen Negro painters. Efforts are being made by the League at the present time to organize Negro carpenters.

The Negro mechanic in St. Louis is faced with an almost insurmountable difficulty, that the building trades unions in this city are very strong and deeply entrenched and are determined to keep Negroes out. Negroes have met with every legitimate requirement from the standpoint of training, experience, and qualifications, but despite provisions in the constitutions of the unions against discrimination, there are ways in which the Negro is excluded.

White mechanics refuse to work with Negroes on union jobs, although their real reason is never given. Contractors who might willingly hire a journeyman Negro mechanic holding union membership in another locality, will refuse work on the grounds that he does not need any more men, or that he is using only the men who have worked for him before, whereas actually he fears that if he employs the Negro, his white employees will suddenly become ill, or have to take care of some personal business, or for any number of other fictitious reasons quit work. On the other hand, the League is aware of many instances where white union men have worked with Negro mechanics on open shop jobs for less than union scale.

A Negro mechanic who applies for membership in a union may be kept out if he is blackballed by the members. In a city like St. Louis where traditional attitudes are so deep-seated, it is easy to see how prejudice may operate to keep Negroes out of the unions when the final decision depends upon the approval of a $^2/_5$ or $^3/_4$ majority of the membership. Furthermore, when an applicant's qualifications must be passed upon by an examining committee, that committee reserves to itself the right to determine whether the applicant is qualified. Naturally, it can arbitrarily decide that a man is not qualified, no matter how well trained he actually may be. A short time ago to the League's knowledge, several Negro painters who are unquestionably capable workmen applied in person to the painters' union and after a superficial oral examination were rejected."

Thus, although there were no constitutional provisions excluding Negroes from membership in the building trades' union of St. Louis, colored artisans were, in fact, kept out of the organizations. Due to this local situation, Negroes have not been allowed to obtain employment as skilled workers on Federal Buildings. The construction of these projects is carried out under a closed-shop agreement and Negroes are excluded from the locals which enforce the closed-shop.

While this development has been going on within the ranks of the labor movement, the Negro worker has formed certain attitudes towards unionization. He has come to believe that labor unions usually oppose the economic interests of Negroes. This follows from the fact that every union seeks to establish a closed-shop or as near a closed-shop as is possible. Since American unions have largely excluded Negroes, the closed-shop has meant an arrangement under which there are no job opportunities offered black workers. There have been other occurrences during the past fifty years which have tended to strengthen the Negro's feeling of opposition towards unions. In the past, practically every important entry that the Negro has made into industries previously closed to him has been through his activity as a strike-breaker. Thus, at the very time when unions symbolized few job opportunities for Negroes, strike breaking, scabbing, and unorganized status represented greater job opportunities for them.

There can be no doubt that the nonparticipation of Negroes in the American labor movement was fundamentally harmful to colored workers. It allowed them to be exploited as a submarginal group and it accentuated the racial discrimination to which they ordinarily are subjected. At the same time, failure of the American unions to attempt seriously to include Negro workers greatly crippled the bargaining power and strength of these unions. For the Negro, however, there were certain benefits of a pragmatic and short run nature to be gained from non-union status in the period prior to the NRA.

The NRA has deeply altered this situation. Article 7A of the Act declares that "employees shall have the right to organize and bargain collectively through representatives of their own choosing" and shall not be restrained from joining any labor organization with which they wish to affiliate themselves. The National Labor Board was created to facilitate the functioning of labor clauses of the NIRA. Up to the present time this Board, which hopes ultimately to have mandatory power, has rendered certain decisions which indicate the temper of its policy. In the first place, the board feels that there should be employment of men who were formerly on a strike against a plant. There are indications of the possibility of certain categories of strikes being outlawed. Indeed, the right to strike has been deeply modified. These tendencies indicate that there will be fewer strikes in the future and the strike-breaker will have less chance for permanent employment. This in itself has taken away the chief compensation offered to Negroes as unorganized workers. If unions persist in discriminating and often excluding colored workers from their membership, the new trend of events will translate such action into the exclusion of Negro workers from all desirable jobs in areas where labor is well organized. Unless specific safeguards are set up, Negro wage earners will suffer. There is need for special protection of this minority group.

S O U R C E   NYA, Division of Negro Affairs, Reel 8, frame no. 0001, in *NDABA*.

97. *"The Inter-Departmental Group Concerned with the Special Problem of Negroes: Report of the Agricultural Committee." National Youth Administration, Division of Negro Affairs, ca. Jan. 1937. Discusses the impact of the depression and New Deal programs on black sharecroppers and tenant farmers; concludes that racial violence intensified as the price of cotton dropped and forced blacks off the land.*

The Effects of the Depression on the Negro Farmers of the South

The recent depression has been extremely severe in its effects upon the South. The rural Negro—poor before the period of trade decline—was rendered even more needy after 1929. Many tenants found it impossible to obtain a contract for a crop and were left stranded without any economic resources. It is also evident that many Negro as well as white farm owners lost their property. As the competition in earning a livelihood increased, social unrest grew and racial prejudice became more severe, to the extent that racial friction and lawlessness increased in many sections of the rural South. A study of lynching over a period of forty years reveals that as cotton prices go down, the number of lynchings increases. A study of racial relations during the depression verifies that conclusion.*† In addition, there are evidences of the breakdown of the plantation system during the years of depression. Many rural Negro schools have been closed during the last few years.

The most severe situation confronting the Negro farmer has been that facing the share cropper and farm tenant. The difficulties in the production of cotton involved losses to the landlords. These, in turn, were translated into greater dependence, less security and lower standards of living for the tenants. Since the share croppers were least powerful to resist the hardships of economic depression, they have suffered greatest from the chaos which has permeated southern agriculture.

A most instructive picture of the situation is reflected by the treatment of the Negro farmer under Federal aid offered prior to the initiation of the Recovery Program. There were many abuses in the administration of this aid which are instructive as indication of what can happen to colored farmers under any program of relief. The most complete picture of the situation is that presented at the conference on the Economic Status of the Negro, held in Washington last May.‡ The following summary is drawn from a report of the findings of that conference, as written by Dr. Charles S. Johnson:

Under the Hoover administration, Federal aid was available for farmers in the form of feed, seed and fertilizer loans. The report includes the following general statement concerning the administration of this and other Federal farm relief measures: "Although well conceived as an aid to relief, they have not in practice escaped abuses of a notorious character insofar as Negro farmers are concerned. Not all of them have always been exploited, but the existence of abuses on so large a scale seems inexcusable in the administration of Federal service in such desperate emergencies. Re-

---

The Tragedy of Lynching, by Arthur Raper.
†According to Monroe N. Work, editor of *The Negro Year Book*, the lynching figures from 1928 through 1933 are as follows:

Year	Lynchings Prevented	Persons Lynched
1928	11	24
1929	10	27
1930	21	40
1931	63	13
1932	34	8
1933	37	28

‡Charles S. Johnson, *Economic Status of Negroes*.

sponsibility for a measure of this may be placed upon the unfortunate imperatives of the social system which regards the exploitation of Negroes as more or less a 'normal' condition."

The feed, seed and fertilizer loans have been variously administered. Although in a few belt areas the tenants received and spent their loans according to the intent of the law, the planters often got control of the tenants' checks. "As a matter of fact, the landlord virtually forces the tenant to deliver the check to him; the landlord explains to the tenant that he will not waive his rent to the government—one of the requirements for the loan—unless the tenant agrees to bring the check to him when it comes." The report goes on to show that when the check came, it was delivered to the landlord and the latter often took the money and deposited it to his own account, issuing cash back to the tenant as he felt the tenant needed it. For this service the planter usually charged eight per-cent interest. "Thus, the tenant pays double interest—six per-cent to the government for the money and an additional eight or ten per-cent to the planter for keeping it for him! This practice is common in the upper part of Georgia Black Belt."

The report continues that in other instances the planter secured the money from the tenants upon its arrival and they repayed it to the tenant in feed, seed and fertilizer at credit prices. Thus, it was the farm owner rather than the tenant who profited from the government loan. This practice was fairly prevalent in the central Alabama Black Belt. There have been instances where Negro land-owners have not been allowed to spend the cash which they secured through loans from the government.

There were violations of the Feed, Seed and Fertilizer Loan Service in 1931 which were so flagrant, according to the same report, as to occasion court proceedings. Some of these cases came to light when tenants received receipts from the government for the repayment of loans of which they had no knowledge.

In concluding the experience of the Negro tenant under those forms of Federal aid, the report of the conference makes the following statement: "The planter class appears to be proceeding upon the assumption that the landless farmer must be kept dependent. The property-less tenants in turn have gotten all they could out of the owners before settlement time. Both are hard pressed, but the planter has a scapegoat."

In addition, the report cites instances of flagrant abuses of the Red Cross service. In some cases, planters evaded their agreements for advances to tenants, say: "Let the Red Cross feed them." In one community, the administrator of the Red Cross service is reported to have charged his tenants for the flour and cloth which he "secured" for them.

The report concludes the discussion of relief with the following statement: "These abuses of the relief intended for the farmers reflect the weight of social tradition on the matter of the Negro and the least protected workers, perhaps, more than they reflect purely agricultural problems. It becomes a matter, in this instance, as in many others of the same order, of insuring the protection of this class of workers from abuses which are part of the history of race relations in the section, before their normal plight as farmers can be effectively remedied."

Effect of the Recovery Agencies upon Negro Farmers of the South

The Agricultural Adjustment Administration

When the New Deal was extended to agriculture, one of the most important features of the program was the plan for acreage reduction. In the case of cotton, there was to be a forty per-cent reduction. The cultivation of cotton gives rise, perhaps, to more employment among Negroes than the production of any other product. Naturally, therefore, a program which proposes to reduce materially the amount of this production affects Negroes.

According to the *Administrative Rulings and Instructions Relating to the 1934 and 1935 Cotton Acreage Reduction Plan* * and the *Questions and Answers Covering 1934 and 1935 Cotton Acreage Reduction Plan,* * the program provides for direct payments to owners and cash tenants. In the case of managing share-tenants, the rental and parity payments are to be divided equally between the owners and managing share-tenants. The share cropper or share-tenant is to receive a full proportionate part of any parity payment made under the contract but all payments will be made to the producer and he is under contract to pay the share cropper and/or share tenant. In addition, the land owner is required to adjust the acreage reduction as nearly ratable as practicable amongst tenants on the farm and to maintain the normal number of tenants and other employees on the farm. Both of these requirements are to be carried out "insofar as possible." Further, all tenants are to be allowed to continue occupancy of their houses on the farm, rent free, for 1934 and 1935 *unless any such tenant becomes a*

---

*United States Department of Agriculture, Agricultural Adjustment Administration (Production Division), December, 1933.

nuisance or a menace. Access to fuel for home consumption for tenants is to be allowed without cost to the tenants; an adequate portion of the land rented to the Secretary of Agriculture is to be given tenants to grow food and feed crops for home consumption; the reasonable use of work animals and equipment, in exchange for labor, is to be given to cultivate the land used by the tenant subsistence, and pasture for domestically used live stock is to be granted.

There is evidence to the effect that the Negro *farm owners* producing cotton have generally received fair treatment under the cotton reduction plan although there are occasional irregularities. But since only 11.2% of colored farmers were owners in the 104 counties of the South with greatest number of Negro farmers, and 56.4% of all Negro farmers in thirteen leading southern states were croppers in 1930 (the proportion of Negro share-tenants is much greater in the chief cotton producing areas), the effect of the cotton reduction program upon colored farmers is largely concerned with the fate of the share-tenant. In spite of the safeguards established by the cotton acreage reduction plan, there is evidence that the tenant farmer is not receiving the full measure of protection intended by the plan. In certain instances, the letter rather than the spirit of these protective measures of the cotton crop reduction agreement has been carried out.

Dr. Calvin B. Hoover of the Agricultural Adjustment Administration, in his report on *Human Problems in Acreage Reduction in the South,* gives the following account:

> Various undesirable effects and instances of hardships to individuals have occurred in connection with the cotton acreage reduction program. In some cases these were due to the nature of the cotton contract itself, sometimes to its misinterpretation and sometimes to its violation. These undesirable effects and hardships may be summarized as follows:
>
> 1. There have been a considerable number of cases in which tenant farmers have not received the full amount specified by the 1933 cotton contract.
> 2. The operation of the acreage reduction program creates a motive for reducing the number of tenants on farms. The acreage reduction contracts have within them provisions designed to prevent this motive having effect but the system of enforcement of these provisions has been inadequate.
> 3. The percentage of the rental payments paid to share tenants and share croppers for land withdrawn from cultiva-

tion in accordance with the 1934 cotton contracts is less than in other contracts.

4. The way in which the 1934 cotton contracts have been drawn has produced considerable confusion in the classi-fication of types of tenantry. Upon this classification the division of benefit payments by Government between landowners and tenant depends.

The displacement of Negro tenants (as was the case also for whites) began before, and grew throughout the depression. Thus, at the time of the announcement of crop reduction program, there were many families without arrangements for renting crops—some without shelter. Since the new program has been announced, there have been fewer opportunities for contracting for a crop and this condition has become more grave. Where landlords have kept their promise and have maintained the number of their families, they have often changed the families and substituted smaller families for their former tenants. Often managing share-tenants have been reduced to share croppers despite the fact that the Administra-tive Rulings and Instructions prohibit such action. This has allowed the owner of the farm to receive the full payments from the acreage reduction plan. It has also materially reduced the status of a large number of Negro cotton producers.

In instances where tenants have not been displaced, they have been given only shelter and fuel. They have no contract to make crops, no in-come and no certain means of supplying themselves with food and cloth-ing. If they do receive these, it is because their landlord chooses to give them to the tenant and their continued supply rests entirely in the hands of the giver.

Although there has been but little increase in complete displacement of tenants in the South, the fact that they are remaining is not deeply significant. In many instances landlords are willing to allow their former tenants to live in houses and cabins (for which there are no other possible occupants at this time). The already exploited Negro is rendered more impotent to resist unfair treatment by this peculiar situation. Thus, it is the inability to secure a crop—the contract which provides for advances of seeds, subsistence and equipment, rather than physical displacement—that is most crucial. The tenant in the South—and the Negro tenant in particu-lar—is being separated from his means of earning a living. The tenant needs not only relief but social and economic rehabilitation.

It is difficult to estimate the amount of livelihood displacement the depression and the recovery program have created in the South. Mr. Brown of the State Federal Emergency Relief Administration estimated that in the Eastern part of North Carolina (twenty-three counties) alone, there were some 9,302 farm tenant families who, for the year of 1933, had no arrangement with any landlord to make a crop and had no other employment sufficient to earn a livelihood. These families were managing to live in their former abodes, on neighboring farms and in unoccupied buildings of every description. Their subsistence was obtained through meagre relief, CWA jobs and occasional day labor for their landlord or for a neighboring landowner.

Mr. Brown's summary of conditions in one county of a southern state will serve as an illustration. The North Carolina Federal Emergency Relief Administration and the Institute for Research in Social Science have made a survey of the situation in Greene County, North Carolina. The picture presented by this county is representative for the Eastern part of the state and furnishes what seems to be a slightly favorable pattern for the South generally. In 1930, the county had a population of 18,656 divided almost equally between whites and Negroes. There were some 3,260 farm operators. Their distribution was as follows:

Nature of Farm Population of Green County, N.C.

STATUS	WHITE	NEGRO	TOTAL
Full owners	439	77	516
Part owners	40	26	66
Managers	2	0	2
Tenants	1,306	1,370	2,676
Cash tenants	22	6	28
Croppers	714	1,004	1,714
Other tenants	570	360	930

There were over 325 displaced tenants in Greene County in January, 1934. The survey concerns some 265 of these—84 colored and 81 white. The survey has classified these families in the following manner:

Classification of Displaced Tenants in Greene County

CLASSIFICATION	COLORED	WHITE	TOTAL
Suitable for replacement	114	64	178
Too old, physically unable to farm	28	4	32
Widowed or deserted, no male provider	7	0	7

Have rented a crop for the coming year	35	13	48
Totals	184	81	265

The average farming experience for these tenants was 13.8 years for Negroes and 13.6 years for whites.

A most instructive table which shows length of time without tenant status follows:

Period of Displacement of Families in Green County

LENGTH OF TIME WITHOUT TENANT STATUS	NUMBER OF FAMILIES		
	COLORED	WHITE	TOTAL
Less than a year	14	13	27
One year	18	8	26
Two years	21	19	40
More than two years	42	13	55
Never had tenant status, always farmed as a day laborer	5	5	10
Totals	100	58	158

These data present the gravest problem facing Negro farmers today. At the present, these livelihood-displaced Negroes—as well as whites—are existing at the mercy of their landlords. They have no security or protection from the worst form of arbitrary treatment. Besides, they have no means of earning sufficient to support themselves and their families.

The Farm Credit Administration

While the crop reduction program of the AAA has reduced the managing share cropper to a share cropper in some places, has occasionally displaced tenants and universally rendered it more difficult for those without a crop to secure contract for the same, Negroes have not received the maximum relief possible under the provisions of the FCA. This has been due to a combination of circumstances. First, the ignorance of the rural colored dwellers (enforced by the inadequate school facilities) has made it impossible for the black farmers to avail themselves of all possible benefits. Secondly, they are penalized by their traditional fear of white associations. In some instances where colored farmers have attempted to participate, local administrative practices have limited their benefits. In 1930, 69.4% of Negro-owned farms had dwellings valued under $500 and 90% of them had dwellings valued under $1,000. The Negro farm owner is, therefore, predominately a small farmer. The FCA is intended to include such producers. In the South, the Negro has experienced great difficulty in securing adequate loans upon his property under the FCA. Where loans were made to colored farm owners, the amount of the advance has frequently been too small to meet the needs of the farmers. Although a part of this difficulty is due to the recent deflation, evidence indicates that much of the situation is the result of racial discrimination.

Investigation of the situation in Mississippi has shown that the difficulty presenting itself to Negro farmers has been one of appraisership. The local appraisers for the FCA are often most unsympathetic in their treatment of Negro-owned farms. Thus, in Jones County, a Negro farmer who asked for $3,000 on his improved farm of 120 acres was given $800. His white neighbor across the road from him received $900 on 37 acres. The nature and state of repair of the buildings was about the same in both instances.

The Federal Emergency Relief Administration and the Civil Works Administration

In the operation of rural relief, the Negro has suffered because of the administrative policies of local authorities. A recent investigation showed that the allocation of CWA jobs and the approval of projects had been generally discriminatory. The actual execution of these matters was often in the hands of county committees. Certain of the more important members of these committees were county office holders elected by the local voters. Since the white population controls the political situation, the administration of the committee was executed in a manner which was designed to please the voters. Seldom was any county committee member free from the influence of local pressure. The same situation existed where the administration was in the hands of a prejudiced or "controlled" official. The result was that projects directly benefiting the colored population and Negro employment and relief have been considered only after the white population has been taken care of. This condition was most grave in those rural areas where control is concentrated in the hands of a few influential persons.

In local communities of several states, plantation owners have brought their hands to the CWA and the FERA offices and demanded jobs and relief for them. The landowner has been sufficiently powerful to enforce his request and relief has taken the form of a subsidy to the plantation owner.

Conclusions

The condition of the rural Negro in the South has been presented above. Colored farmers of the South were victims of economic exploitation, lawlessness and poor educational facilities in the years prior to 1929. Since the depression their condition has become worse and attempted relief has not effectively remedied the situation. Indeed the maximum benefits possible under the various Federal agencies for recovery have not been enjoyed by the great majority of Negroes. This has been largely the result of the failure of local administrators to carry out the rulings transmitted to them. It may be said that the smaller the administrative unit and the greater the degree of local control, the worse the conditions to which Negroes are subjected.

(signed)
The Sub-Committee on Agriculture of the
Inter-Departmental Group concerned with the special problems of Negroes

E. H. Shinn, Chairman
Extension Studies
Department of Agriculture

Henry A. Hunt
Assistant to the Governor
Farm Credit Administration

Bruce L. Melvin
Chief of Section
Subsistence Homesteads Division
Department of the Interior

Forrester B. Washington
Director of Negro Work
Federal Emergency Relief
    Administration

Clark Foreman
Adviser on the Economic Status
    of Negroes
Department of the Interior

S O U R C E NYA, Division of Negro Affairs, Reel 8, frame no. 0001, in *NDABA*.

---

98. *"The Marianna, Florida, Lynching. . . ." Report of Walter White, secretary, NAACP, to Harod L. Ickes, secretary, U.S. Department of Interior, 26 Nov. 1934. Offers a detailed, moment-by-moment account of the lynching of Claude Neal, and describes the tension and violence that followed.*

The Marianna, Florida, Lynching

A Report of an Investigation Made for the National Association for the Advancement of Colored People, 69 Fifth Avenue, New York, by a White Southern College Professor into the Killing of Claude Neal by a Mob on October 26, 1934.

On October 19th, 1934, Claude Neal, 23, of Greenwood, Florida was arrested by Deputy Sheriff J. P. Couliette for the murder of Lola Cannidy, 20, also of Greenwood, Florida. Neal, when arrested, was working on a peanut farm belonging to Mr. John Green. He was taken in custody with another man whom investigating officers believed to be involved in the murder to the woods and questioned. It is alleged that a confession was wrung from Neal and that he assumed entire responsibility for the crime. Sheriff W. F. Chambliss, of Jackson County, who was at the Cannidy home at the time of the arrest, was apparently aware of the lynching spirit which was beginning to rise throughout the little farming community, and ordered Neal to be taken to Chipley, Florida for safe keeping, a distance of about 20 miles. With Neal were arrested his mother, Annie Smith and his aunt, Sallie Smith. . . .

The Lynching of Claude Neal

According to a member of the mob with whom I talked, Claude Neal was lynched in a lonely spot about four miles from Greenwood, Florida, scene of the recent crime, and not in Alabama as it was first reported. After Neal was taken from the jail at Brewton, Alabama, he was driven approximately 200 miles over highway 231 leading into Marianna and from there to the woods near Greenwood, where he was subjected to the most brutal and savage torture imaginable.

Neal was taken from the Brewton jail between one and two o'clock Friday morning, October 26. He was in the hands of the smaller lynching group composed of approximately 100 men from then until he was left in the road in front of the Cannidy home late that same night. I was told by several people that Neal was tortured for ten or twelve hours. It is almost impossible to believe that a human being could stand such unspeakable torture for such a long period.

Due to the great excitement sweeping the entire northern section of Florida and southeastern Alabama and to the great number of people who wanted to participate in the lynching, the original mob which secured Neal from the jail at Brewton, evidently decided that if all the niceties of a modern Twentieth Century lynching were to be inflicted upon Neal that it would be unwise for a larger mob to handle the victim. They preferred that his last hours on earth be filled with the greatest possible humiliation and agony. However, the word was passed all over north—eastern Florida and Southeastern Alabama that there was to be a "lynching party to which all white people are invited," near the Cannidy home Friday night. It is also reported that the information was broadcast from the radio station at Dothan, Alabama. I talked to at least three persons who confirmed this statement.

A member of the lynching party with whom I talked described the lynching in all of its ghastliness, down to the minutest detail. After talking with him I went immediately to my room and tried to recall word for word all that he had told me. The story of the actual lynching as related to me and later corroborated by others is as follows:

> "After taking the nigger to the woods about four miles from Greenwood, they cut off his penis. He was made to eat it. Then they cut off his testicles and made him eat them and say he liked it." (I gathered that this barbarous act consumed considerable time and that other means of torture were used from time to time on Neal.)
>
> "Then they sliced his sides and stomach with knives and every now and then somebody would cut off a finger or toe. Red hot irons were used on the nigger to burn him from top to bottom." From time to time during the torture a rope would be tied around Neal's neck and he was pulled up over a limb and held there until he almost choked to death when he would be let down and the torture begin all over again. After several hours of this unspeakable torture, "they decided just to kill him."

Neal's body was tied to a rope on the rear of an automobile and dragged over the highway to the Cannidy home. Here a mob estimated to number somewhere between 3000 and 7000 from eleven southern states were excitedly waiting his arrival. When the car which was dragging Neal's body came in front of the Cannidy home, a man who was riding the rear bumper cut the rope.

> "A woman came out the Cannidy house and drove a butcher knife through his heart. Then the crowd came by and some kicked him and some drove their cars over him."

Men, women and children were numbered in the vast throng that came to witness the lynching. It is reported from reliable sources that the little children, some of them mere tots, who lived in the Greenwood neighborhood, waited with sharpened sticks for the return of Neal's body and that when it rolled in the dust on the road that awful night these little children drove their weapons deep into the flesh of the dead man.

The body, which by this time, was horribly mutilated, was taken by the mob to Marianna, a distance of ten or eleven miles, where it was hung to a tree on the northeast corner of the courthouse square. Pictures were taken of the mutilated form and hundreds of photographs were sold for fifty cents each. Scores of citizens viewed the body as it hung in the square. The body was perfectly nude until the early morning when someone had the decency to hang a burlap sack over the middle of the body. The body was cut down about eight-thirty Saturday morning, October 27, 1934.

Fingers and toes from Neal's body have been exhibited as souvenirs in Marianna where one man offered to divide the finger which he had with a friend as "a special favor."

Another man has one of the fingers preserved in alcohol. . . .

The Marianna Riot of October 27.

After Neal's body had been removed from the courthouse square most of the members of the mob dispersed. Although Saturday is a "big day" in Marianna when the rural folks comes to town to trade there were not as many Negroes in the town on the day following the lynching as usual. The entire week had been one of terror and consequently all those who could remained away from the town. The feeling was very tense in Marianna between the Negroes and whites and the Negroes who came in kept pretty much to themselves.

Toward noon a white man struck a Negro who sought to defend himself and in the struggle with the white man hurled a pop bottle at him. By this time a crowd had gathered and at the sight of a Negro resisting a white man the crowd flew into a frenzy. The Negro finally tore himself away from the mob and ran across the street and into the courthouse where he was given protection by a friendly group of white men. The mob clamored for another victim but they were held at bay by a machine gun. Being unable to secure their intended victim the mob began a systematic attempt to drive all Negroes from the town. I am reliably informed that this mob was led by a young man from Calhoun county who has money and comes from a *good* family. The mob apparently started from the west side of the Plaza and began driving Negroes from the streets and stores where some were engaged in buying and selling and working for white employers. An observer stated that, "the mob attacked men, women and children and that several blind persons were ruthlessly beaten." Another observer said: "They (the Negroes) came from the town in droves, some driving, some running, some crying, all scared to death."

In several instances the mob met resistance on the part of the white employers of Negro labor. A Negro porter was serving a white customer in front of his employer's store. Before he knew what was happening the mob was upon him. With a knife he slashed his way thru the mob and gained the front door of the store. His employer locked him in a room and kept the mob away with a shot gun. A woman who was caught downtown with her maid almost single handedly drove the mob away from their intended victim. After emptying the streets, stores, places of business, hotels, etc. of Negroes the mob started into the residential section to drive out the Negro maids. Some women sent their maids home, others hid them in closets. One man whose wife shielded her maid from the mob said, "Saturday was a day of terror and madness, never to be forgotten by anyone."

Lack of Police Protection

During the rioting the city of Marianna was completely without police protection. I was told that members of the mob searched the town for members of the police force and threatened to beat them up if they were found. One observer said, "The United States army couldn't have stopped that crowd Saturday morning." When Mayor Burton realized what was going on and that the city was at the mercy of the mob he tried personally to deputize some special officers but was unable to find anyone to serve. He later sent a friend out to find some men who would serve. This man finally returned and said that he could not find anyone who would serve.

National Guards Called

At this juncture the Mayor called Governor Sholtz in Tallahassee. In response to the mayor's request a detachment of National Guards arrived from Apalachicola about 4:30 Saturday afternoon and gradually dispersed the mob. The guards patrolled the streets of the town and particularly the Negro section. The mob retreated before the guards but left the parting warning that they would, "be back Saturday to finish up what we started."

On the following Saturday the police force was increased by about twenty men. Several Negroes were attacked early Saturday morning by white men who were arrested and placed in jail. A drizzling rain began about 9 A.M., followed by a downpour about 11 A.M. which probably prevented another "day of terror and madness" in Marianna.

Lola Cannidy

On the afternoon of October 18, 1934, Lola Cannidy, 20, daughter of Mr. and Mrs. George Cannidy, farmers near Greenwood, Florida, disappeared from home. It is alleged that Lola Cannidy told her parents that she was going to "water the pigs" and attend to some other chores about the farm. The family took no particular notice of her absence when she failed to return in the late afternoon. She had been seen by her brother, who was working in a nearby field, talking to someone on the farm. When she failed to return in the evening her parents called her sister in Tallahassee to find out if Lola was there. When they were unable to locate her in Tallahassee and she did not return home, a search was begun for her in the community. Early on the morning of October 19, her body, fully clothed, was discovered by an uncle, John King, a short distance from the Cannidy home, badly mutilated about the head and arms and partially covered with brushwood and pine logs.

Sheriff W. F. Chambliss of Jackson county was called to the Cannidy home and an investigation was begun immediately. A watch, ring, a piece of clothing and a hammer were among the things discovered near the place where Lola Cannidy came to her death. Among the first homes in the community to be searched was that of Annie Smith, mother of Claude Neal, who lived just across the road from the Cannidy home. The officers investigating the case claim to have found some bloody garments in the home.

Several boys claimed that they saw Claude Neal near the scene of the crime that afternoon and that he had some wounds on his hand which he said he received while repairing a fence.

Claude Neal Arrested

A search was immediately begun for Claude Neal. He was arrested on the peanut farm belonging to John Green. When Neal was arrested he told officers that another man, Herbert Smith, was associated with him in the crime. Smith was later arrested and he and Neal were taken to the nearby woods and questioned. I am reliably informed that Neal had been in a fight with Herbert Smith on the Saturday previous and that in the fight "Herbert had whipped him." In order to "get even" with Smith, Neal sought to involve him in the case. Smith later related the entire incident to an informant who described Smith as being literally scared to death. Neal finally admitted that Smith had nothing to do with the crime and that he alone was involved. Smith was subsequently released by the officers.

Claude Neal and Lola Cannidy

Claude Neal and Lola Cannidy had always lived in the same neighborhood. Mrs. Smith's home (Neal's mother) was just across the road from the Cannidy home. Neal had played with the Cannidy children and when he was large enough to work, worked on the Cannidy farm. For some months, and possibly for a period of years, Claude Neal and Lola Cannidy had been having intimate relations with each other. The nature of their relationship was common knowledge in the Negro community. Some of his friends advised him of the danger of the relationship and had asked him not to continue it. Miss Cannidy, it seems, desired to break the relationship existing between herself and Neal and the fatal meeting was prearranged for the purpose of arriving at some understanding. At the meeting in the woods Miss Cannidy told Neal that she did not want him to speak to her again and that if he did so that she would tell the white men in the community on him. (Should Miss Cannidy have "told on him" it would have meant certain death.) When she told Neal that she wanted to "quit" and further threatened to "tell on him," he "got mad and killed her." Neal later told a friend what had happened. Neal is reported to have told the friend, "When she said she didn't want me to speak to her and then told me that she'd tell the white men on me, I just got mad and killed her."

Was Claude Neal Guilty?

When I first arrived in Marianna I heard that there was serious doubt as to Neal's guilt. The rumor was that a white man had murdered Lola Cannidy, had taken the bloody garments to Neal's home to have them washed and had later laid the murder on Neal. Knowing how often innocent Negroes are framed by guilty white men I gave particular attention to the theory. I was unable to find any substantial support for this theory among the Negroes in the Greenwood community. It is entirely possible that due to the great terror under which Negroes all over this section of Florida are living that they were too frightened to say or do anything which might cause them to become victims of another mob as had so recently descended upon them. Feeling was running so high during the period of investigation that it was not safe for a citizen to ask too many questions about the lynchings. Naturally it was difficult for an outsider to carry out a thorough investigation of every particular. The account of the murder came to me from the most reliable sources including white and Negro informants. I still have some doubts in my mind but I accept the story as told as the most plausible and reliable account which I received. . . .

Conclusions

It is evident from these findings that:

(1) The mob intended to lynch Claude Neal from the beginning,
(2) That the nature of the press reports confirmed their intention,
(3) That the statements occurring in the local press incited to lynching,
(4) That the local officials and the Governor of the state must have been aware of the probability of lynching, and
(5) That, insufficient protection was given to the prisoner.

S O U R C E NYA, Division of Negro Affairs, Reel 8, frame no. 0001, in *NDABA*.

99. *"More Senators Lining Up Behind Anti-Lynch Bill." News release, Press Service of the NAACP, ca. Apr. 1934. Discusses growing support for a federal antilynching law and a variety of civil rights struggles that engaged the NAACP during the period.*

More Senators Lining Up Behind Anti-Lynch Bill

Continuous Pressure Needed to Get Bill to Vote As Passage Seems Assured Once It is Up; White House Said to Favor

Washington, April 2—Continuous pressure on each senator is the crying need for the passage of the Costigan-Wagner anti-lynching bill.

Voters should write their senators asking them to become active in getting the bill up for a vote, as well as voting for it once it comes up. A new tabulation of senators here yesterday showed that without a doubt the bill can be passed if it is brought up.

The edge has been taken off the bitter fight which southern senators would have waged upon it by the growing sentiment in the South, and especially the resolution of the powerful Woman's Missionary Council of the Methodist Episcopal Church, South, which passed a resolution March 12 unanimously endorsing the bill.

Senator Bennet C. Clark of Missouri has written the St. Louis branch of the N.A.A.C.P.: "I am heartily in favor of the proposed anti-lynching bill."

Senator L. J. Dickinson of Iowa has written the Des Moines N.A.A.C.P. branch: "If the Costigan-Wagner bill comes to a vote I expect to vote for it."

Both these Senators were recently reported as opposed to the bill.

Oswald Garrison Villard has written thirteen senators asking them to vote for the bill and has received definite pledges thus far from half of them that they will vote for the bill.

Senator Nye of North Dakota writes: "I shall give the bill my most earnest support."

Senator Shipstead of Minnesota writes: "I expect to support it."

Senator Cutting of Arizona writes: "I intend to vote for the Costigan-Wagner anti-lynching bill." Senator David I. Walsh of Massachusetts writes: "I am in strong sympathy with the Costigan-Wagner bill. I have always supported anti-lynching bills."

It is understood here that the White House favors the passage of the bill. Telegrams and letters to President Roosevelt asking him to insist to the leaders of Congress that the bill be passed before Congress adjourns will be exceedingly helpful at this stage of the fight. . . .

Editorial of the Week

Jubilee of N.A.A.C.P.

**From *America* (A Catholic-Review of the Week)
February 24, 1934—New York City**

The National Association for the Advancement of Colored People, the "N.A.A.C.P.," celebrated its twenty-fifth anniversary as an organization on Lincoln's birthday, February 12. During the entire period of its history the Association has battled for Negro rights, particularly in the civic field. It has been the major agency in arousing the sentiment of the country against lynching. It fought, successfully, against the Louisville segregation ordinance of 1914. In 1925 it carried the case of the Arkansas peons before the Supreme Court of the United States, and won an historical decision therefrom. It was instrumental in preventing the Senate of the United States from confirming the appointment of Judge Parker. In the meanwhile, its branches have grown to 378, in the North, West, and large centers of the South. At the present moment the Association is conducting an appealing campaign for its work: "a penny for every Negro in the United States." The N.A.A.C.P. has been severely criticized for its militancy, and will probably continue to be. However, it is not the policy to impede the work of those who resort to more peaceful methods. Its advocates observe that, in point of fact, the more conservative movements in behalf of the Negro would not achieve what they have accomplished were there not the more militant group in the field to bear the burden of controversy: indeed, that the Negro has obtained little in the United States that he has not had to contend for. From the Catholic point of view, militancy is as Christlike as peace. In His life, the Saviour illustrated both policies; and the story of

Blessed Roch Gonzalez, in this issue, shows the sanction that His Church puts upon a genuine battle for human rights. Catholics can wish success to the N.A.A.C.P. . . .

S O U R C E   NYA, Division of Negro Affairs, Reel 8, frame no. 001, in *NDABA*.

C. LIFE HISTORIES: WORK, FAMILY, AND COMMUNITY

100. *Interview by Jeff Norrell of George Brown, 30 Aug. 1981. Discusses work at the Sloss-Sheffield Furnace in Birmingham (now one of the nation's leading industrial museums); relates various aspects of the work process, managerial practices, and changing technology.*

QUESTION: How long did you work here at Sloss?
ANSWER: I started here in 1929.
QUESTION: How old were you when you started?
ANSWER: We didn't have an age situation at that time. If you were big enough they'd hire you, and if you worked well they'd keep you.
QUESTION: When did they start bringing in Brazil ore to use here?
ANSWER: I can't remember the date, the company got together on bringing in this ore here. It was the Tennessee Coal and Iron Railroad Company at that time. The company was later bought by U.S. Steel. U.S. Steel, U.S. Pipe, Republic, and Sloss. They had the franchise on this ore being brought in here. This ore would make better pig iron and better steel than the old iron we had.
QUESTION: Did they change over when you were working for Sloss?
ANSWER: They changed over under U.S. Pipe but it was the same thing. This place operated according to how people would buy iron. As long as they could make a sale on pig iron they had the work force to do it. When they got to the place where they didn't need any pig iron, what we'd do was bank

Street musicians in Harlem in 1943. The hard times brought on by the depression provided inspiration to a generation of black blues artists. Courtesy of the Library of Congress.

the furnace. When you'd bank the furnace, they'd set there for six months and all they'd do was come over here get the boilers and stones hot and get everything in operation, put the wind back over the furnaces and blow back up. We use to open it up for awhile and run it and bank it.

QUESTION: Do you remember periods when it was inactive here? What years or about when it might have been when you had to bank it for a long time?

ANSWER: When I came here we had two furnaces here on First Avenue. We had two furnaces in North Birmingham, and we had two furnaces in Sheffield. That is why it was called Sloss-Sheffield Steel and Iron Company. You had three places that was operated by Sloss Sheffield Steel and Iron Company.

QUESTION: So you would have periods when there wouldn't be any demand for pig iron?

ANSWER: During that particular time it was the Depression days and there wasn't any work for any of us. Then they got an order for a good bit of pig iron they'd call us back. We'd come back and we'd work probably until that order was out and they would put so many thousands of tons of pig iron on the ground. That's how we would operate. As long as they got enough pig iron to take care of the customers, it was too expensive to operate and they'd have no need to operate.

QUESTION: Well, during the Depression would they cut you off completely or would you come and, like, work a day a week? How would you do when things were real slow?

ANSWER: They were pretty nice about that. What they'd do, they had something for you to do. I have worked one day a month, I'd work sometimes one day a week. If they had anything for you, they'd call you and give you a chance, because they know you had to live. In those days the company had quarters to live in.

QUESTION: Where were your quarters?

ANSWER: Well, I never did live in the quarters but we had them. All around the garage, all where the general office is, all out in this area. If the company needed you, you stayed in those houses. If they cut you off they wouldn't put you out but if you lived there and failed to come out and work, well, they wouldn't let you live there then. You had them in North Birmingham for two or three blocks. Blast furnaces had to have people where to get a hold of them in cases of emergency, or if they need you right quick, they had to have someone around.

QUESTION: What is this right here?

ANSWER: This right here is what you call a granulator. A man operates this granulator where the slag runs out of the furnace. It runs into the hole. That chain wheel turned all those wheels and drug that slag there into a receiving hopper. Up under the bottom you've got a clutcher and it fall out of that clutcher into a belt. Another belt at the bottom takes it over and dumps it into a car ready to be chopper. That's what you call pulverized slag. Then you've got a different type of slag, unpulverized—like that lump slag over there. When it comes out of the furnace the iron goes to the bottom and the slag comes to the top. It runs out of the pit and the iron runs in the ladle. That's what you call flushing the furnace. Flushing the furnace to get rid of the slag but they had a order for it so they used the pulverized slag to make concrete blocks out of it.

QUESTION: Who would order the slag?

ANSWER: Well, different companies, for concrete blocks and various things.

QUESTION: Didn't they make fertilizer out of the slag too? Fertilizer to put on the crops?

ANSWER: The concrete buusiness as far as I know. They could use it for anything they wanted.

QUESTION: What was down that long way?

ANSWER: A casting shed. They used to make pig molds under the shed. They used to mold them by hand. Molds to pour the iron in. They used to mold them in the sand but they had to handle them by hand. Then they would get all the pig molds out of there to be dumped into various cars and be shipped like that.

QUESTION: Is that the real size of one of them?

ANSWER: Well, that's a good question you asked. That size pig that you've got there was made from a machine. The pig molds that we used to make into the sand molds were much larger. We were lucky enough by the help of the good Lord to find one or two around here to let the public see whenever we are ready.

QUESTION: How much would one of these pigs of iron weigh?

ANSWER: Well, they come in different sizes. You might have a company to say he wanted to make small sizes but so many pounds for perspective purposes. Well, the man on the pig machine would pour them that way, you see? But making them on the regular size like that one, they would be about sixty or seventy pounds. Some companies wanted small pig molds.

QUESTION: When you made these pigs in the sander over here, would a man have to lift it once it got dry and cooled off? Would a man have to lift it and put it somewhere? Did you have any mechanization?

ANSWER: Well, Naw. That's what we had to do by all manpower. We had to mold in the sand, take them out of the sand, pick them up, no crane, and load them by hand into cars and be shipped like that.

QUESTION: Well, let me get it straight now. Here at Sloss Furnace you just made iron. You didn't make steel. This was not a steel furnace, but an iron furnace, right?

ANSWER: This was what you call a hot blast furnace.

QUESTION: Anybody making steel could have bought this pig iron from you and then reprocessed it, right?

ANSWER: Yes, they buy the pig iron and keep it in that type of furnace and mix it into steel.

QUESTION: What is this over here?

ANSWER: That's a stove. If we were going to start this furnace up we would have to build a fire in those four stoves, get those stoves as hot as you could get them. The boilers on the rear end would do the same thing. You'd get the blowing room ready, you'd get the furnace ready.—you talking about starting it up. Every man would be on his job getting them ready. I could name them for you. When you get everybody in place and the Superintendent tell them, "Man the engine and start moving it!" Throwing hot air out of the stoves. It starts blowing them in hard. You make the steam on your boilers continue to run. You start to melting your ore and you getting hotter and hotter until all the things going. When you get the furnace to operating, it operates itself. All you got to do is keep feeding and that's the way it operates.

QUESTION: Are you saying you heated the ore on this part (melted) and did it go over there or what?

ANSWER: No, your hot air and pressure would be coming this way. That pipe holds quite a bit of pressure, hot air is so hot until it melts that ore or anything you put into it.

QUESTION: So this is where the cooking actually took place right here?

ANSWER: Right up on that wall. It's called a hot blast furnace, it blows pressure in and it gets so hot until it holds so many degrees. I think that furnace runs about two hundred and fifty to two hundred and seventy-five pressure for heat and you know that's quite a bit of pressure for heat.

QUESTION: Would they use coke to heat that iron?

ANSWER: Oh, yes.

QUESTION: What would they use over here?

ANSWER: What we used over there to keep the stove in operation comes out of here. When you get it in operation the furnace produces its own goods, goes to a gas washer out of the gas washer, through that pipe back over the stove. You've got a place to heat the stove and keep them hot. We keep things operating on the boiler around here.

The gas off the furnace heated anything we could use for certain purposes, that's what you call a "down turner." When it gets to operating that type of gas that we got will come in that pipe and then in the "down turner." That long pipe is the gas washer. It washes that gas and comes in another pipe.

The water would have it processed and it would come out of that pipe and into the stove and then reuse it. It wasn't quite as high as this natural gas but it was the gas that we used.

QUESTION: Where did the coke go in?

ANSWER: When we get up there I'll show you where it goes in.

QUESTION: What did a millwright do?

ANSWER: He tends to all these pipes up here and does whatever is necessary in case of an emergency. This, where we are now, is the bottom of number one furnace. We were speaking while ago about the conductors pipe, this is where your gas travels in. Your hot air comes in here and goes down in this blow turner and blows into there, and this air is so hot, red hot.

Right in the middle of this pipe, if you wanted to look in and see how it was operating, it had something like a piece of plastic and you could see how it was melting.

QUESTION: When you say stock you mean coke and iron ore, right?

ANSWER: Right, this is what I mean. If you say limestone in one bin, Brazil ore in another, African ore in another, any type of ore being ordered to be put in the bin had to be put in whenever they were told to be put in.

Whenever one got ready to put it in the furnace, the supervisor could walk up here and pick up a piece of slag and say, you've got the wrong thing in it. And if you put the wrong thing in it, you would have phosphate iron.

QUESTION: Tell us again a little bit more about the different kinds of ore. What were the characteristics about the "Red Mountain" ore.

ANSWER: Well, the "Red Mountain ore I don't know too much about it. Sloss-Sheffield had, when I came here, had ore mines in Bessemer. I got some right here, it was a pretty good grade of ore.

Sloss had an ore mine in Sheffield, good brown ore. Then we had one in Russellville, then they had brown ore scattered around.

This company had quite a few ore mines. In those days all these companies were digging and producing and using their own material. As time went by they found out they could make a better grade of iron with South American ore. I guess that's why later on they went to closing all the ore mines. I don't think you've got one operating in Alabama.

QUESTION: They went to the South American Ore because it had a higher grade of iron in the ore, right?

ANSWER: They learned they could buy it over there cheaper than we could dig it and deliver it here.

QUESTION: They would basically let the stock off over here on the track. How would they move it from over there into this furnace?

ANSWER: By your skip car. The skip car go on that track and the man puts it on the scale car and brings it on down here and dumps it in the skip car and the skip car takes it to the top of the furnace. When it gets up to there, then it goes into a receiving hopper, and if he's not ready then it stays in there until he gets ready and he pushes a button and opens one bell.

When you open one bell, you close another. It still holds the pressure in the furnace.

QUESTION: How hot would it get in there?

ANSWER: Too hot for me. It would be so hot until you couldn't stand around here.

QUESTION: Would it be anybody standing around here when it was really cooking in there?

ANSWER: Somebody was gonna be standing by it or kneeling near it.

This furnace had to be nursed like a baby. You've got to know what to do with it.

QUESTION: How hot would it be out here?

ANSWER: Maybe hot enough for you to fall out. I've fell out here. See, when this furnace is casting you've got over two thousand degrees.

About one hundred tons of pig iron goes in that ladle there when it's in liquid form. You've got to get somebody to operate it. Then you've got two troughs. You've got to get somebody to get it down these troughs.

Come around here and I'll show you exactly how it works. This trough has to be prepared, has to be mixed with sand. The trough has to be all the way to the far end.

QUESTION: What does the "mud-gun" do?

ANSWER: The "mud-gun" stops up that hole. Two men have to stand over here with an air drill and drill that hole out in the furnace to get that iron out of it.

After they drill that hole then the iron starts shooting out. When it gets to shooting out there the trough starts building up. After it builds up, it levels here.

The first thing to come out of this trough right here would be slag. Over in the runner, over in the pits. Reason why your slag would come first would be cause your iron is heavier than your slag. Your slag would come to the top.

QUESTION: Tell me again, how would they drill a hole? What was up there, what was stopping it up?

ANSWER: That hole that's up there, after they drill that hole, when they get ready to stop that hole back up, the stone man would operate this "mud-gun." This "mud-gun" would turn it all the way around in this hole and that little lever right there, he'd close the door and the weight of it, that little motor on the block would pump that mud in the hole and it would automatically close up.

QUESTION: How would they drill a hole in it?

ANSWER: You could do it. You've got a little air drill, three men would drill it out.

But whenever it got hard, that's your mud right over there, mix it with coal. There's your mud mixer over there. When you'd get your mixer fixed up like that the hotter it'd get, the harder it would stay in there. They would hold that iron an pressure in there.

QUESTION: George, it must not have been as hot as it could be right here when they drill a hole in there.

ANSWER: Well, you didn't care nothing about it you had to get the iron. See, the way you cast is, you cast so many hours when after the first cast you got two men to take care of it.

You've got a "cable" man to take care of this, you got a "fall" man to take care of this over here. Then you've got a stone man, his job is to operate the stones out here. Plus you've got the superintendent.

QUESTION: How hot would it get when this thing is going full blast?

ANSWER: Regardless of how hot it is, it's your job. It would be over one hundred degrees in this particular place, but in working on the blast furnace every bit of it was dangerous.

Each man accepts a job that's got to be done. If he's going to do it, it's three hundred degrees. The man would come out here and help you if you got in trouble but your job is to be a keeper. The keeper tends to this side of the furnaces and helps the fall man. All work is in teams.

If it runs up to five hundred degrees well, that man's got eight hours of work that he's got to do. That's the way blast furnaces operate. It don't operate on how hot it is or how bad it is. That's what it takes to produce pig iron.

Then, when they get through they may have a resting period sit down and rest two or three hours. We've got shacks on the other side that they'd go over and get out of the weather.

QUESTION: How long would it go like that? Would it go like that for eight straight hours?

ANSWER: No! No! If you'd let this furnace go like this for eight straight hours you'd burn it down.

QUESTION: How long would you burn it?

ANSWER: Oh, that would be determined by the type of ore and the material that you put into it. You had to measure to get certain amounts of iron, then you'd flush your slag out of it.

Your problem is the melting. If you're melting some type of iron like maybe two and one-half or three percent foundry iron or something like that which produces a heap of iron, they may have a shorter breakage or making hot iron may take a little longer but you get less iron out of it. It may be harder to handle.

QUESTION: Tell me the difference.

ANSWER: The difference between a hot iron and a cold iron is: a hot iron makes less iron but it's a higher grade and it costs more money to produce. But it's a hotter iron that you can't hardly get out of the furnace, then when you get it in the runners you can't hardly make but small amounts at a time. Now, cold iron you can make quite a bit of that.

QUESTION: Is hot iron a stronger iron?

ANSWER: Well, if it's high manganese iron, high sulfur and low sulfure, then the high quality and low quality, whatever degree of iron it is about two and one-half or three percent high iron.

Some grades of iron doesn't make much of it but it costs more money.

QUESTION: Which job did you have? Did you work around in here?

ANSWER: I have but not regularly. I was always a borrowed man. I never did like to be around this heat here. But whenever they wanted me to do something I never said no. Any job I done what I could and various people taught me what they could about it and I always appreciated that. That's why I learned as much as I possibly could, not knowing, I'd ever be able to live this long, this day in this site. That's why I wanted to see this furnace preserved to see it fixed so people could come out here. Sloss Furnace Association, they worked hard all the way through. This is our second president we've got. Our first president had to leave and Jim Walters and I have been working together for quite a while and he'd done great things.

I am hoping that people will come out and find what this old historic landmark is, under the supervision of Jim Walters. The people will sit back and say what they'll do. Come on out and let's all get together and see what we all can do. That'll be one of the best things in the world if you want to make some history in the city of Birmingham.

QUESTION: When you came here to the Sloss Furnace in about 1929, what would a man just coming in here most likely make?

ANSWER: Back when I came here you made thirty-two cents an hour when you could and that was big money. Thirty-two cents an hour was great.

QUESTION: Were ya'll working an eight-hour day then or what?

ANSWER: Naw, it would at least be ten hours or twelve hours. Unless they didn't need you at all, just didn't have nothing for you to do.

QUESTION: On the sight here, were some of these jobs here reserved for white men and some for black?

ANSWER: Well, in those days the superintendent, the shopkeeper, and the foreman were white. Before I came here it used to be about eighty-five percent black. You had to be almost a mule to do this kind of work out here. . . .

QUESTION: Was there a lot of noise?

ANSWER: Yes, there was so much noise till you worked by signals. When you changed stoves, you could hear it on Red Mountain, over in Mountain Brook.

QUESTION: Did any of the furnaces ever blow up while you were working here?

ANSWER: No, they never blew up. One might get hot, one might burn out or burn through, but we was always lucky enough to get the wind off that furnace in some kind of way where it wouldn't blow up.

Each man knew what to do. One would always look out for the other one. That's the way we operated here. You've got to know something about it, you've got to watch the other worker.

Everything around the blast furnace is dangerous, nothing is safe around here, nothing is easy around here. In order to make it go, you must maintain the interest in it.

SOURCE Oral Interviews, Birmingham Collection, Department of Archives and Manuscripts (Birmingham Public Library).

101. *"Virgil Johnson, An Old School Colored Farmer." Interview by W. O. Foster, 22 Nov. 1938, Chapel Hill, N.C. WPA interview; discusses life on the farm from slavery to the Great Depression.*

"I jest got in," Virgil's wife, Rachel, told me when I knocked at her door. "Come on in and I'll call 'Budge'; that's my husband; his name's really Virgil. I'm not here much. I work down at Mr. James Johnson's. His mother's there; she's ninety-one and has broke her hip. I goes down there about six in the morning and comes home about two for a couple of hours; then I goes back and works 'till seven. Here's Budge now."

"How am I doin'?" Budge said. "I'm sixty-seven years old, born in 1871. Too old to farm much more. I was born two hundred yards from here; 'ceptin' seven years, I've always lived with the Johnsons."

I notice you have the same name as the Johnsons. Did your people belong to them before the war? "Yes, my father was a slave on their place and never left them. I heard my parents tell of slavery days and how they hid the hams and the horses and cows when the Yankees came through.

Some of the boys around here can't remember the World War. It looks like we'll bring on another war for them real soon."

Budge noticed that I was interested in the baby carriage across the room and anticipated my question. "No, that don't belong to us. Our daughter lives with us; they has a two months old baby. I been married twice. First wife died after her first baby. Then I married Rachel here and we had five more; but all of 'em is married now. Daughter keeps house for me and her husband works for a contractor. He's been working lately at Chapel Hill and Duke. I keep on messin' around on the farm but I tell my son-in-law to keep on at public work 'cause there ain't no money in farming. I likes to have my own mule and buy my fertilizer; then I gits three-fourths of the cotton and two-thirds of the corn and wheat. Everything else I raise is mine. I didn't git no allotment for tobacco; they let me have four acres of corn and two acres of cotton. Last year I made a bale of cotton on two acres. Old man boll-weevil cut in on me this spring and I raised only about two hundred pounds. This year I done all the plowin' and hired only three days of choppin'. Wife and daughter don't work on the farm none. I'se only got one hog. A varmint got thirty of my chickens one night so I quit raisin' 'em. My daughter canned a lot of things last summer."

Budge lives about seven miles north of Chapel Hill near the railroad tracks. He has four rooms. We sat in the living room before a wood fire. The Johnsons are glad that the fireplace projects so far into the room because it gives forth so much warmth. This is the only chimney in the house and has to draw for the three stoves in the two bedrooms and the kitchen-dining room. In one corner of the living room was a sewing machine, a double bed of strong iron frame, a dresser, and a broken-down phonograph. Two rockers and three straight chairs completed the furniture of the room. I saw what appeared to be a life insurance policy projecting from behind a mirror and asked about it. Budge said "that's a straight life policy I got with the New York Life Insurance Company; won't anybody get anything as long as I live." He said he didn't carry as much as a thousand dollars but didn't seem to want to state the amount.

"We are members of the Mt. Sinai Baptist Church," Budge told me. "No, I don't vote. I used to until they fixed the franchise up. About forty years ago I was votin' and they passed a law making the voters explain the constitution and they put in the grandfather clause. I couldn't fit in with that; knew it was just an excuse to keep the niggers from votin', and I ain't voted since. If I was to vote today, I'd vote for Roosevelt. I don't care if he is a Democrat, he helps the poor man and the farmer. They say that Hoover told 'em over the radio that the jobs should be given to the whites and the colored people could go rabbit-hunting. People can't live on rabbits. Hoover don't care for the workin' man and he said they's no better than dogs. Roosevelt has held cotton up to nine cents and if they gives up the allotments, it will drop to four cents."

"Ever since the war, the colored folks has looked on the elephant as the animal that helps 'em. But I'm coming to believe that the elephant may be all right in Africa but the American niggers had better stay close to the American mule. I honors Lincoln for freein' us. But the Republic party has changed. The G.O.P. stands for the rich man. They jist counted on the colored man voting right and didn't do nothing for us. Roosevelt is for all the poor folks, white and black. You know, as well as I do that they ain't one rich nigger in a thousand. If the Democrats keeps bein' friendly to the poor, there soon won't be one Republican in a thousand colored people. Some of the colored peoples tries to hide it that they's votin' for Roosevelt. I don't vote for him but I talks for him and I don't care if I do git scolded for it. The best friend a colored man has is a white Democrat. Just as sure as most of my race gits to votin' Democratic the South is goin' to give 'em back the vote. Northern Republicans don't like us colored people except at a distance. When they moves down here they don't know how to treat us. The only white people that is interested enough to git along with us is the ones that has lived here all their lives. I tells my colored neighbors that the sooner they forgit the Republicans the better off they'll be.

"Lot of colored people moved up North lately. They makes more wages but pays higher rent. Some of the rich folks like to work 'em until they's through with 'em. When they is out of work a northern man won't even give 'em a meal. What's the good of calling you 'mister' if they won't give you work and won't help you when you's hungry. I tell 'em they can go to Chicago or Detroit, wherever they is, but I'm er-staying right here. As long as there is any brush near by I can get wood to keep the house warm. I'm old but I can still dig my food out of the ground. I've always been able to buy or beg enough clothes to make me warm. Mr. Johnson's place is home ter me.

"This here insurance won't make the old lady rich but she won't starve when I'm gone. She can work for Mr. Johnson a long time yet. Then our chillun will keep her from want. We will come in on that pension for old folks soon. Mr. Johnson says Congress is likely to jump it up some more next year. If they wants the money to keep movin' tell 'em to give it to us old folks. We'll keep it movin'. We'll spend each check long before the next one gits here. People over sixty ought to give up their jobs in the cities and let the young fellows have them. Then the boys could marry early and quit their meanness. The girls wouldn't need to work so much neider, case they could git husbands earlier. Then we would have the old fashioned family with lots er chilluns round de door. Looks to me like the country is on de way out of de woods. Wish I could live to see the new day de new deal is goin' to give us. You are young enough to see the reapin' of what's being sowed now. Some of the seed has done come up and I can tell that the people is gittin' in better shape. But the next twenty-five years will see a new country. Wish I could be here to see the sun come up on the new day. . . ."

SOURCE Federal Writers Project #3709, in the Southern Historical Collection (University of North Carolina Library, Chapel Hill).

102. *George Burris, black servant, interview/narrative with Mary Brown, Charlotte, N.C., Aug. 1939. WPA interview; recalls sharecropping life in South Carolina; discusses casual labor, child rearing, superstition, religious beliefs.*

"I was born down in South Carolina in June 1905, I don't know the date because it was never written down no where. I disremember what Ma told me about it, but I knows one thing I have been hungry a lot of times.

"Pa was a sharecropper, and he had a house full of younguns. There were so many of us we could not get to the table at two settings. It seemed I always had to eat at the last table and there was nothing left except some cold bread and a few meat skins. Pa raised a lot of cotton, and looks like he ought to have made a lot of money 'cause he made us younguns work from sun up till dark, sometimes 'twas so dark us couldn't see us hands 'fore us faces.

"Us had all kinds of chickens, and one time us had a mule and cow, but you know how it is with pore ole niggers. Every year the white man would come 'round with the year book and sorta figure up how we stood. Well, sometimes he would give us a little money, and Pa would git out his little 'bacco sack and stick it right down in there; all hell and high water couldn't git him to part with one cent, on account of he was saving it to be buried with. Then the next year when the man would come back, he would tell us that we hadn't made nothing that year, and then he would say, 'If it wasn't for your wife and chilluns I'd run you offen this place.' Then he would take the calf that Pa had saved for a young cow.

"All the money we ever had to spend at all, we had to go out and work by the day for it, and in them days us got twenty five cents a day and had to board ourselves outten that. I stayed around home till I was about grown. I wanted to go with the gals a little like the rest of the boys was doing, so I says to myself, 'I'se gwine to leave these ole folks and go out and work for wages so I can git some money.' I soon found out it won't what it was cracked up to be, and I was mighty glad to git back to my mammy and daddy.

"Pa kinder got to what that white man was doing, 'cause everytime we would git a cow calf raised up that would be the time he would come 'round and tell us we hadn't made nothing and go off leading the calf. One year Pa give me the calf, and I told them that was one calf the white man wouldn't get. In the fall I seen him coming, he and Pa just talked and talked, then I hears Pa tell him, 'I ain't got no calf; it 'longs to Jim.' The man says, 'I don't care who it belongs to, you and your bunch of good-for-nothing niggers owes me money and I am going to take that calf 'twill about pay you out.' I waited as long as I could and thought maybe Pa could talk him outten the calf, but when I seen him going toward the stable with a rope I got me a fence rail and run him offen the place. He cut a shine but it made no never mind to me. I had worked too hard over that calf for him to take away from me. He made us move right out.

"Then we had a time looking for a home. Every time we thought we had one the man would come at the last minute and tell us he was 'sorry but another family had jest moved in.' One night Pa come in as drunk as a fool, he said we had to git outten that house in the morning. He told us that another man had promised him to send his mules and waggin for us the next morning at sun up. Sure nuff when the sun come up the waggins was there. I ain't never going to forgit about Ma's dadblamed ole broom straw. She rung off some for her brooms that winter and we was so busy gitting the things on the waggins we forgot about it; do you know she made us go back and git it?

"The first year at the new place things went fine. That fall Pa got one hundred and forty five dollars in money and he loosened up and give us younguns some for the first time in our lives. I ain't never going to fergit what went with my money either. I went to town and got me some moonshine with part of it, then I got me the pruttest yaller gal in town and stepped out. I was too drunk to know just what happened. In a few months her Pa come to see mine and told him if I didn't marry that gal he was going to blow my brains out. I was one more scared nigger in this world, I asked Pa what to do, he told me to go on and marry up with her, that she was from a smart family and could help in the field after the baby was born. She come in that house and cleaned it up, wasn't no dirt nowhere in it, but when her time come she couldn't birth the baby and they both died. She was one more smart woman and I hain't never cared for no other woman from that day to this.

"When settling time come that fall the man told us we hadn't made nothing, and I reckon he was right for he stood for the coffin I buried my wife and baby in. He took a nice little bull yearling that I had raised too. I got so I didn't want to live in the house that Julia died in so I begged Pa to git another place next year, so we moved up in Cook County. We had our meat and corn, so we got the man's waggin and led our cow along behind it. Ma hadn't used all of her straw and you know she had me to put that daggone ole straw on them waggins agin?

"We made nothing the first year in Cook County; in the fall the man come and took our cow away from us. He was one mean man in this world. Ma was sick and needed milk then, more than ever, but that man didn't care nothing about that. He told us if we didn't make nothing the next year he was going to take them mules back. All of us chilluns was about grown then and we didn't care if he took the ole mules, we wanted to move to town anyhow.

"Ma died that summer and Pa give the man the mules and we moved to Riverton. We won't here long till Pa died. We was looking for some clothes to put on him and found his ole 'bacco sack and in it was $64.00. I was one proud boy in this world. We put Pa away and then had money left.

"I've hated so many times that we ever moved to Riverton to live. I've got seven sisters and there ain't nary one of them married and they all got big families. I tried to tell them they won't living right, but they won't lissen to me, and now they are working themselves too death trying to take care of all them younguns their dadies won't help none.

"I've been working from one place to the other; I don't make much. You see I jest room and always try to git me a job where I can git my meals. I work at boarding houses and they pays me $3.00 a week. I wash dishes, dress fish and chickens and all that kinder stuff. One lady I worked for didn't pay me at all, and when I asked her for it she grabbed a shovel and come down on my head, she beat me so bad I had to leave. I ain't been back yet to see if she would pay me.

"My sister left this youngun here for me to take care of while she went out to see if she could git some work. He is the meanest youngun I ever saw. His name is Booker T. 'Cuse me Miss, I got to see where he is; he was asleep when you come but I can see right now he is going to keep me busy the rest of the time. Good God Almighty, boy, I thought you was a goner that time, you run right out in front of that car, if the man hadn't stopped when he did you'd been a dead nigger. A town ain't no fitten place to raise younguns nohow.

"I ain't been long got outten jail. A boy come by me and asked me to hold his gun for him. I took it and put it in my pocket. In a few minutes the Law come after me. When my trial come up I didn't have nobody to go my bail and I had to serve ten days in jail. They shore is hard on the niggers; when they takes them to jail they won't let you say one word, if you do they puts you right smack under the jail.

"I'm a member of the Baptist Church, I wouldn't go down there and join Bishop Judah's church. I ain't going to say nothing against him, 'cause he can put spells on you. I know when he went to Rock Level and they run him outten there he told them there was going to be a storm, and in about a week they had a storm that took the trees up by the roots; blowed down houses, even took the roof off the hospital. Then a lot of business houses was burned to the ground. I wouldn't have him put no cusses on me for nothing in this world.

"This is something I'm wearing around my neck to keep the witches from riding me. I can't tell you what is in it 'cause if I did it wouldn't do me no good. Yes, I believes in haints. I was living in a house one time where a woman died and she hainted me. One night I was fast asleep and she liked to choked me to death. The next morning they told me it was something I had et. In a few more nights she come again, and I grabbed her and said, 'Kate you ole sorry devil if you don't go away from here and let me alone I'm going to blow your brains out.' When they moved my bed outten that corner of the house she didn't bother me no more. All you has to do when haints bother you at night is move your bed and they won't look for you. The reason they git after you is because your bed is setting right where their bed was setting when they dies. Since I learned that I don't have no more trouble 'cause I moves my bed right then.

"I wants to git my teeth fixed, they don't ache none but every cullud person I sees has got some gold in their mouth. Somebody told me I could buy some gold teeth at the dime store. Is you ever seen any there? I think they makes a body look plumb stylish with gold in their mouth.

"I don't want to farm no more, I'm in the service now and I'm going to stay, ain't going to help my sisters no more. From now on I am looking after Jim."

SOURCE Federal Writers Project #3709, in the Southern Historical Collection (University of North Carolina Library, Chapel Hill).

103. *Oral History, Minnie Davis, retired teacher. Interview with Leola T. Bradley (edited by John N. Booth), 29 Aug. 1939, Athens, Ga. WPA interview; discusses childhood experiences, education, and life as a schoolteacher and ex-schoolteacher during the depression era. Revealing also for the role and racial presumptions of interviewer.*

. . . "I don't know exactly where I was born. Dat's one thing I never did ax about, but I think it was in Greene County. Anyhow I've lived most of my life right here in Athens. My mother before me believed in chillun gettin' learnin'. My white folks taught me to read, and my white folks' chillun taught me to write. Yes, mam, I went to school too, and I had as good education as there was for people of any race in dem days. Den I went to normal school; all teachers had to go to dem special schools. In 1881 I graduated from Atlanta University. I wasn't but seventeen when I went to teachin' in a little country school, and pretty soon I was teachin' right here in Athens. I kept up me teachin' for 48 years.

"I was a good sort of girl. Course I was full of fun, but I didn't run 'round and give my mother a whole passel of trouble like some. No, mam! No, mam!" She shook her head decisively, and continued: "De young folks today ain't a bit worse'n dey've allus been! It's just dat dey do things diffunt-like. Course girls is more clothes-crazy, and dey use more powder and paint. And den dey's all got to have dey hair straightened dese days. Go barefooted like us used to? No, dey don't do dat now. Dey wears silk stockin's now to make de legs look pretty. I loves de young people though; dey's so free and open-minded. Yes, honey," she sighed, "You can straighten out kinky heads, but you can't get de crooks outen old bodies like mine.

"School-teachin's a fine callin'. If you can lead somebody in de light of learnin', den you've done somepin' fine. I taught in de grades—de little chillun. Lawsy me! Ain't dey sweet? You know, chillun ain't bad like some folks say; dey's jes' worrisome, dat's all. You have to humor 'em and den some—jes' 'bliged to. Many's de time I've had little fellows to come to school, and maybe de very fust day dey gets homesick for dey mammies. I wouldn't scold and try to force 'em to stay in school. No, mam! I'd jes' say to one of de older chillun: 'Here, take dis here child home,' and wid a pat, I'd tell de little-un, 'Now, honey, go on home to your mammy and ease your little heart, den when you feels like it, come on back to school.' And nine times outa ten, dey'd be back de next mornin'. Bless deir little hearts! Dey ain't bad, and dem what went to school to me didn't have de white folks' worrisome call of, 'Come back here and be punished.' " Millie caught her breath and continued: "Whippin' was stylish in dem days, but it ain't now. I made 'em stand up lots 'stead of beatin' on 'em so bad. De superintendent wouldn't let us keep 'em in after school. Yes, yes, dey throwed spitballs just as bad den as dey do now. Dey didn't teach no singin' in school dem days. I can't sing, and if a body can't sing, dey jes' can't sing. Now-days de teachers is all s'posen to sing and teach singin'," she chuckled, "but dey can't do all dey's s'posen to.

"I'm proud of my teachin' record. When I look around and see so many of my old pupils in high positions, I feel like teachin' is de grandest thing a body can do. Sometimes I get down sick and some of my old pupils drops by and gives me a dollar, or maybe fifty cents, and it makes me feel mighty good. Den if de money don't come I don't worry, cause Miss, if you trust de Lawd everything will be all right. Besides, people get tired of being nice, 'specially when times is so hard.

"I didn't worry 'bout money when my husband was livin'. He had a newspaper and he done very well. I sold it after he died. Den I saved a little money, but Lawsy me, de doctor got most of dat. Dey can sho' get your money, but dey's good. When I don't have de money dey comes right on.

" 'Sides teachin', I've done a lot of public work. Durin' de war I worked in de Red Cross. When de soldier boys would come through on de trains I'd go down to de depot and help serve coffee and little things to eat.

"I even vote sometimes when somebody comes to carry me down to de votin' place. But, honey, I'm too old and my brain gets too muddled to worry over such things as politics. Dey says our President is a very fine man. 'Cording to my notion dey's some things good about him and some bad. I aint' got nothin' 'gainst our governor, but jes' let me tell you right now, if he hadn't promised to help de old folks and to give free school books he never would have been elected. I don't have to look to de governor for nothing—my city gives me my livin'. I draws thirteen dollars and thirty-three cents every month for bein' a retired school teacher.

"Politics is like churches—some of de folks pulls one way and some another. No, honey, I don't worry none over politics. I'm too old and my brain gets tired too easy. I didn't ask for no old age pension, and I don't want it.

"Som folks might think I get lonesome. Well, I don't. I visit 'round de neighborhood a little and read a lots. My eyes does fairly well, 'cept dat my glasses needs changing bad. Looks like I can't get enough money ahead to buy me no new specs."

"Do you own your own home, Aunt Millie?" I inquired.

"Yes, Miss, s'cusin' some taxes dat's due on it. I'm thankful I've never knowed what it was to have to keep movin' around.

"Sometimes I think it would've been fine to have some chillun of my own to get grown, but when I look around me at some of the s'periences of dam dat's raised families, I jes' don't know. My love for chillun has been poured out on other folks' little-uns, and big-uns too. One thing sho', I don't believe in no birth control. No, mam! De Lawd give me two babies: den He decided to take 'em.

I has a man roomer. Po' thing, he's 65 years old, out of work, and ain't got nowhere to go. He's a good barber. Yes, mam, he sure is, but like lots of folks, he jes' ain't got no job.

"I never had no idea of gettin' married again. When my husband died, I says to myself: 'I'll jes' live by myself until I die.' . . ."

SOURCE Federal Writers Project #3709, in the Southern Historical Collection (University of North Carolina Library, Chapel Hill).

104. *Oral History, Lucy Reeves, former school teacher and supervisor of a U.S. Government Employment Office. Interview with Geneva Tonsill (edited by Maurice Russell), 21 June 1939, Atlanta, Ga. WPA interview; recollections of childhood, family life, and development of Atlanta's black community.*

Mrs. Reeves was sitting on the porch as I entered her yard.

"Come right in," she called. "I was expecting you. I have just finished reading the book, 'These Are Our Lives,' which you left for me to look over. I began reading it immediately after you left yesterday. It was so interesting that I read most of the night and began early again this morning. It's really a wonderful book. While I was reading it I pictured myself giving a similar history for I was reminded of many interesting things that have happened in my life and I had somewhat of an outline of what I was going to say to you. You know I was an interviewer for several years and having done this type of work I knew just about what I was going to say, but now that I am actually being interviewed I find it rather difficult to talk about myself."

She invited me to sit on the porch of her spacious two-story home, where it was very cool and comfortable, although the day was hot and sultry. The porch was shaded by large trees through whose branches the wind blew making it a delightful place to sit. The house is located on a very busy street in the midst of the leading colored business district of the city. Our conversation was often distracted by the roar of busy traffic. After a few minutes idle talk, Mrs. Reeves began her story:

"I was born in Clark County. The first recollection of my childhood was a big rambling two-story house, surrounded by lilac, crape myrtle, hollyhock and snowballs. There was old-fashioned boxwood and tiny bluebells. Hyacinths and narcissus grew all around, and there were rose bushes of many varieties, as my grandmother, by whom I was reared, was fond of flowers. She had a large scuppernong arbor and I recall the pleasure I got out of swinging on the vines. We had peach and apple and cherry trees, and also blue damson plums such as I have never seen since. My grandmother had cows, and to preserve milk and butter, as ice was a luxury in those days, she had the well enclosed with a sort of house where she would hang the pails of milk and butter to keep cool.

"My childhood was indeed a happy and pleasant one; even now I can see the old home place as it was then. I read recently that the Federal Housing Authority was taking over that section of town to build a Housing Project. It seems such a pity that the old homes that Negroes have lived in for half a century, or more, are to be torn down. They need to stand as landmarks—landmarks of a thrifty people who prided their homes, even though they were humble shanties, and who had such a struggle acquiring those homes.

"My grandmother ran a restaurant; in the front she served the white customers and in the back, the colored customers. She would go from Athens to Jackson County for supplies. She raised her own hogs and would kill four and five at a time. She had a spinning wheel and would spin all of the cloth for our clothes. She was an industrious woman.

"I recall quite vividly having a large cup which I used as a bank, as my grandmother's customers gave me many nickels and dimes when they would come to her restaurant. I remember filling the cup and how proud I was when it was filled. Even today I am proud of her teaching me to save the nickels and dimes for it instilled in me a great principle from which I have profited greatly.

"My grandmother used a one-horse wagon and an ox-cart as a means of conveyance. She would drive fifteen miles to buy what she needed and I would go along with her. Once we were on our way to town and we had to cross a creek and before getting across the ox suddenly balked and dumped us in the creek. It is wonderful the progress that has been made in transportation today.

"I suppose you do not want to hear so much about my childhood experiences but to me it is interesting. Of course, you need not write all I am telling if you don't care.

"I'll tell you of an incident that happened when I was very small, which affected me throughout my childhood and even now: I was suffering with toothache and my grandmother carried me to the doctor who, during those days, pulled teeth as well as practiced medicine, for dentists were not many. While I sat in the chair awaiting the doctor's preparations, he went in a closet where he kept supplies, and as he opened the closet door a skeleton fell out. It scared me nearly to death and even now I have a horror of doctors' offices.

"My mother was born in Jackson County. She married at the age of fourteen years. She was very religious and strict. We all had to attend church services and there is a pew in the church that even today is known as our pew. Mother was a great lover of young people. She taught a class of young men and women. When she died, I have never seen as many young men and women and boys and girls weep over a bier. Her family belonged to the family of Dr. Crawford W. Long, the great scientist who is credited as being the first to discover anaesthetics. Ours was a thrifty family; always owned our home. I have never rented. The place grandmother purchased housed five generations and the family is still in possession of the home.

"Grandmother would sing to us and make figures with her hands on the wall. I remember a song that made us scream with laughter. One of the verses went something like this:

'Buckeye rabbit boo, buckeye rabbit boo
The rabbit skips and the rabbit hops
The rabbit bit my turnip tops
All that grieved my heart and mind
He bit my water-million vine.'

"Once grandmother visited her folks in Jackson County. A niece, of whom she was very fond, died. She seems to have had a premonition before she received the news and hurried to Athens, arriving after the funeral. She was told that the niece had called for her repeatedly before she died. Grandmother was much upset. When bedtime came she was told she could sleep in the niece's room, but she refused to do it and instead went to bed in the room with the children on a cot. She couldn't sleep, just seemed restless. She lay awake for a long time and then suddenly she was conscious of the door opening softly. She thought one of the children was coming in but as she lay there waiting for the person to come in, to her amazement no one came in. The door just closed and she felt a presence in the room. Well of course she was scared but she didn't scream, fearing she would disturb the children. Finally a hand, cold as a block of ice, touched her cheek, caressing her gently, as a mother would have caressed a child she loved. It seemed that each stroke said, 'I am glad you are here and to see you.' She was paralyzed with fear but as silently as the sensation came it left and she heard the door open and close again very softly. The next morning she told the family she was going back home for she did not wish to experience another similar thing and for months after she got back home the cheek which the hand had stroked was cold. She said she didn't believe in ghosts but she was never able to get the incident out of her mind, for she was not dreaming or asleep when it happened.

"Grandmother reared us and mothered us and during our childhood never allowed us to be left in the house alone at night. She instilled lofty ideas in the four of us that have followed through the years. She taught us to 'find a way or make one' and that 'a good name was better to be chosen than great riches.' She was proud of her ancestry and taught us to be, teaching us never to bring shame on the family name. *I* am proud of my heritage, too, from the paternal as well as the maternal branch of the ancestral tree. Though my forebears were slaves, that situation instilled in my folk a sense of self-respect, honesty and family pride, that nothing has been able to efface. Grandmother spoke lovingly of 'Mars' Crawford. Her family never worked in the fields. Her father belonged to Jonas Long (brother to Crawford W. Long) and he was an overseer of the other slaves.

I shall never forget my grandfather, John, who was tall and so straight, nearly or quite six feet. He wore his hair long, a broad brim black hat, white shirt, long black coat, black bow-tie and in appearance he resembled Abraham Lincoln. I was a very small girl when he would visit my mother. They would go to town and wherever they went he was the center of attraction. The more forward folks would ask if she were his daughter and he would laugh and tell them 'that was what her mother said.' He, his mother and sister were sent from Richmond, Virginia, as slaves. 'Granny Mary,' as his mother was called, would never talk much about her family; she never mixed with the other slaves and lived in a little house built especially for her. She was very fair complexioned. She did the sewing for her mistress. The tale was handed down to us of how her mistress cut her hair and made her wear a tar (sic) cap for several weeks to ruin it because it was long and beautiful, but when it grew back it was more lovely than ever. Another tale was told us of her helping in the kitchen with the cooking. Biscuits were not given the slaves but were made for the white folks. Her mistress would always come in the kitchen, roll and cut the biscuits. However, after her mistress would leave the kitchen she would take the biscuits out of the pan, re-roll them and cut them and have more biscuits than she could eat. At Christmas time her mistress would give each slave two and one-half yards of material to make a dress. Of course that was not enough and she would take the new material and combine it with old cloth—anything she could find—and strut out. Once her 'Marster' asked her what was the reason she had old and new material in her dress. She told him that she was afraid she would fall in a ditch, as her Mistress gave her only two and one-half yards of cloth, and that made only a tight dress. Consequently she got more. She always told me she got what she wanted. I wanted to know how she did it and she would say:

'I always remember there are only two kinds of folks in the world, the cotched and the uncotched. In other words, you get what you can get by with.'

"I was told of how the soldiers, during the war, would come to the homes of her Marster and Mistress and 'ramshack' the premises looking for valuables and food. Her mistress on one occasion gave the slaves her valuables, silver, jewelry and all that was valuable, to hide. She recalled hiding it and although they could have gone back later and gotten the valuables for themselves, they did not. It remained as they hid it and after it was safe to return the slaves always gave it back as it was given by their owners. Even ham, flour, meal and other foodstuffs were hidden under planks that were torn from the slaves' little shanties and replaced, for safe keeping. It was always returned to the mistress intact.

"After completing high school, I went to Tuskegee in 1895–98. After that I went to Birmingham, Alabama, and taught in the public school eight years. I married and came to Atlanta during the riot. That was terrible.

The whole city was in a turmoil of frenzy and hate. Negroes were afraid to poke their heads out of the door. I remember, quite vividly, my husband and I lay in bed and saw crowds of white men stop the street car near my house, pull helpless Negroes off the car and beat them unmercifully. The streets were crowded with Negroes, running pell mell from crowds who were after them with bricks, sticks, and anything that they could get their hands on. A lame boot-black, an unoffensive, industrious boy, at work shining a man's shoes, was dragged out and cuffed, kicked and beaten to death in the most unspeakable and horrible manner. Yes, and the mob went into a barber shop where respectable Negro men were at work, shaving white customers, and just pulled them away from the chairs and beat them. Street cars were stopped and inoffensive Negroes were thrown through the windows or dragged out and beaten. They demolished Negro shops and restaurants and robbed stores kept by white men. Not a criminal was touched by the rioters; its victims were law abiding and industrious citizens. Yes, I remember how many were killed. Two white men and ten colored men were killed and ten white men and sixty colored men were injured. It seemed that the demons of torment were turned loose. At that time we had two government railway mail clerks living at our house who couldn't get home from the depot, and they were protected in the government mail room. I never wish to see another riot and the happenings of this one has left an indelible impression on my mind that will never be erased.

"I have lived right here for thirty-three years. All of my children were born here. My husband died in 1927, twenty-one years after our marriage. He worked with the United States Government as a mail clerk for forty years. He was a clerk-in-charge thirty-eight years and carried mail two years. Oh Lord! I don't know what else to say about him, he being dead." She seemed hesitant to discuss her husband further and a bit of sadness crept into her voice, but she did say, "Of course, I could say more but guess I'll let it go at that. He was, however, a man of keen business sense and before his death made provision for his family's future."

At this point a man out on the sidewalk interrupted the conversation to comment on the sky-writing stunts of an aviator who was advertising a soft drink. He said the aviator received $75.00 a day for his stunts. Mrs. Reeves answered him. "Well, that is one $75 I do not envy for I would not go up there and do that for $7,500. The ground suits me for stunts." She turned back to me and said, "Gracious me, what will men do next? Air planes and radio are wonderful. I often wondered when I was small what was meant by the term: 'And there will be no more sea' and I could not understand how the sea would be done away with but now that we have planes to hop over the universe as they do I have lived to learn the significance of that statement, for with planes and radio, there is no more sea. They have made all countries seem like next door neighbors—one continent can converse with the other, or one can get a plane and hop from one to the other over night. What would our forefathers who used horses and oxen say now if they would come back to see this new day; they would, I know, feel it nothing less than a miracle.

"When my husband died I took over the responsibility of the home, or rather it fell on me. At that time my youngest son was fourteen and the oldest nineteen. The youngest had just started to high school and the oldest was a sophomore at college. They continued their education, completed the college course; then the oldest boy spent one year on his Master Degree. They both are teachers." She beamed with pride as she added, "My youngest son is quite an athlete. He won many trophies in baseball, basketball, and football. My daughter married young and is the mother of two boys. She is a graduate of Home Economics at the Atlanta School of Social Work. She has held several supervisory positions in the Federal Relief Administration and is an outstanding modiste. My oldest son has made contributions to several leading magazines and was won several prizes for short stories and poems. His musical ability is remarkable. He plays a violin, wind instruments, and the piano. He is director of the children's orchestra at the school where he teaches."

As we talked we were interrupted many times by people who passed directly in front of the house, which is located only a few feet from the street. Both white and colored greeted her as they passed, which indicated that she was well known and well liked in the community.

"Well, what about your occupational experiences?" I asked. She laughed and said, "That is right; ask me what you want to know now for I was taken up with telling about my childhood days; I forgot this was an interview. Well, I had charge of a Government Employment Office and also served as an interviewer during FERA. Of course, I've already mentioned that I taught school several years." Thus summarily disposing of her occupational life she went on to other subjects. She mentioned the fact that she had seen her immediate vicinity emerge from "a shambling residential section, with few stores scattered here and there, for Negroes, to a hustling thoroughfare, with businesses of great magnitude—bank, drug store, daily newspaper plant, dry goods and department stores, undertaking establishments, beauty salons and many others."

"There were only two little tracks of the Georgia Power Company in the car barn over there, and now they occupy almost two blocks, housing the street cars that run in this vicinity. I have seen the city advance from smaller cars to the larger ones and busses, and now trackless trolleys. I have seen the street lamps with lights that reminded me of lightning bugs give way to brilliantly lighted boulevards. I have seen small brick structures grow to huge towering skyscrapers. Or, to put it this way, I have seen Atlanta put on the map." . . .

s o u r c e   Federal Writers Project #3709, in the Southern Historical Collection (University of North Carolina Library, Chapel Hill).

105. *Oral History, Lizzie Mercer, unemployed. Interview with Annie A. Rose, May 1939, Macon, Ga. WPA interview; discusses the impact of unemployment and underemployment on black families.*

. . . "If'n you wants me to tell you 'bout myself and all I kin sho say I'se having a mighty po time. I'se poly all the time, done had a misery fer twenty year or mo'." As she spoke she held up her gnarled, twisted hands from which dry skin was peeling. "dat's pellagra," she explained. "I done had it for 'bout twenty year and it looks like I won't never git well. It comes out on my hands an feets but I'se sore all over my body. Lots of times I has to stay in bed, and I'se jest as weak as a cat. It ain't so bad in the winter time but in the summer I suffers all the time.

"My husband died 'bout ten years ago, and I sho been havin' a po' time ever since. I ain't got no health and I ain't got no money. I'se 'pendent on my chillen fer my victuals an' my clothes an' a place to sleep." Though Sally is only 56 years old the disease from which she suffers has wasted her frame and taken toll of her strength until she appears much older.

The house in which she now lives is a three-room frame cottage with a small front and an even smaller back porch. It is one of more than a dozen houses exactly the same in appearance on a narrow, rain-washed alley in a section that houses a large number of negro families. For this house they pay eight dollars a month and proudly boast of the fact that the house has a bath room and electric lights. A narrow hall runs from the front to the back door down one side of the house and leading from the hall are two bedrooms and a kitchen. Both bedrooms are furnished with two iron beds each, rickety chairs and odd pieces of furniture. From a highly varnished radio in the front room came the voice of a commentator, speaking on the current European situation.

"Turn that there radio down or shet it off," shouted the youngest daughter who had joined us on the veranda. "It's been a-running full tilt ever since five o'clock this morning and this white lady can't hear what us says and we can't hear her neither. Ain't no body listening to that man talk no how." So, with the house considerably quieter, the feeble old woman resumed her story.

"I married me a good man," she said. "The best man on earth," echoed the daughter. "I says that," continued Sally, "cause I knows there ain't many good ones now. I was married to him most thirty years and ifn he ever done what was low down I don't know nothing 'bout it. He was a Methodist preacher, could read the Bible good and knowed most all of it by heart. He went to school when he was a boy but he didn't near finish. He preached hard and raised his chillen in the fear of the Lawd but I'se sorry to say they done strayed from the path. But he sho done his duty and I done mine and I hates to see 'em serving the devil now 'stead of the Lawd."

Sally has never learned to either read or write but she and her husband insisted on all the children attending school regularly and the mother is proud of the children receiving an education. "I wish I could read," she continued, "it would come in mighty good now when I ain't able to work none but I ain't never had the time to learn. Soon as I married the chillen started coming and they kep' me busy all the time. It's kinder funny 'bout my having chillen," she continued, "I had eight—one of 'em died bout five years ago—and I ain't never wanted nary one. Folks that wants chillen can't git 'em and folks that don't want 'em gits em. My husband wanted chillen, though. He was sho a chillen man. He used to say the Lawd sont 'em. I didn't say nothing cause he never 'lowed me to talk sassy but I used to think: 'Well, the Lawd may be sending 'em but you sho is helping Him and I ain't never heard the Lawd axin' me does I want 'em.' " She laughed in her cracked, thin voice and continued, "Well, they's here and I'se always done my best by 'em but I ain't gonna say I wanted 'em cause it ain't so."

"I knows how you feels, Ma," her daughter interrupted. "I got one kid but that ain't saying I'm gonna keep on cause I sho ain't. 'Course, I ain't married now—I been married but if I does git married again I ain't aiming to have no chillen." Mercer, the daughter, is at present unemployed. She was laid off in September and has been unable to work since. For several years she was employed by a local concern making crocus sacks and bags for cotton pickers. She made $5.95 a week, working 48 hours a week. At the time thirty-five women were employed at the same place. When the Wage-Hour Bill went into effect the wages of the workers were raised to $11.00 per week. "That jest lasted one week," Mercer explained, "then they said if they kept on paying that much they'd have to shet down. So they let us all go but five and them five is trying to do all the work and they gits jest $5.95 a week."

The oldest daughter who lives in the little house has a place as cook; for this she is paid $3.00 per week. Her son, a twenty year old boy, makes $7.00 a week for running an elevator in a hotel from eleven P.M. till eight A.M. At present these are the only two in the house of eleven people who are working. Jerry, the son, strolled out on the porch, a straw hat set jauntily on his head, a lighted cigarette in his hands. He was dressed in a bright blue shirt, dark green trousers and tan shoes. "Yessum," he said, "I likes my job all right but I likes my trade better. I'm a painter by trade but I can't get steady work at painting. I runs the elevator at night in the hotel. My job's all right in the winter when there's more folks in the hotel but in the summer the trade falls off and we don't get paid as much. I keeps right busy most all the time; I gits all the drunks, it looks like but they don't bother me much. They mostly jest laughs or sings and sometimes when they gets to feeling real good they tips me, though us elevator boys ain't supposed to get tips. I got me a paint job fer this morning, gonna paint some wood work fer a white lady. I likes to paint." And he strolled down the street, his hands in his pockets as he whistled a tune.

As Jerry walked away two grown girls joined us on the porch. One, a very light mulatto, stood in the doorway, busily chewing gum. She was dressed in a cotton print dress, a blue felt hat, green sandals with extremely high heels and white sox. The rest of the negroes were so black that I looked at this girl in amazement. "She ain't none of my chillen or grand-chillen. She lives down the street," said Sally in response to my wondering expression. "I ain't never had none that color cause I ain't never changed pappys on 'em." Four or five doors away a mulatto woman on the steps of a house screamed out demands that Loretta, the mulatto girl, come home. "Will you jest tend to half my business and let me tend to the other half?" was the impertinent reply shouted by Loretta. "That's my ma," she explained, "She all time butting into my business." Here she laughed loudly and calmly took her seat in the swaying swing with the other girls. Sally's feeble voice had as little chance of being understood over those of the younger girls as it had had when the radio had been turned on full blast.

The whole household evidently felt flattered over my visit, several talking at once. Isolind, the girl about fifteen years of age, is in the ninth grade at school. She explained that she was absent from school in order to attend a track meet in the afternoon. She plans to go to Ballard if she is able in another and learn to be a teacher. Loretta is now a pupil at Ballard. Her ambition is to become a stenographer and get a job in Atlanta.

On being asked about their recreation they said, "We dances and goes to the movies and plays ball." There is a large hall near in which dances are held twice a week. These are popular and well attended.

"We don't never go to church, hardly," they confessed. "It's jest too poky and slow. We goes night times to the 'Sanctified Church.' But we ain't sanctified; we jest goes for the fun. All time there's a crowd there and them folks sho is hot. They sings and shouts and jumps up on the seats and in the aisles. They carries on thataway till 'bout eleven o'clock at night. Lots of folks goes to their own church and then comes on by the 'Sancti-fied' after their church is out. They say they is living without sin, says they don't eat no pork or a heap of things but the next day they goes on and does jest like the rest of us folks. They sho is crazy, but they puts on a good show.

"My uncle had a brother; his wife was sanctified. She had it so bad that she said she could walk on the water like Moses. She took all her chillen and went down to the river, she went down there singing, saying she was gonna walk on the water. She started in the river, pulling the chillen with her but they jerked away and wouldn't go. She went right on in that river, jest a singing. She walked all right; she walked right plumb to the water, into it and down to the bottom of the river. She was as dead as a door nail when they pulled her out. Ma, tell the white lady 'bout the time you started to join 'em," said Mercer.

"Well, I didn't never join 'em, but I thought lots about it," Sally said. "They said they could live in this world without sin and if I could live without sin I wanted to do thataway; it would be jest like being in heaven now. So I went to the meetings but my husband, he didn't like it; he said it were a sin to go the meetings and he told me to keep away from them folks. But I went on and didn't say nothing to him about it. Then one of his church members joined the Sanctified—yessum, she joined on a Sunday night, she went to Milledgeville on Monday and she died on Tuesday. She sho did. My husband, he say, 'Now, you see what happens to them folks what leaves their own churches and fools with them things.' So I never did join 'em but I sho would like to live without sin; I sho would," she wistfully said.

"It seems like to me," said Loretta with a loud laugh, "that living without sin, no sin at all wouldn't be much living. 'Twould be a mighty drabby living. You couldn't never have no fun, couldn't go to no dances, go to no picture shows or nothing. You couldn't do nothing but jest work and sing and shout. And I ain't gonna shout fer nobody. I'd look like a fool, jumping around and flinging myself all over the place. But I guess I ain't never had religion. I did have a touch of it 'bout a year ago—there was a good looking preacher here in a tent meeting. He could sho preach and man, was he a good-looker. If he had stayed long enough I might have got religion, but I spec he was married, anyhow."

All the members of the little household are firm believers in the wisdom of insurance. The grown members all have a straight life policy with a premium of ten cents a week. Sally belongs to a lodge, "The Daughters of Jerusalem." The dues are 25¢ every three months and she is supposed to receive a dollar a week when she is sick in bed. She said that on one occasion she was sick for such a long time that they cut her pay to 25¢ a week. This lodge is also a burial society. All the members have to attend the various funerals dressed in their robes or pay a fine of one dollar. To hear her tell of it, it must be a grand sight to attend a funeral of one of the members and it is no little consolation to her to know that she will be buried in such a fine style. In fact, one gathers in talking to her, that most of her dreams as she sits and suffers from pellagra is of the fine funeral she will one day have.

s o u r c e Federal Writers Project #3709, in the Southern Historical Collection (University of North Carolina Library, Chapel Hill).

CHAPTER IV

World War II, 1940–1945

A. INTRODUCTION

Historical Context

African Americans gained new industrial opportunities as the nation mobilized for war and called men into the military in rising numbers. It was during this period that African Americans regained a foothold in the industrial economy and broke the "job ceiling" at the level of semi-skilled and skilled jobs. The movement of African Americans into defense industry jobs was nonetheless a slow process. Employers, labor unions, vocational training schools, and governmental agencies all discriminated against blacks and undermined their participation in the war effort. Unlike their response to World War I, however, African Americans refused to simply "close ranks," support the war effort, and postpone their own struggle for full citizenship and recognition of their rights at home. They now used the war emergency to wage a "Double V" campaign for victory at home as well as abroad. Their campaign received its most powerful expression in the militant March on Washington Movement, which led to the federal Fair Employment Practices Committee.

As the nation mobilized for war in the years after 1939, African Americans bitterly complained of racial discrimination in the defense effort. The president of the huge North American Aviation firm informed African Americans that they would be considered for janitorial jobs only. "While we are in complete sympathy with the Negro, it is against the company policy to employ them as mechanics or aircraft workers." Despite the interracial work of the Congress of Industrial Organizations and the Communist party, skilled black workers—plumbers, bricklayers, carpenters, electricians, cement finishers, and painters—continued to face exclusion from labor unions either by "constitutional" provision or by some form of "ritual." Moreover, since many defense industry jobs required additional training for large numbers of white as well as black workers, the U.S. Office of Education financed such programs, but failed to ensure access to African Americans. When asked why blacks were not trained and employed in defense industry jobs, training school supervisors, unions, and employers conveniently passed the buck back and forth.

In the armed services as well, African Americans faced limitations on their efforts to serve in new capacities requiring skill and training. Blacks were admitted into the U.S. Army in large numbers, but were placed in segregated service and labor units. At the war's outset, the Marine Corps and Air Corps barred blacks completely, while the Navy and Coast Guard accepted them as messmen and other similar service positions only. Still, by war's end nearly one million black men and women had served in the armed forces, nearly three-quarters in the U.S. Army, followed in numbers by the Navy (and Coast Guard) and Marine Corps. Nearly 500,000 of these African Americans saw service overseas. Although some broke the

military assignment ceiling, served in the Air Corps as pilots, and received medals of honor, most served in transportation corps, port battalions, truck companies, and construction units.

Racial discrimination in the military was deeply rooted in shifting patterns of class and race relations at home. Under the impact of World War II, another 1.6 million blacks moved into the nation's cities. The percentage of blacks living in urban areas rose from less than 50 percent in 1940 to nearly 60 percent in 1945. Western cities like Los Angeles, San Francisco, and Seattle now joined established northern and southern cities as major centers of black urban population growth. As the black urban population increased, race relations deteriorated and violence broke out in several cities. In some cities, contemporary observers often described patterns of race relations as resembling an impending "race war." Much of the violence centered on the so-called Zoot Suit Riots, in which white sailors and civilians attacked young African American and Latino men who wore a new style of clothing—broad felt hats, pegged trousers, and pocket knives on gold chains. African American and Latino youth were assaulted in Los Angeles, San Diego, Long Beach, Chicago, Detroit, and Philadelphia.

The most serious racial conflicts occurred in Harlem and Detroit. In August 1943, a policeman shot a black soldier and touched off the Harlem riot, which resulted in at least five deaths, 500 injuries, hundreds of arrests, and $5 million in property damage. The confrontation in Detroit left behind even more deaths, injuries, and arrests. On 20 June 1943, a race riot broke out at the city's Belle Isle Amusement Park. Only the arrival of federal troops put down the violence, which resulted in 34 deaths, 675 injuries, nearly 1,900 arrests, and an estimated $2 million in property damage. In both the Harlem and Detroit riots, most of the deaths, injuries, and arrests involved blacks, while the damaged property belonged almost exclusively to whites.

Racial violence in Detroit and elsewhere was intertwined with the growing residential segregation of African Americans in cities. As it had in the depression years, federal housing policy reinforced patterns of residential segregation. Such housing policies, along with restrictive employment

---

Protesters outside the Democratic National Convention in 1940 carry signs calling for an end to discrimination in the armed services. Courtesy of the Schomberg Center for Research in Black Culture and the New York Public Library, Astor, Lenox and Tilden Foundations.

---

practices and discrimination in the military, helped to aggravate black-white relations in urban America and fueled the underlying forces leading to racial conflicts during the period.

Unlike World War I, African Americans resisted racial discrimination in the defense program by launching a militant "Double V" campaign against social injustice at home and abroad. Popularized by the *Pittsburgh Courier,* the "Double V" campaign enabled African Americans both to declare their loyalty to the war effort and to struggle for equal rights at home. The NAACP and other civil rights organizations escalated attacks on what they called "racial bias" against blacks in the military and industrial establishments. The African American quest for social justice gained its most potent expression in the emergence of the militant March on Washington Movement (MOWM).

Spearheaded by A. Philip Randolph of the Brotherhood of Sleeping Car Porters, the MOWM was launched in 1941 following a meeting of civil rights groups in Chicago. By early June, the MOWM had established march headquarters in Harlem, Brooklyn, Washington, D.C., Pittsburgh,

Detroit, Chicago, St. Louis, and San Francisco. March officials urged African Americans to fight for jobs in war industries, integration into all branches and assignment classifications in the armed forces, and abolition of Jim Crow in all government departments. The official call exclaimed that "The Federal Government cannot with clear conscience call upon private industry and labor unions to abolish discrimination based upon race and color so long as it practices discrimination itself against Negro Americans."

Although Roosevelt resisted the movement as long as he could, the MOWM finally produced results. Roosevelt met with black leaders A. Philip Randolph and Walter White of the NAACP on 18 June 1941. A week later, 25 June 1941, F.D.R. issued Executive Order 8802, banning racial discrimination in government employment, defense industries, and training programs. The order also established the Fair Employment Practices Committee (FEPC) to implement its provisions. The FEPC was empowered to receive, investigate, and address complaints of racial discrimination in the defense program.

Executive Order 8802 proved to be a significant turning point in African American history. It linked the struggle of African Americans even more closely to the Democratic party and helped to transform the federal government into a significant ally. African Americans used the FEPC to broaden their participation in the war effort, but it was a slow process. The AFL unions and the railroad brotherhoods did much to hamper this process, but the unions of the CIO often supported the FEPC claims of black workers and helped them to break the job ceiling. At its annual convention in 1941, for example, the CIO denounced racially discriminatory hiring policies as a "direct attack against our nation's policy to build democracy in our fight against Hitlerism." A year later, the organization established its own Committee to Abolish Racial Discrimination and urged its affiliates to support the national policy against discrimination.

The FEPC played a key role in facilitating the movement of black workers into defense plants. The proportion of employees in war production industries who were black increased from less than 3 percent in March 1942 to over 8 percent in 1944. Although black workers faced ongoing

Cadets in the U.S. Army's first all-black air unit, the 99th Pursuit Squadron, were trained at Tuskegee Institute in Alabama. More than six hundred black pilots were trained there during the war. Courtesy of the Everett Collection.

obstacles in their struggle for skilled, managerial, and clerical positions, by the end of World War II they could claim the CIO, the Democratic party, and the federal government as important allies in their struggle for social change. The "Double V" campaign for victory at home and abroad, the March on Washington Movement, and the growing use of the federal government to secure equal treatment all helped to write a new chapter in the history of African Americans and set the stage for the modern Civil Rights Movement during the postwar years.

Documents

This section focuses on the emergence of the federal Fair Employment Practices Committee and the proliferation of complaints of racial discrimination in the defense program. Subsection IVB addresses racial inequality in war industries and the armed forces. The documents cover the experiences of black men and women in a variety of places, but we offer the Norfolk Navy Yard as a case study. These selections reveal widespread dis-

crimination in defense industries, the special problems of black women, and the diverse ways that African Americans used the war emergency and the FEPC as levers to increase their participation in the industrial economy and secure full citizenship rights at home and in the military. This section offers particularly illuminating documents of black men and women who wrote about experiences in the military.

Subsection IVC highlights the incidence of racial violence and the increasing political militance of blacks themselves. Documents cover the Zoot Suit riots, expressions of black consciousness in new literary publications (*Negro Quarterly* and *Negro Story*), and inter- and intraracial debates about the impact of war on American and African American life. The subsection concludes with the *Negro Story* editor's query, "What Should the Negro Story Be?" The responses illuminate the ongoing quest of African Americans to define and redefine themselves during the industrial age.

B. EMPLOYMENT, DISCRIMINATION, AND DEFENSE INDUSTRIES

106. *"Hate Strikes." Article in* Race Relations, *Aug. 1943. Covers white workers striking against the employment of blacks and other minorities in Detroit, Brooklyn, and Sparrows Point, Md.*

Hate Strikes

Someone has coined the term "hate strike" to refer to a strike by a group of workers in protest against the hiring or upgrading of workers of another ethnic group. It seems to be an apt term. The Department of Labor reports that between March 1 and May 31, 101,955 working days were lost in strikes attributable to racial bigotry. They were chiefly strikes protesting the upgrading of Negro laborers. Within the two months following the time covered by this report at least $1^{1}/_{2}$ times as many days have been lost in exhibitions of intolerance.

An angry mob of whites chases a black man (indicated by the arrow) through the streets of Detroit during a 1943 race riot that left twenty-three people dead. Courtesy of the Everett Collection.

Detroit Michigan

A strike involving 20,000 workers and lasting nearly a week—ending June 5th—occurred at the Packard Plant when 3 Negro workers were promoted to skilled jobs. The United Automobile Workers (CIO) which bent every effort along with the War Manpower Commission and the War Labor Board to end the dispute, claims that definite evidence has been turned over to the FBI to show that the Ku Klux Klan played an active part in this strike against industrial democracy. Albert Deutsch reports listening in on a telephone call by an investigator to the caretaker of the Forest Social Club. This club is alleged to be a blind for the KKK. The caretaker told of the "good work" being done at Packard in ridding "that white man's plant" of the "black alligator bait." (GP, NP)

On July 27th the white women working on the night shift at the Timken Gear and Axle Company walked out in a strike demanding that they be provided with separate toilet facilities from those used by the Negro women. When management refused to give in to their demands they returned to work within the hour. Only four accepted management's

challenge to leave if they could not use the facilities along with their fellow-workers. (ANP)

Brooklyn, NY

Two of the three shop stewards who led a strike against the promotion of a Negro fellow-worker at the Acme Backing Company, during the week of June 7th, have been expelled from their union, the Coke and Chemical Company's Union of the CIO. (CN)

Sparrows Point Maryland

When a riveters school was opened at the Sparrows Point plant of the Bethlehem Steel Company during the last week in July, eight whites and three Negroes were admitted. The riveters—all white—demanded that the school be closed. When management yielded and the Negroes employed in the plant saw their opportunities for promotion going out of the window, 800 of the latter staged a protest. Again management yielded. Seven thousand Negroes and whites massed in opposite corners of the yard, and only the company police prevented violence. The Industrial Union of Marine and Shipbuilding Workers (CIO) worked out an agreement with management to re-open the school and place all promotions on a strict seniority basis, regardless of race. The agreement was unanimously accepted, and work was resumed on August 3rd under the surveillance of state, county, city, and company police along with Federal troops.

Industrial Violence

Chester, Pennsylvania

Four Negro workers were seriously wounded, one fatally in the race-angled industrial violence that broke out in the Sun Shipbuilding Yard No.

The SS **Frederick Douglass** *was built by an integrated workforce at the Bethlehem-Fairfield shipyards in Balitmore. Courtesy of the Library of Congress.*

4 on June 16th. The violence came in disorders following the infraction of a slight company rule by the workers involved. However, it had a deeper significance, for it came at a time when a hotly disputed election campaign for a bargaining agent for the workers was under way. The contest was between the Sun Ship Employees Association, which the NLRB has held to be a company union, and the CIO Industrial Union of Marine and Shipbuilding Workers. It was also a struggle between two philosophies of Negro leadership. One group, representing the philosophy of "working with 'the best people,' " meaning management, tried to influence Negro workers to vote for the company union. The other group, advocating co-operation with organized labor, worked to get the workers in the yard to vote for the CIO. The CIO maintains that the guards who shot the men were hired by the company to intimidate the workers. In the election the following week—one of the most closely contested in NLRB history—the CIO won by 25 votes. The company stated that the workers in the all-Negro yard were responsible for the union victory. George Weaver, direc-tor of the CIO's National Anti-Discrimination Committee, has been sent to Chester to work with the Union on a program of racial amity and trade union education among the Negro workers. (NP, GP)

s o u r c e "Hate Strikes," *Race Relations,* Aug. 1943.

107. *"Introduction of Jim Crow to the Northwest."* Article *in* Race Rela-tions, *Aug. 1943. Discusses the firing of black workers at the Kaiser Shipbuild-ing Yards in Portland, when they refused to join an all-black auxiliary.*

Introduction of Jim Crow to the Northwest

Portland, Oregon—Because they were unwilling to join a segregated auxil-iary of Tom Ray's anti-Negro local Local 72 of the Boilermaker's Union (AFL) 300 Negroes were fired from their jobs at the Kaiser Shipbuilding Yards in Portland, Oregon, during the last two weeks in July. Other than paying dues, the members of such an auxiliary would have no trade union functions. All decisions would be made by the main local, which is lily-white. The FEPC has asked that the Negro workers be reinstalled pending an investigation. Ray was strongly opposed to the hiring of Negroes in the beginning—even using the familiar "marry your sister" argument to keep them from being hired.

There Is Unity of Thought . . . Unity of Purpose Is Possible

"This incipient race war must be calmed down and eased off. It is a matter for strong treatment only as a last resort. The enemy's effort to split the nation into separate racial and factional groups must be foiled by human understanding and temperate action. The many must not be made to suffer for the violence or disloyalty of a few. It is a job of bringing this great national family into closer union and harmony, regardless of racial origin or color or anything except the essential bond of American loyalty." (Corinth, Mississippi, *Corinthian*, June 28, 1943)

"In a war waged for freedom, decency and the preservation of democracy, race troubles, riots and killings here at home are disgraceful, shameful. Moreover, they give our enemies great quantities of propaganda ammunition to use against us. 'The Americans preach equality, democracy, justice, while at the same time they are oppressing and killing colored people on the streets of American cities.' That is the assertion made by the axis radio speakers, and what can we say to refute it? For it is true. All too true." (Danbury, Connecticut, *News-Times,* August 3, 1943)

S O U R C E "Introduction of Jim Crow to the Northwest." *Race Relations,* Aug. 1943.

108. *Letter from Eleanore E. Sawyer, Philadelphia, to A. Philip Randolph, Brotherhood of Sleeping Car Porters, 28 Apr. 1942. On employment discrimination against black women at the aircraft factory of the Philadelphia Navy Yard. Demostrates the use of established black networks to reduce perceived wrongs.*

Dear Mr Randolph: First may I introduce myself to you. I am the daughter of a Pullman Porter George W. Sawyer of the Philadelphia District. Miss Eleanore E. Sawyer.

Upon my first opportunity to write to you may I extend my congratulations to you for the work that you have accomplish for the Pullman Porters. Although I do not know much about the Pullman work, I enjoy reading the news of the Black Worker.

Mr Randolph, I have a problem which I think you would be interested in. It is the problem of discrimination among the Negroes in the line of Defense. Probably no one else has discovered it in the Naval Aircraft Bldg (75) in the Philadelphia Navy Yard. The reason why I have so much interest in breaking up the discrimination in that bldg I am anxious to get employment. No matter who it is if they are anxious to get employment they will take notice of things which are important to the Negro Race.

The Civil Service Commission here announce the needs for Junior Property and Supply Clerks. The examination is still open. On April 7, 1942. I taken the examination for Junior Property and Supply Clerk. On April 21, 1942 I received a report of my rating. "Rating (78) Average Percentage (80). According to this statement I am eligible for the job.

On April 27, 1942. I received a letter from the Naval Aircraft Factory in the Philadelphia Navy Yard to be interview for a job. On April 28, 1942. I went to the Naval Aircraft, Factory Buildings (75). Upon my arrival in the Supply Department along with other white women, I notice out of the vast number of employees there were no colored girls or men.

After being interview for the job the interviewer told me that if I was selected for the job I would be notify within three days. Upon my arrival back to the door, a white woman whom was interview at the same time I was, was given employment. I was turned down because I was a Negro yet I have the same ability to do the same work.

Mr Randolph will you kindly take this matter into consideration. If you can do something for me not only for me but for the rest of the Negro Men and Women who might be turned down the same way as I was turned down. They might not take it into consideration as seriously as I have and realize that the matter of discrimination will not be broken until we fight to brake it down.

I will be glad to have any of your advice at once or any action that you may take in this building in the Philadelphia, Navy Yard, for me.

May I have a reply at your earliest conveniences.

SOURCE John H. Bracey and August Meier, eds., *The Papers of A. Philip Randolph* (Bethesda, Md.: University Publications of America, 1990) (hereinafter cited as *PAPR*), Reel 14, frame nos. 0311–0312.

109. *Letter from George E. Demar, secretary, Pittsburgh Urban League, to P. T. Fagan, area director, War Manpower Commission, 25 May 1943. Discusses racial discrimination against black women in a variety of Pittsburgh area companies, including the American Bridge Company.*

Dear Mr. Fagan: After Harold Parker had been refused employment as a machinist's helper and complaint was made by the Industrial Department of the Urban League of Pittsburgh, The American Bridge Company, Ambridge Pennsylvania, shipbuilders, in a statement submitted by the Company to the President's Committee on Fair Employment Practises April 2, 1943, said:

> "Non-whites are used in every part of the plant and are upgraded as their skill and knowledge warrants. Some are training as welders, and shipfitters; others work as burners, erection machinist helpers, fitter helpers, etc. The number of non-whites is now approximately 1000."

With this statement by the Company one might assume that all is well at the American Bridge Company; that Negroes, both men and women, are hired and upgraded in accordance with Executive Order 8802 and the War Manpower Commission's warning that all manpower is needed at its best skill for the full utilization of the nation's labor supply. Such assumption of victory hiring practises would not include all the facts.

During the last three months at the Ambridge and Leetsdale plants, white women by the hundreds have entered training and the employ of the Company, as welders and as burners. They have been employed in the plate shop, also in the clean-up gangs of the ways and docks. But in all, only five Negro women have been hired—to clean the lavatories.

When Mr. Riley, Manager of the Company's employment service, was approached each week for a period of six consecutive weeks, various reasons were given for the failure to hire Negro women in production. Said Mr. Riley, "It is impossible for me to hire until Mr. Oscar Seidel, the General Superintendent, asks for Negro women to be hired, but I will employ as many as he (Mr. Seidel) says."

May 10, 1943, R. L. Carter, 6363 Shakespeare Street, East End, and Houston Dargan, 3450 Webster Avenue, both members of the United Steel Workers' Union obtained an audience with Mr. Seidel. Mr. Seidel said, "We had expected to complete two buildings: in the buildings two janitresses will be needed. The buildings are not complete so that we have no need for Negro women. We will use Negro women where they will fit in."

The American Bridge Company needs welders. This is evidenced by their ads in the newspapers and the fact that the night shift at Connelly Trade School has been given over to prospective American Bridge Company welding trainees. After eight days training such trainees are being taken into the employ of the Company. But please note:

Evelyn Andrews, 2H McKees Rocks, Terrace, McKees Rocks, Pennsylvania; 5 feet five inches; weight 124; single; a high school graduate with more than 200 hours, April 16th, in welding at the Connelly Trade School; with ability to weld flat, horizontal, vertical and overhead; highly recommended by her instructor, Mr. Phillip Miller; and who now returns to the Connelly Trade School each Friday night for refreshing, so as to keep her touch; on May 14th, in answer to an advertisement by the Powers Piping Company, Beaver Avenue, North Side, Pittsburgh, Miss Andrews talked to a Mr. Frick. She was told the Company was obtaining welders for the American Bridge Company. When she inquired as to whether or not Negro women were employed by American Bridge Company, Mr. Frick said that he would have to call the plant and talk to Mr. Boyer; after an hour, and after the plant had been contacted, this message was left—" The

American Bridge Union did not allow them to hire colored female help."

Other women have repeatedly sought employment and/or training at the American Bridge Company. Mr. Baer interviewed May 3, 1943:

Thelma Olston, 590 Herron Avenue; aged 32; weight 185; two years high school; was asked if she would be willing to do any type of work; when the reply was in the affirmative, she was told that the Company was not taking anybody in the schools, but that he would let her know in about ten days.

Lillian Williams, 718 Herron Avenue; age 22; weight 115; ninth grade education and in addition 300 hours machine shop training was told the Company was taking only Erection Machinists; in reply to the question of any type of work the answer was affirmative; was told he would let her know.

Mildred Tucker; 720 Adelaide Street, age 22; weight 154 education—first year high school, was told after she said she would accept any type of work; "he would let her know."

Naomi Smith, 537 Herron Avenue, age 20; weight 120; 2 years high school; one month forge shop training; husband in the Army was chided "you do not want to work do you?"—he would let her know.

The above named women visited the Employment Offices at the plant at least three times; were given the same story; white women by the dozens of all ages, shapes and sizes were being employed but there was no place for Negro women.

So keenly have the Negro men employed by the Company felt the slight given Negro women that Sunday, May 16th, 1943 they held a meeting at the North Side Elks to try to find what could be done. There were suggestions of work-stoppage to bring to the Company's attention the feelings of the race involved; the men involved are ready and willing to accept the democratic way of doing things; even as they struggle for top production in the interest of "The Four Freedoms" and victory. . . .

These Negro women have come to realize that advertisements for help, the need for skilled workers, the need for training, the need for American citizens to push the war effort as proclaimed over the radio and through the press does not mean Negroes, particularly women. . . .

It appears to me Mr. Fagan; to workers of the American Bridge

Company; to citizens of the State of Pennsylvania; to community organizations, such as the Citizens' Coordinating Committee with its sixty-two affiliated organizations; that a thorough investigation of American Bridge Company's policy and practises is needed in the interest of the proper use of women and manpower. In this war effort there should not be considerations of race, creed, and/or national origin. It should be remembered that Negro women are American workers too. May we depend upon you as the Area Manpower Director to right existing situations after investigation of the actual work conditions which prevail not only at the American Bridge but at other plants in this area. We must work for victory even as all races are dying for victory. Mr. Director, we should make Executive Order 8802 a fact.

SOURCE *PAPR,* Reel 14, frame nos. 0361–0364.

110. *Letter from George Douglas, Sr., to U.S. Civil Serv. Com., 7 Nov. 1942. Charges discriminatory dismissal from Norfolk Naval Yard; claims discrimination in assignment of leading men. Claims supported by others.*

Dear. sir i am writeing. you. to. inform. you all. that. i am. being. discharged because. i am. Colered. they. claim. my. work. is. not sadisfactery its only. my. face. its no. time for. race preagherty. god dont like that. the men. all wants. me. for. their lead. man. they say. they had to show. all. the lead men that. they had before i come. but i. showed them i had. 4 years exspearance. as lead. man. before i came. there. now i beg you all to give me. a. job as lead man. some where in the navy. Base army. Base. or. navy. yard. withe the same ratings. the men all. send. you on therir Page numbers and names. i. taken. out a $750. bond. very truely yours

SOURCE FEPC Papers, Norfolk area, Boxes 630–40, Record Group 228 (National Archives, Regional Branch, Philadelphia (hereinafter cited as FEPC Papers).

111. *Letter from George Douglas, Sr., to George M. Johnson, assistant to chairman, FEPC, 28 June 1943. Douglas informs FEPC officer that he was the only leading black man on base but was soon relieved of his job.*

Dear mr. johnson. your. honor. i received. both of. your. letters and. was very glad to hear from. you.
i was. the only colored leading man. at the base. and. when. i got there mr mackfowler. give me card to a. white leading. man. and told him to put me heading. i let him. keep the card. awhile and. then i told him. that card you has belong. in my pocket and he give it to me
2) the men. told me as soon as i. got that that the did not have colored leading men there. and. i began to notice that way they acted. and i soon.

found out they dident want any colered. leadingmen there and. when they
discharged me. they asked me. if i wanted to take a. jobe as. stevedor. and
they would. pay. me 94 cent and after awhile they would rate me to $1. i
had left my leadeing mann. job in. baltimore and came here. and had gret
heavie exspences. and was. and as bieing $7.50 a week war bonds
3) i am. not geting. but 94 cent yet and. if you pleas. give me a. job in the
navie yard. or. see that i ger a fair deal i give. up my job in Baltimore
where i was leading 4 years. and 16 years exspearance as. stevedore. and.
its hard.

SOURCE FEPC Papers.

112. *Letter from L. A. Moyer, U.S. Civil Service Commission, to George M.
Johnson, assistant to chairman, FEPC, 4 Sept. 1943. Informs Johnson that
Douglas was discharged as leading man because of inefficiency, provides details,
and admits no blacks then employed as leading men.*

Dear Mr. Johnson: Further reference is made to your letters of June 19,
and July 24, 1943, in regard to the case of George Douglas, Sr. who has
alleged that the Naval Operating Base, Norfolk, Virginia, has discriminated against him because of race in removing him from the position of
Leadingman Laborer.

You are advised that the Commission had been informed that Mr.
Douglas was employed as Leadingman Laborer on September 1, 1942,
and that on November 9, 1942 he was discharged from this position because of inefficiency. The earlier report received by the Commission had
indicated that Mr. Douglas is a meek individual, of good character, but
lacking in leadership. Statements were made by several Quartermen Steve-
dores to the effect that Mr. Douglas does not possess leadership and
seemed to be unable to organize a gang; that he lacked the proper knowledge of rigging and ship work in general; and that his lack of education
was a handicap in that he could not absorb instructions and give directions.

According to the report, when Mr. Douglas was discharged as Leadingman Laborer he requested that he be rerated down to the position of
Stevedore and this was granted.

Relative to the inquiry of the President's Committee as to whether
there are Negroes employed as Leadingmen, the Commission has been
advised that at present there are no Negroes employed as Leadingmen
Laborers at the Naval Operating Base. The Assistant Foreman at the Base
stated, however, that if efficient colored Leadingmen Laborers could be
found they would be willing to employ them. He stated further that one
other Negro had been employed in this capacity in the past and was no
longer employed there.

By direction of the Commission:

SOURCE FEPC Papers.

113. *Letter from J. H. B. Evans of the FEPC to George Douglas, Sr., 20 Sept. 1943. Includes report of the Civil Service Commission, alleging inefficiency as the cause of Douglas's dismissal from his job as leading man. Shows the somewhat bureaucratic routinized handling of complaints.*

Dear Mr. Douglas: With further reference to your complaint that you were discriminated against on account of race because you were removed from the position as Leadingman Laborer at the Naval Operating Base at Norfolk, Virginia, we have received from the Civil Service Commission a report on their investigation from which I quote:

> You are advised that the Commission has been informed that Mr. Douglas was employed as Leadingman Laborer on September 1, 1942, and that on November 9, 1942 he was discharged from this position because of inefficiency. The earlier report received by the Commission had indicated that Mr. Douglas is a meek individual, of good character, but lacking in leadership. Statements were made by several Quartermen Stevedores to the effect that Mr. Douglas does not possess leadership and seemed to be unable to organize a gang; that he lacked the proper knowledge of rigging and ship work in general; and that his lack of education was a handicap in that he could not absorb instructions and give directions.
> "According to the report, when Mr. Douglas was discharged as Leadingman Laborer he requested that he be rerated down to the position of Stevedore and this was granted."

If you desire to make further answer to this explanation or have additional facts which would indicate that you were discriminated against on account of race, please write this office.

SOURCE FEPC Papers.

114. *"Protest of Workers." Petition and letter, 29 Sept. 1943. Black work gang at Norfolk Naval Yard signs petition to secure George Douglas as their leading man; petition certified by notary public.*

Dear mr. evans. i received your letter tonight after i got home i am sory i did not get. it intime to go and see. mr. carter but i worked. until 5 oclock. i could told him a. lots.

if i had the privelege of being a leadman. at the navie yard or. some where.
in the government inployment. you could see. i am fit for a leadman
i had 16 years exspearance in loading and unloading ships in baltimore..
and 4 years. stevedore ladman. and i left that job and came here they dont
want no. clored leadman here. i am 58 years of age. it goes very hard with
me the way i was treated god dont like it

now mr evans. i beleave you. will agree with me on this i beleave you will
do right. i am. a colored man. i am. a sad man hart broken. i left my good
job and came here if i had known. it was like it is at the base. i would have
put in for a job in the navie yard
i would be glad if i could talk with you
my rateing. is too small. for. my exspences i was promosed $1. an our and
only gets 94. cent my exspences. is great i am bieing a home in baltimore
and i pay to the goverment $5 a month. there. and pay $7.50. a week for.
war bond. and. mr evans pleas give this mater a close studie

Protest of Workers

THIS IS TO CERTIFY THAT: The following names, and their Check Numbers,
consisting of the men who were workers in the gang of George Douglas,
Sr.; a Leading Man, Labor Stevedore; at the Naval Operating Base, Norfolk, Va, in protest of actions taken, in removing him from his former
position as follows:

6819 Flod Alston,
6803 John E. Holley,
6808 Leroy Banks,
6813 Charles J. Roberson,
6823 Mosses Osborn,
66821 Charles Hall,
6809 William L. Jarvis,
6806 Henry F. Moore,
6814 Henry Robinson,
6820 William M. Mayo
6815 Walter Jenkins,
6816 D. Crump,
6823 David Wilson,
6812 Howard Sumler,
6818 Robert E. L. Elliott,
6804 Charlie Wright,
6807 Milton Foreman,

We want Mr. Duglas, George,
for our Lead Man.

Signed by the Whole groupe.

6805 Bell Z. Hill,
6811 Willie F. Steed,
6817 James Williams,   /s/ George Douglas Sr.
6810 James Scales,   George Douglas, Sr.

NOTE:

This instrument and signatures was viewed by a Notary Public.

State of Virginia
County of Norfolk

ON this, 6th day November, 1942, personally appeared, one George Douglas, Sr. personally known to me to be the same person, who presents the above written instruments, and swears to the same to be true to the best of his knowledge and belief and signed the same in my presence.

/s/ J. B. Eaton
Notary Public

(Seal)
My Commission Expires Oct. 28, 1943

S O U R C E FEPC Papers.

115. *Memorandum of Julius M. Gardner, War Manpower Commission, to Frank E. Hook of FEPC, ca. Oct. 1943. Reports inability to meet with George Douglas during visit to Hampton area.*

TO: Mr. Frank E. Hook
         Regional Director
         Region IV
         President's Committee on Fair Employment Practice
From: Julius M. Gardner
         Sr. Field Representative
         War Manpower Commission
Subject: Complainant, Mr. George Douglas, Sr.,
         1535 Wilson Road, Route #6, Norfolk Virginia, against the Naval Operating Base, Norfolk, Virginia.

During my visit in the Hampton area, I was unable to contact the above complainant. He did not keep the appointment as Mr. Joseph H. B. Evans instructed him, in a letter dated September 27, 1943.

I am returning the file regarding the above case.

Enclosures—10

S O U R C E FEPC Papers.

116. *Final Disposition Report from J. H. B. Evans, regional director, FEPC, to Will Maslow, director of Field Operations, 14 July 1944. George Douglas case closed because of "lack of efficiency and ability to command" and failure to keep appointment with FEPC officials.*

A. Chronology: Date of discrimination: 11/42
Date of filing complaint: 11/17/42
Date of personal contacts with complainant: none
Date of docketing: 9/1/43
Date of first contact with party charged: none
Date of personal visits to party charged: 9/29/43
Date of closing: 12/2/43
Date of submission of FDR: 7/14/44
Type of final disposition: Merits

B. Description of party charged: Government agency, adjunct of Navy Department given to the repair and salvaging of Naval Aircraft.

C. Summary of complaint: Mr. George Douglas, Sr. the complainant, a Negro, alleged that he was unfairly discharged from his job as a Leadingman Laborer, solely because of his race. Mr. Douglas wrote a very poor letter of complaint and must have sent it to the Civil Service Commission, which agency furnished FEPC with a copy. The letter stated that he had had 4 years experience as a leadman before his employment at the Naval Base.

D. Background: Numerous complaints against the Base have been filed. There had been none previous to Mr. Douglas's.

E. Date and type of final disposition: Dismissed on merits—12/2/43

F. Reasons for action taken (if other than satisfactory adjustment): The Civil Service Commission requested a report from the Fourth Civil Service Region at Winston-Salem. After quite a lapse of time, FEPC was sent a copy of the Civil Service's report. It stated that Mr. Douglas had been employed as a Leadingman Laborer on September 1, 1942 and discharged for inefficiency on November 9, 1942. It also stated that Mr. Douglas is a meek individual of good character, but lacking in leadership; that he does not seem to be able to organize a gang and lacked the proper knowledge of rigging and ship work in general, and his lack of education was a handicap in that he could not absorb instructions and give directions. The report further stated that when Mr. Douglas was discharged as Leadingman Laborer, he requested that he be rerated down to position of Stevedore and this was granted.

FEPC endeavored to establish personal contact with Mr. Douglas through Mr. Julius Gardner of WMC. An appointment was made for an interview. Mr. Gardner went to Norfolk, but Mr. Douglas did not keep the appointment.

In view of the report as to Mr. Douglas' lack of efficiency and ability to command and organize a gang and his failing to keep the appointment made for him the case is closed on merits.

SOURCE FEPC Papers.

117. *Letter from Miss Cathrose Norwood, Norfolk, Va., to FEPC, 10 Aug. 1943. Complains of inability to secure job at Norfolk Naval Yard, despite training as electrical welder, because of discrimination. Norwood sees the FEPC as an ally, highlighting the improving relationship between black workers and the federal government.*

Dear Sir:

I feel it my duty to write you concerning my present troubles in the government service.

My troubles is that, I have been trained by the government for a job as an electric welder. After having five months training in this particular business, I have been turned down. I have talked with all of the leading officers in the Norfolk, Navy Yard where I was in training, but the same answers, to every question I asked, came from each one.

Instead of being given a job as a welder, which I'm well fitted for & know that I am, I was given a discharge.

Now, I fell it your duty to help me in getting this job since I have spent so much of my time trying very hard to do something to help win this war.

My help is needed in the yard, but for some reason, the don't seem to want we to have credit for the part I play in winning this war. How do they ever expect to win the war, if they don't give we, as well as others, the considerations we are here for.

There has always been too much destintion made between the two races of people down south any way. And I can truly say, that until these people learn to treat every man alike, victory is no where to be found.

We hate to loose our country, but if they wont let us do our part and give us honor for what we try to do, then, there is nothing before them but a lost country.

You people know for yourselves, that if you were in my place now, you would demand what you were there for.

After all, I feel that if I buy bonds to help win the war, I should have the consideration I am here for. I know my help is needed, & I need the job. So please do all you can for me.

s o u r c e FEPC Papers.

118. *Letter from Miss Cathrose Norwood, Norfolk, Va., to President Roosevelt, 10 Sept. 1943. Describes discrimination in training and job placement of black women. Like a number of Americans, Norwood believes that F.D.R. will take note of her complaint.*

Dear Mr. Roosevelt: I feel it my duty to write you concerning my present status. I have done all I could thinking things would work out without consulting you, but nothing seems to work out.

I have written two letters to the committee on fair employment, but no answer has been received. That has been a month ago.

Mr. Roosevelt, I have been trained by the government as an electric welder. Before I started this trade, it was explained to me in full details that my job awaits me at the completion of my course. Everything has worked out . . . altogether different. I have tried every way I knew to get what I studied for, but every way was a failure.

My training began March 1, 1943 at the N.Y.A. Academy— Norfolk, Va. under the instruction of Mr. C. C. Goodwin. There I had eight weeks training in electric welding. After completing those eight weeks, I was sent to the Norfolk Navy Yard, where I was kept in training twelve more weeks under the instruction of Mr. Stephens. After finishing those weeks, I took my test and passed the first one. I was then kept in school two more weeks after passing my test.

White girls who came into the school after I did, finished and went out before I did. I was called one of the best in the class, but I cant see how they could come in after I did and go out before I.

Oh well, I can't see but one thing, that's because I am colored. That's the trouble with our country today. Our whites don't want to give the blacks what belong to them, for fear they might equal the whites.

Now Mr. Roosevelt, the reason I am writing you is because I have failed to get the consideration that was promised me.

After finishing my trade, all I got was "take what we give you or get out." So I kindly steped out with pleasure, leting them know that I was one negro who wasn't a fool.

After wasting my time trying to do something to help my country, that's what I have gotten. I think it's very unfair. After all, you asked us to take these trades and promised us jobs after we finished. So now, I think it's time you were doing something about the matter.

My case isn't the only case. There are quite a few others, but I am merely talking for myself.

After all, I feel that if I buy bonds to help win the war, I should have the consideration I'm here for.

So, will you please do all you can to help, and let me hear from you real soon.

SOURCE FEPC Papers.

119. *Letter from L. A. Moyer, U.S. Civil Service Commission, to George M. Johnson of FEPC, 11 Mar. 1943. Discusses efforts to place Rebecca Watson in a position as a graduate nurse at the Norfolk Naval Hospital.*

Dear Mr. Johnson:

Reference is made to your letter of February 27, 1943, in which you request that the President's Committee on Fair Employment Practice be informed if and when the name of Miss Rebecca Watson, 1306 Outten Street, Norfolk, Virginia, is again submitted to the Norfolk Naval Hospital for consideration for appointment to the position of Graduate Nurse.

The Commission desires to advise you that the necessary steps have been taken in noting the records so that this may be done.

By direction of the Commission:

SOURCE FEPC Papers.

120. *Letter from Rebecca Watson to Mrs. Franklin D. Roosevelt, 20 May 1943. Seeks the First Lady's help in getting a job as a nurse at the Norfolk Naval Hospital.*

My Dear Mrs. Roosevelt;

I'm asking your information as to what I can do concerning a position which I applied for in Civil Service as a graduate nurse, General Staff duty, and was rejected after reporting to the Naval Hospital in Portsmouth Va. from all view points on account of race discrimination.

After writing Mr. H. C. Hull of what happened in detail, he answered confirming my statements, and said that my name would be placed at the head of eligibles, so that I would recieve first consideration on account of the positions lost to me.

I recieved a letter from the Naval Department denying the report that the Civil Service Commission had found true, and that I would be given consideration due to merit and fitness should my name appear or is certified for appointment at the Naval Hospital.

I answered, and made it plain that I wrote Mr. Hull of the case at the Portsmouth Naval Hospital because I did not want my name removed from the list of eligibles for a reason that was no fault of my own, and I would appreciate a position in Hampton or Newport News or at Freedman's Hospital in Washington.

The last letter I recieved doesn't promise anything definite, and why should I be discarded altogether just because I'm colored, when I have to make sacrifices to aid the government.

Mrs. Roosevelt I am proud to be an American, which can be said for the whole race, Our Fathers, brothers and uncles are giving everything they have along with the rest. So when it comes to consideration why do we have to be treated so differently. We buy Bonds, those of us who are defense workers aren't asked whether or not we will or want to, but so much is taken out the hard earned salary even before we see it.

We helped to put the second war loan over and not only that we are still in there cheering and rooting for this government that's supposed to be for the peoples.

I have an uncle who was in World War One, Ellis Duncan, S. N. 3,638,993 did his bit, and says if he were called he'd do the same thing all over again, because it would be helping America.

You see Mrs. Roosevelt these are the reasons we want equal rights but yet we have to fight to be treated with a little fairness.

Moreover I need a job, am doing private duty at the present with the Tidewater Nurses Services Bureau Medical Arts Building, Norfolk, Va. but would like something steady.

Mrs. Roosevelt, please don't think I'm trying to stir up any racial matters, with this dreadful war on our hands, things are bad enough.

I talked to Congressman Harris of Norfolk Va, concerning the matter three weeks ago, but I don't know if he's gotten around to my problem. Inclosed [sic] please find the copies of the letters sent me by Civil Service Commission and the Naval Department from Washington D.C.

Will be very grateful for any information you might be kind enough to give.

SOURCE FEPC Papers.

121. *Letter from George M. Johnson, assistant executive secretary, FEPC, to Rebecca Watson, 5 July 1943. Acknowledges receipt of letter that Watson forwarded to Eleanor Roosevelt; requests more information on charges of discrimination.*

Dear Miss Watson:

Your letter of May 20 to Mrs. Roosevelt has been referred to this office for acknowledgement and consideration. You state that you have not been able to secure employment in line with your qualifications in the Federal Government, and you inform her of your complaint against the Naval Hospital at Portsmouth, Virginia, where you were discriminated against because of your race in your efforts to secure employment as a graduate nurse in that institution.

You mention in your letter that you received a communication from the Navy Department denying that you had been discriminated against because of your race. It is requested that you immediately furnish this office with that communication or an exact copy thereof. Upon receipt of this, we may be in a position to make a further investigation into this matter.

SOURCE FEPC Papers.

122. *Final Disposition Report of J. H. B. Evans, regional director, FEPC, to Will Maslow, director of Field Operations, 19 Aug. 1944. Reports on the Watson case, which closed as "other" because it could not be closed on "merits" or "satisfactory adjustment," since Miss Watson refused to withdraw her complaint against the Norfolk Naval Hospital at Portsmouth, Va.*

A. Chronology: Date of discrimination: 9/42
Date of filing complaint: 11/6/42—by references from CSC
Dates of personal contacts with complainant: none
Date of docketing: 8/1/43
Date of first contact with party charged: 1/21/43
Date of personal visits to party charged: 5/2/44–8/26/44
Date of closing: 9/19/44
Date of submission of FDR: 9/19/44
Type of final disposition: Other

B. Description of party charged: Navy Department Facility

C. Summary of complaint: Miss Rebecca Watson, the complainant wrote to the Civil Service Commission on October 28, 1942, and stated that more than a month ago she had been certified to the Norfolk Naval Hospital at Portsmouth for appointment as a Nurse—(General Staff Duty). She further stated that when she appeared, the officer whom she was instructed to see was out when she appeared and she was referred to the Chief Nurse, who told her she had not been instructed to hire colored nurses, but she might if she cared to do so, wait to see the officer. When he finally arrived he read and reread the form she presented him and said he didn't quite understand. He then left and conferred with the Chief Nurse and returned and told Miss Watson that there were no vacancies.

Miss Watson's letter to the Civil Service Commission caused that agency to institute an investigation which resulted in a finding that Miss Watson had been refused employment by the appointing officer at the Naval Hospital solely because she was a Negro, and as a consequence the Commission had placed her name at the top of its list of eligible Graduate Nurses in order that she might receive first consideration for appointment for the number of considerations lost as a result of having been passed over by the appointing officer at the Naval Hospital at Portsmouth.

D.   Background: This is the first case filed against this facility.

E.   Date and type of final disposition: 9/19/44 "Other"

F.   Reasons for action taken (if other than satisfactory adjustment): At this stage FEPC actively stepped into the picture and wrote Asst. Secretary Bard asking him to inform the Committee of the action taken by the Navy Dept. The reply to this was to the effect that at no time had any departure from a strict adherence to the instructions in Executive Order 8802 been directed or authorized and that appointing officers and others had again been directed to exercise particular care in avoiding the occurrence of either or actual or implied discrimination as to race, creed, color or national origin. The letter concluded with a statement that if Miss Watson's name were again presented she would be given consideration solely on the basis of her fitness. This was reported back to the Civil Services Commission and that agency was asked to inform the committee if and when her name was so referred.

The Commission, on November 9, 1943, notified the Committee that Miss Watson's name was submitted in February 1943 to the Federal Security Agency for consideration for appointment in the U.S. Marine Hospital in Norfolk. She was reported as considered but not selected. In this letter the Commission also notified that Committee that Miss Watson's change of her statement as to the place in which she would be available, or would prefer employment, had never been communicated to the Civil Service Commission; and that the Commission understood that the Nurse positions in Naval institutions are now filled by nurses who have been Commissioned from the Navy. In the meantime Miss Watson received a letter from the Navy Department's director of personnel informing her in the same manner as Asst. Secretary Bard had informed the Committee. Region IV subsequently inquired of the Commission whether Miss Watson's name had again been submitted. Later, by phone call, one of the examiners in Region IV learned that [the] Civil Service Commission intended to establish a new list of eligibles. The method agreed upon to do this was by circularizing those who had not been selected and determine their present availability.

Region IV then asked the Navy Department to state its policy in the matter of hiring nurses for its hospital and was told that the Department used only enlisted personnel.

There followed a letter from the Committee reviewing the circumstances of the case for the benefit of Admiral F. G. Crisp who had succeeded to the post of Director of Civilian Personnel in Shore Establishments, and requesting redress for Miss Watson in the form of granting her a commission in the Navy or any other form of redress which the Department might consider. It was made plain to the Admiral that Region IV was anxious to settle the case on regional level without resort to the Committee and the Secretary of the Navy.

Subsequently Examiners Roche and Houston had a conference with Admiral Crisp on a number of other cases which had been filed against various Shore Establishments. During this conference it developed that the Navy's policy had always been to use only enlisted personnel in nursing capacities. This one instance of a call for referral of civilian personnel was an emergency, caused by the delayed arrival of an enlisted assignee, and was the only occurrence of its kind within the memory of Admiral Crisp, Captain Sprung and Commander Thomas, both of whom were also present.

Another fact not previously known to FEPC was developed at this conference. That fact was that after Miss Watson had been refused employment the appointing officer of the Facility appointed a white person who had been referred at the same time. The appointee only worked eighteen days before her services were terminated. There has not since been an occasion to need the services of a civilian nurse and the officers were unanimous in expressing their beliefs that there will be no such occasion in the future.

The negotiations in behalf of Miss Watson have very definitely reached an impasse. The case cannot be closed as Satisfactory Adjustment. It cannot be Dismissed on Merits. There was no question of Jurisdiction. It was not withdrawn by the complainant.

In view of the fact that the circumstances which brought about the original referral no longer exist, and doubtless will never exist again, there is no alternative but to close the case as Other.

Mr. Will Maslow, Director of Field Operations

SOURCE FEPC Papers.

C. RACIAL CONFLICT, WAR, AND CHANGING POLITICAL CONSCIOUSNESS/IDENTITY

123. *"The Bitter River." From the* Negro Quarterly, *Fall 1942. Poem by Langston Hughes on the sad state of race relations and social justice in the south during World War II.*

The Bitter River

by Langston Hughes

(Dedicated to the memory of Charlie Lang and Ernest Green, each fourteen years old when lynched together beneath the Shubuta Bridge over the Chickasawhay River in Mississippi, October 12, 1942.)

There is a bitter river
Flowing through the South.
Too long has the taste of its water
Been in my mouth.
There is a bitter river
Dark with filth and mud.
Too long has its evil poison
Poisoned my blood.
I've drunk of the bitter river
And its gall coats the red of my tongue,
Mixed with the blood of the lynched boys
From its iron bridge hung,
Mixed with the hopes that are drowned there
In the snake-like hiss of its stream
Where I drank of the bitter river
That strangled my dream:
The book studied—but useless,
Tools handled—but unused,
Knowledge acquired but thrown away
Ambition battered and bruised.
Oh, water of the bitter river
With your taste of blood and clay,
You reflect no stars by night,
No sun by day.
The bitter river reflects no stars—
It gives back only the glint of steel bars

The pastor of the Church of God in Christ in Washington, D.C., preaching during a service in 1942. The black church and religious traditions played a major role in the African American struggle for full citizenship. Courtesy of the Library of Congress.

And dark bitter faces behind steel bars:
The Scottsboro boys behind steel bars,
Lewis Jones behind steel bars,
The voteless share-cropper behind steel bars,
The labor leader behind steel bars,
The soldier thrown from a Jim Crow bus behind steel bars,
The 15c mugger behind steel bars,
The girl who sells her body behind steel bars,
And my grandfather's back with its ladder of scars,
The old slave's back with its ladder of scars
Long ago, long ago—the whip and steel bars—
The bitter river reflects no stars.

"Wait, be patient," you say.
"Your folks will have a better day."
But the swirl of the bitter river
Takes your words away.
"Work, education, patience
Will bring a better day."
The swirl of the bitter river
Carries your "patience" away.
"Disrupter! Agitator!
Trouble maker!" you say.
The swirl of the bitter river
Sweeps your lies away.

I did not ask for this river
Nor the taste of its bitter brew.
I was given its water
As a gift from you.
Yours has been the power
To force my back to the wall
And make me drink of the bitter cup
Mixed with blood and gall.
You have lynched my comrades
Where the iron bridge crosses the stream,
Underpaid me for my labor,
And spit in the face of my dream.
You forced me to the bitter river
With the hiss of its snake-like song—
Now your words no longer have meaning—
I have drunk at the river too long:

Dreamer of dreams to be broken,
Builder of hopes to be smashed,
Loser from an empty pocket
Of my meagre cash,
Bitter bearer of burdens
And singer of weary song,
I've drunk at the bitter river
With its filth and its mud too long.

Tired now of the bitter river,
Tired now of the pat on the back,
Tired now of the steel bars
Because my face is black,
I'm tired of segregation,
Tired of filth and mud,
I've drunk of the bitter river
And it's turned to steel in my blood.

Oh, tragic bitter river
Where the lynched boys hung,
The gall of your bitter water
Coats my tongue.
The blood of your bitter water
For me gives back no stars.
I'm tired of the bitter river!
Tired of the bars!

SOURCE "The Bitter River." From the *Negro Quarterly*, 1, no. 3 (Fall 1942):
249–51.

124. *"The Social Front: Summer Madness." Article in* Race Relations, *no.
1 (Aug. 1943): 6–7. Discusses "Zoot Suit" riots in Los Angeles, major riots in
Beaumont, Tex., Detroit, and Harlem, and other conflicts in Newark, Charleston, S.C., and Houston.*

World War I taught that a great national crisis could fan old racial animosities into open and destructive violence. Race riots were expected at the end of World War II, but not at the end of the North African campaign. July and late June brought a sudden, "premature" epidemic of open racial violence, in race rioting, minor outbreaks, aborted riots, industrial-racial violence, soldier-racial violence, a high wave of police brutality and racial clashes in the congestion of transportation. Of these the Detroit riot was the most serious, but the others were no less significant for their underlying implications.

Race Riots

The "Zoot-Suit" Riots in Los Angeles

Allegations in the press to the contrary notwithstanding, all evidence points to the fact that the beating administered to young Mexicans and Negroes by white American sailors and soldiers, with the apparent encouragement of the local police, constituted a type of race riot. Although the Los Angeles City Council, with adroit indifference to the more serious underlying social factors, passed an ordinance making the wearing of a zoot suit a misdemeanor, it seems clear that the selection of victims was on an ethnic rather than a sartorial basis. For among the victims of mob action by service men (who were described in the local press as "avenging their buddies") were several Negroes and youths of Mexican extraction who wore Army and Navy uniforms. The facility with which anti-Mexican and anti-Negro feeling was incited was due in part to the fact that, according to Carey McWilliams, throughout 1942 and particularly after August, the Los Angeles press never failed to mention a Mexican arrest, a Mexican juvenile delinquency problem, a Mexican "crime wave."

The Beaumont, Texas Riot

Two deaths and 75 injuries, in addition to thousands of dollars in property damage, resulted from the mid-June rioting in Beaumont, Texas. The occasion for the riot was an alleged rape attack on a white woman by a Negro. White mobs entered the Negro section of the city and tried to raze it to the ground, and almost succeeded. War production came to a standstill, business establishments were closed, and martial law was finally invoked in order to quell the riot. The day following the major violence and bloodshed it was announced that a physician's examination had thrown serious doubt upon the veracity of the woman's statement that she had been raped. Notable about this outbreak were the numbers of white youth involved, the extent of Negro property damage, the lack of active Negro resistance, the courage of one Texas ranger who stopped a mob by evidence of trim intent to enforce law observance, the laudable example of a southern State's Attorney condemning racial violence, and the later offer of some white citizens to contribute to a rebuilding of the destroyed business places of the Negro victims. (FR, GP, NP)

The Detroit Riot

The most serious of the outbursts of rioting occurred in Detroit, Michigan during the week of June 20th. Into a situation that has been charged with racial tension for serveral years came a fist fight and two rumors. The former occurred on a bridge leading from the Belle Isle Amusement Park and followed several minor incidents between whites and Negroes that had occurred throughout one of the summer's hottest days. One of the rumors was intended for the ears of whites to the effect that a Negro youth had shot a white woman on the bridge. The other, circulated in the Negro community, was that a white man had thrown a Negro woman and her baby into the river. In the two days of active rioting that followed, 34 persons were killed, 461 were injured, and approximately 1800 were arrested. Property damaged in looting, burnings and vandalism is estimated in terms of millions of dollars; while over a million man-hours were lost to war production.

Of the 34 fatalities, 25 were Negroes, and of these 17 were killed by police. There was some looting, but there was also evidence, from photographic coverage and the sworn testimonials of eye-witnesses, that police abetted the rioters. The Police Commissioner's report listed 211 Negroes and 250 whites as injured, providng the prosecutor with the argument that the major riot guilt rested with the Negroes. However, fewer injured Negroes than whites had access to public hospitals, which in fact provided the basis for the racial statistics on injuries.

Poor and nonexistent housing, lack of recreational facilities, active anti-Negro propaganda, lack of confidence in the police on the part of white rioters were important factors contributing to the tension and adding to the ferocity of the riots. In the name-calling that has followed, all sorts of scapegoats have been discovered to account for the outbreak. The most recent list of "instigators" of the riot (August 1) is that of Prosecutor William Dowling, which gives first place to the "yellow" Negro press and the National Association for the Advancement of Colored People. This is, in a sense, like accusing the witness and the prosecutor for responsibility for the crime. (FR, GP, ANP, NP)

Harlem

The shooting of a Negro military policeman by a white New York City policeman, who accused the former of interferring in the arrest of a disorderly Negro woman, precipitated an outbreak in the world's largest Negro community. Five persons were killed, several hundred were injured, and property damage to businesses in the community was estimated at $5,000,000. Although the soldier sustained only a slight injury, the rumor spread rapidly that he had been killed. Active rioting followed the throwing of bottles into a crowd of persons who were demonstrating outside the hospital to which the soldier was first taken. The riot was handled adroitly by the police, the Mayor, and the Negro leaders of the community. It never actually became a *race* riot. Aside from a few minor incidents, white civilians were not molested, and there were no organized raids on white neighborhoods by Negroes or on the Negro area by whites. As in the 1936 outbreak in Harlem, the main acts of aggression were against property. Photographs taken during the rioting show Negro and white persons chatting amiably. White and Negro soldiers who were sent into the area to clear the streets of soldiers were greeted with cheers. . . .

Minor Outbreaks

Newark

Following a track meet in Newark on June 3rd, a group of white and a group of Negro boys returning to the city on the bus got into an argument. This incident set in motion rumors which spurred bands of Negro and white boys to roam the streets looking for victims of the other race. In the youthful gang warfare that followed, a Negro boy of 15 was stabbed to death and several white and Negro boys were injured in the stonings, stabbings and fist fights that raged in the city for the next few days. (GP) . . .

Rumors of Riots That Did Not Happen

Charleston, South Carolina

Rumors of an impending race riot spread over Charleston during the last week-end in June. It was reported that Negro soldiers were stopping all cars carrying whites through the Negro section and threatening the occupants' lives if they did not leave the area. Actually, a crowd of Negroes had gathered to watch a purely intra-racial fight. Three cars that passed through carrying white passengers were hailed, but there is no record of the occupants of either of them being threatened. All beer parlors and liquor places were closed, and police dispersed all crowds. The people of Charleston breathed more easily. This was the second serious riot rumor in the city in an eight-month period. The first involved workers in the shipyards. (GP)

Houston, Texas

June 19th is "Juneteenth" to Negroes in Texas—the day on which they celebrate emancipation from slavery. For several weeks before the last "Juneteenth" celebration, rumors were current that Negroes were storing arms for wholesale rioting. In this instance leading Negro and white citizens decided to meet the situation head on, rather than to avoid or ignore it. An interracial committee put on an active campaign to combat the rumors. The campaign was climaxed by a full-page advertisement in a leading Houston daily paper calling upon the white citizens to disregard the rumors. The riot did not occur; and Negroes of Houston celebrated the "Juneteenth" in peace. (GP, FR)

SOURCE "The Social Front: Summer Madness," *Race Relations,* no. 1 (Aug. 1943): 6–7.

125. *Letter from black marine to A. Philip Randolph, ca. 1943. Offers a detailed discussion of discrimination against blacks in the U.S. Marine Corps.*

Mr. Randolph

To start with, please excuse this informal way of addressing you.

My problem is, like 30,000 other colored marines, just this: We want to know why our boys cannot become officers in this our democratic marine Corp. Why our boys can only serve in labor or service battalions. Why Washington, the birth place of our colored marines must be converted. To convalence camp for white marines.

I will start with my entrance in the U.S. Marines and try to give an accurate account of the different action and reactions. I arrived at camp LeJeune New River, N.C. the 15th of Oct. 1942. The training was tough but strictly regulation. We were put into different schools according to our choice and educational qualifications. I stop here to add that up until Feb of 43 our colored marines were not draftees. But all enlisted men, and of these men they found negroes of the highest qualifications. Out of first 1500 men 1000 were college grads. or senior college men all seeking advancement and adventure like myself. These black Marine were an experiment, Elenor Roosevelt's babies so we were bandied with kid gloves. Feb.

our first left for over seas. This outfit was made up of the fellows that had doped off in the Marine Corp consequently meriting shipment over. Why they were looked upon this way is because of main outfit the 51st was still in training. This first outfit to move over had no special qualification so they were destined to become a service batallion.

Well every month from that time on the least little thing the men done that was wrong they found themselves in a service Battalion going over. These Battalions left at the rate of one a month comprising of from 100 to 300 men. Those that remained were being charmed into the steward's branch or cooks division in the promise of quick ratings. In the mean time our 1500 men of high educational qualifications were covering up and being shown as the colored Marine Corp. All opposing parties or radicals to these treatments were [illegible] sent out with work Battalions [illegible].

Around April of 43 our first outfit left that was not destine for overseas. It was a guard company for Oklahoma. They caught and are still catching hell from the discriminating officers and non-commission officer over them. The boys that had their wives there had to stand by and see them abuse to ease the terrific pressure in themselves. The boys were prohibited from wearing their blue uniforms in [illegible] gave them a good looking appearance in that [illegible] reknown radical "Satchel" he was sent back to N.C. There continued to champion our cause. He is now serving time in the Naval Jail. Pormouth Va. for five years.

In working in the administration building as a corporal, heard of an outfit going to Philadelphia, secured for myself a place as second in command of 100 men. when we arrived last Oct 7, 1943 we were told that we were to be on the working end of this war and if we conducted ourselves right [illegible] men would be sent up from N.C. to Philly. We didn't complain because anything was better than N.C. or service company some where in the pacific. Philly is one of the largest quartermaster outfits and for 8 hours a day all we see is freight cars and vans and whip cracking crackers [illegible] than the ones that [illegible] out to say plain nigger. Yes! We have 400 black steavador marines about 11 sgts 15 corporals and all the rest private first class only to soothe the colored population at Philly to show them that the negro Marines are getting something for their labor (that's a laugh) the majority of the boys live in Philly or near by states so like myself bear with this treatment because after 4:30 we can be ourselves and be with our families. This is why we have not [illegible] before half of our sgts who are suppose to protect us do the opposite to protect their stripes or be busted [illegible] for refusing to drop the men [illegible] radical. We really have no negro representative [illegible] in the Corp. This is why wee appeal to you to help us secure our own representatives with power so they cant be bought or scared. *We want colored Comm. Officers in the Marine Corp* and it is President Roosevelts power to see that we get the same treatment as other branches of the arm services.

Thanks for you help, past, immediate, and future.

S O U R C E *PAPR,* Reel 13, frame nos. 0220–0221.

126. *Letter of protest, Camp Van Dorn, Miss., 1 June 1943. Decries the brutal treatment of black soldiers at the camp and calls for the people of America "To Put An End to Such Wholesale Desecration of the Constitution."*

To Whom it May Concern. This is Not Onley a Letter of Protest Against the Brutal Treatm Ment Of Soldiers of Color in The South. But it is Also A Plea. To the People of America To Do That Which is in Their Power. To Put An End to Such Wholesale Desecration of the Constitution of the United States.

Sunday Afternoon. May 30th. 1943. A Soldier. A Member Of the 364th. Infantry Regiment (Colored). Now Stationed at Camp Van Dorn. Mississippi. Was Brutally Murdered At A Town Called Centreville. Approximately Four Miles From Camp By A. Civilian Sherrff. A Resident of the Town. From the Sworn. Testimonies of Several eyewitnesses to the Crime. the Following information. Was Revealed. And is Being Published. For the Benefit of Those Who Might Be Inclined to Believe. The Articles Which are Published in the Behalf of the. Southern White Gentry.

It Was Learned that Five Colored Soldiers. While Making A Tour of the Town of Centreville. Were Accosted by. Two Military Police. Who Ordered One of them to Button his. Shirt Sleeve. The Soldier informed the M.P. That The Button. Had BeCome Detached. and that He had Not Been Able to Replace It. Were Upon. The Two M.P.s Leaped From Their Car. Brandishing BlackJacks. And one of Them Proceeded to Attack the Soldier. Who had No Button on his Shirt Sleeve. The Remaining Soldiers. Persuaded the other M.P. to Let the Men Fight it out. And, Let the Best Man Win, But the M.P. Obviously Getting the Worse of the. Battle, Noticed the Sherriff of the Town. Mr. Knighten, Coming Up With His Two Deputies, And Called. Mr Knighten, Shoot This, Nigger, The Soldier Then Straightened up, And Said, No. You, Wont Shoot me, Whereupon, Knighten Drew his Revolver, Saying, The Hell I Wont. and Firing Point. Blank at the Soldier. Struck Him Fully in the Chest. the Sherff then Turned to. The M.P. and Asked. Any More Niggers You Wont Killed?, Meanwhile The Deputies Put two of the Other Soldiers to Flight with well Aimed blows to the Head with a sap stick. but took the Other. Two to the Guard House.

Obviously, the unsavory reputation of the 364th. Infantry Regiment. Has Preceded them to this station, Due. Mainly to the fack that this is the Same Regiment which. Figured to Ponminenty in the Thanksgiving Day Riot in of. Phoenix, Arizona, and it is also Quite obvious that the. Civillian Authorities of this Locale have Heard of this. So Called belligerent outfit, and have taken it upon themselves to whip them into submission, and to subjugate them as thy have Done other Negro outfites in the Past.

SOURCE *PAPR,* Reel 13, frame no. 0168.

127. *"Somewhere in the South Pacific." Written by Thomas White in 1945 and sent to his wife. White retired as a major in the U.S. Army; after the war he lived in Cleveland.*

> Somewhere in the South Pacific where the sun is like a curse,
> And each long day is followed by another . . . slightly worse,
> And the men dream and wish for greener, fairer lands.
>
> Somewhere in the South Pacific where a girl is never seen,
> Where the sky is never cloudy and the grass is always green.
> Where the bat's mighty howl robs a man of blessed sleep,
> Where there isn't any whiskey, and the beer is never cheap.
>
> Somewhere in the South Pacific where the nights were made for love,
> Where the moon is like a searchlight and the Southern cross above
> sparkles like a diamond in the balmy tropic night,
> It's a shameless waste of beauty when there's not a girl in sight.
>
> Somewhere in the South Pacific where the mail is always late,
> And a Christmas card in April is considered up to date.
> Where we never have a payday and we never get a cent,
> But we never miss the money because we'd never get it spent.
>
> Somewhere in the South Pacific where the ants and buzzards play,
> And a hundred fresh mosquitos replace each one you slay.
> So take me back to 'Frisco; let me hear the mission bell,
> For this godforsaken outpost is a substitute for HELL.

SOURCE We are indebted to Robert Jefferson, Department of History, Wayne State University, Detroit.

128. *"YWCA Leader Asks President to Abolish Segregation in Armed Services." Article in* Race Relations, *Nov. 1943. Mrs. Henry A. Ingraham, presi-*

dent of YWCA, urges Franklin D. Roosevelt to end segregation in the military because "racial strife destroys national unity at home and renders us suspect abroad."

Sir: Many of us at the National Board of the Young Women's Christian Association have read with great interest your letter addressed to the National Urban League on the occasion of its recent conference in Chicago. We are writing at this time to express our deep appreciation of your having enunciated again some of the profound principles upon which a country like ours is founded, and to which we must increasingly bring truth.

We should also like to take this occasion to urge upon you that you use the power and prestige of your high office, as President of the United States and Commander-in-Chief of its armed forces, to abolish racial segregation in the armed services of the nation. With you, we believe that racial strife destroys national unity at home and renders us suspect abroad. We further believe that until the federal government ceases practices of separation, the efforts of other groups are muted. We have had evidence of this, and should like to cite just one example. When a YWCA group protested seating practices which segregated Negro patrons in an Illinois theater, such segregation being in violation of the Civil Rights statutes of that state, the telling crushing answer received was that as long as the United States Navy could "get away with it" at the nearby Great Lakes Naval Station, there was no cause for the theater management to be too greatly alarmed.

In addition to this, involuntary separations, which always carried with it for the group set apart against its own volition a stigma difficult to bear under any circumstances, becomes a veritable badge of second class citizenship when it stems from the federal government. We believe that this must cease, not only because—as you have so truly said—the integrity of our nation and our war aims is at stake in our attitude toward minority groups at home, but also because if we wish to vindicate the principles of freedom and equality and democracy upon which this nation was based we must solve the problem of race in the United States.

There is nothing in social evolution, we believe, to prove that separation solves such problems, but much evidence that unity does. Our own experience, in attempting to build a fellowship uniting all women and girls, of whatever race, creed or nationality, we are committed to our purposes, has given us practical demonstration of this within the YWCA. On the other hand, the evidence seems to point to the conclusion that many instances of recent clashes between white and Negro service men and civilians have deep roots in the continuation of the undemocratic practice of separation of service people on the basis of race.

Great harm has been done to Negro morale and our democracy has suffered because of the mishandling and mistreatment of Negro Americans in segregated units of the armed forces. We believe that great good would result if you would speak out strongly and clearly against such separation. It is true, indeed, that all true Americans must increasingly accept the responsibilities that go with democratic privileges. We respectfully submit, Mr. President, that your leadership now is vital to our country's future.

SOURCE "YWCA Leader Asks President to Abolish Segregation in Armed Services." *Race Relations*, Nov. 1943.

129. *Lucia Mae Pitts, "A WAC Speaks to a Soldier." From* Negro Story, *Dec.–Jan. 1944–45. Poem reflecting on the role of women in the military and in the defense effort at home; praises the bravery of men but laments that "you did not really want us here." WACs and mule members of the 93rd Army division served at Fort Huachuca, Ariz.*

Dedicated to Lt. Thomas I. Pitts, to the soldiers
At Fort Huachuca, and to all soldiers.

We salute you—
But not with so common a thing as our hands.
Our hands must keep busy working
And we cannot keep them raised
For as long as you need saluting.
It is our hearts that we raise in a gesture of respect—
Quietly and unseen,
But constantly and reverently.

You did not really want us here.
"Women have no place in the Army," you said.
"Women should stay at home and keep the home-fires burning.
We want to think of you as sitting and waiting
For us to come back,
Dressed in the flimsy gowns which were yours alone
And which we remember sentimentally;
Not in uniform like thousands and thousands of others
And so much like our own.
We want to dream of you
As lying down to your rest at night,
Looking up at the stars and the moon above us all
And saying a prayer for us."
Others said, "You were cruel to come in

And push us out to the firing line. . .
Do you know you are sending us out to our death?"

We have swallowed your disapproval
And joined up just the same,
Because there was a job to be done
And we had to do it.
We have tried not to think of things
Like sending you to your death.
We have thought, on the other hand,
Of what would happen to all of us
If you stayed at home . . .
We have come in to share as much as we can
Of your discomfort and your sacrifice.
We, too, march, and soil ouselves with dirty jobs,
And rise with the dawn to put in a good day's work
At the jobs you did before.
When we seek our bunks at night,
Our bodies, too, are weary and sore.
And as we take over and push you from your jobs over here,
We salute you.
With a lump in our throats and determination in our hearts,
We salute you.
We come to do you and our country good.
We believe in you.
We believe it will not be in vain.
You will go forth as men of whom we may be proud,
For whom we shall be glad to have left
The comfort of our homes,
The security of our paying jobs,
The Freedom of action we knew—
For whom we shall be glad to have shared
The sacrifice you make.
We will not let you down.
Though not in the delicate gowns you knew,
Though not sitting, but still waiting.
We shall keep the home-fires burning.
And from the austerity of our Army home,
We will still seek the stars and the moon
And say our prayers . . .

We send you forth,
And as you go marching in never ending files,

With our hearts and the work of our hands
We salute you.

S O U R C E   Lucia Mae Pitts, "A WAC Speaks to a Soldier," *Negro Story* 1, no. 4 (Dec.–Jan. 1944–45): 63.

130. *"They Fight for Democracy." Editorial in* Homestead Daily Messenger, *28 Feb. 1944. This Pittsburgh daily sympathizes with the grievances of a local black youth in an army camp in Tennessee. The editorial produced a flurry of black and white reactions to the issue, also printed below.*

Editorial—They Fight for Democracy

Receipt is acknowledged of a letter from a local negro youth in an army camp in Tennessee. This boy, along with thousands of his race, is training so that he may aid in the nation's fight against aggressors.

Yet he and many of his kind are sent to camps in the south where they are bound by restrictions against their race. His letter contained a mimeographed form handed the negro troops telling them what they cannot do in Tennessee—what the state laws provide in regards to travel in trolleys and buses as well as in hotels, inns, theatres, public houses, moving picture shows, restaurants, places of amusement and other businesses.

What must be the thoughts of these boys when they read these pamphlets? They have gone to a southern camp from the north where they are treated fairly decent. In their new surroundings they are faced with countless prohibitions.

These boys, whether white or black, are Americans. They are willing and eager to take up arms so that freedom and democracy may come through victoriously against our enemies. Yet how much freedom and how democratic are southern states when they tell these boys they must not do this or that for if they do they will be fined.

The contentions in the south are that the whites are so outnumbered that the states must institute these prohibitions if whites are to exist. We believe the southerners really believe this to be a fact and yet we know it is a fallacy. Treat a man, regardless of color or creed, with respect and you get the same kind of treatment from him. Treat him with disdain and with restrictions and he is resentful and rightly so.

If the south is to stand firm in its unreasonable treatment of the negroes then it would seem that negro inductees should be kept out of southern camps. It is the only way we can give our negro troops a taste of real democracy and it is likewise the only way we can retain our self respect.

The self respecting negro is more careful of distinctions between the races than are the whites and that is because he is self conscious. It is easily understood why this is so. From birth it has been dinned into him to keep his place. He is sensitive to a great degree because of this race distinction and he will see that he keeps his place much better than many whites under the same circumstances.

The negro feels he has a cross to bear and our country hasn't made it any easier for him. Yet we expect him to fight for the land that places restrictions all about him. He does fight and he battles gloriously and unafraid. Keep him from the south and place him in camps where his good traits and his qualifications will be recognized no matter what his color and then we will be making strides towards the equality of citizenship that is due him.

3/8/44
Letter Box
Camp Shelby, Miss.
Editor
The Daily Messenger
Homestead, Pa.
Dear Sir:

I read your editorial about the negro in the "Messenger" dated 28, February 1944, and was quite surprised that you would treat the subject as ridiculous as was the Civil War. I grant you, it is a problem, but to condemn the South and think the North is wholly pure in its dealings with the subject is folly. I've been in the South three years, and, contrary to belief in Yankee-land, the negro isn't beaten with a horse whip and lynched at every street corner as is common belief in the North. The South pulls no punches, but it is fair and honest with them. The Southerner is not the hypocrite that you find in the North, where the two races shake hands and pat each other on the back; at the same time each is thinking how he can throw a knife into the others back. The difference between the South and the North is segregation of the races.

And, personally, I think the South is on the right track for you never read of nor witness any race riots as you find in Detroit, New York, and which steam up and down in the city schools of Pittsburgh and on the streets of Homestead. So, what makes you take the stand that the North is the wise-bird and the South the ostrich? Again, ask yourself the question who has the most trouble, the South or North? Ask yourself another question: which of the two negroes, Northern or Southern, is the happier and more content? A little observation soon gives you the answer—Southern negro. With all the Northern mingling, which is supposed to bring outstanding results, it has been the South that has produced the greatest leaders of the negro race. Every time something comes up anymore, people scream "democracy." All right, we have a Superior Court in Washington; since the Civil War this segregation has been going on in the South and has that Court ever declared it undemocratic?

I liken the subject to the setup in our own U.S. Army, where we have the enlisted man and the officer. The two are decidedly segregated, domestically, socially, and otherwise; yet close association exists, understanding and pleasant living exist. But no familiarity exists. And if it did, all would be lost, and the same men would soon hate the officers if the officers were familiar. This same familiarity exists between the white man and the negro in the North, and it is causing the hate and the trouble between the two races in the North today. We have segregation in the Army, yet have you ever heard of resentfulness, disturbances, and riots between officers and enlisted men? On the contrary, the officers and enlisted men you meet every day in your office express mutual respect for each other. The Army today is the greatest living and breathing example of democracy in America, or yes, the world.

Sure, give the negroes equal opportunity, as all men have under the Bill of Rights, but give it to them among themselves. A segregated, united negro race would be more of an expression of democracy than the mingled, broken-up resentful race that you find in the North today. Segregation is the word we must adopt in Yankee-land.

As for bringing the Northern negro Solider to the North, no group of people in this land would be happier to see this done than the Southern whites, because the Northern negro in times will cause the same trouble in the South that he has been causing in the North these many years because of the familiarity of the whites. Familiarity breeds contempt, not love, charity, and good will. So don't be so condemning of another section of the country, for I believe they are away ahead of us Yankees on the negro question.

Too many Northerners think segregation and suppression are the same word. If they will look in Webster, they will read two different definitions or meanings. It is a well-established fact in the Army that the best man to command negro troops is not a Northern officer, but a Southern officer. The Southern officer has much more tolerance and understanding of the negro than the Northern officer, and this is a result of year of mutual understanding of the two races in the South.

To sum this all up, I have been attempting to give you two glaring examples of what peace and contentment exists with segregation; on the other hand all you can give is one example of mingling, and as a result of it, riots and hate and resentfulness exist. Who is correct? Surely not the latter.

Sincerely, your friend

A SOLDIER

3/13/44

Letter Box March 8, 1944

To Soldier, Camp Shelby, Miss.

Sir:

Answering your letter to The Daily Messenger, of March 8, in defense of the editor, Mr. Kline, a true and fair newspaperman printed his editorial on facts presented to him by a negro. His work is to serve his entire district, including all creeds and races, perhaps Soldier, you think he should have printed his editorial on a separate page composed entirely of negro news. He didn't have to print that editorial, he could have thrown the submitted article in his waste paper basket. I believe he realized that the negro is an American citizen.

Soldier, America's destiny is the negro's destiny too. Negroes all over the United States are doing their bit for the victory that must be ours. This editorial is based on a set of rules given to a negro serviceman upon his arrival at a camp in Tennessee. Maybe Soldier, if the rules had been printed, blunt and direct, you might have agreed with those rules. This negro serviceman was stationed in a Northern camp for months, and had no trouble in any way, whatsoever. He was transferred to Tennessee, upon arrival he was given a set of rules (not dealing with his training), but the district itself, which limits his liberties. In order to prevent your misunderstanding, Soldier, as you seem to misunderstand many other things, this serviceman's whole outfit was given these undemocratic rules. Frankly, I don't believe that the War Department has any knowledge of these rules. You have been in the South, so you say, for three years, and in these years have you been told where you can't go, with the exception of Army regulations, where you shall sit in a public vehicle, and after complying to the unfair practices, if this vehicle is to become crowded, you must stand. Even though you are in your allotted place before it becomes so, and say nothing about it, have you Soldier.

It has been said by both white and negro soldiers that the south is still fighting the Civil War. Instead of being accepted as men who are defending American rights, they are treated as though they were invaders. I don't think you have been south long enough to condemn the north, and you only know what happens in your corner.

We negroes comprise one-tenth of the nation's population, I suppose that we should be segregated and given one-tenth of the land to live in.

Do you, Soldier, think that each of the races should be allotted a part of the country in percentage of their numbers and then rise up as a whole when attacked by a foreign nation. Perhaps, Soldier, you think the Negro should fight the battles in the New Britain Campaign and the whites fight in New Guinea. How far do you think the Allies will get, Soldier, if they separate under their own respective commands and fight as separate units instead of fighting together in a common cause.

Speaking of riots, Soldier, you are right about those in Detroit, New York and Pittsburgh, but what about Beaumont, Fort Bragg and those atrocious lynchings. I can assure you, Soldier, that the Negro from the South, who is so fortunate to come north refuses to return to the south except for a vacation or to visit relatives.

Segregation in a nation the size of America is ignorance and only presents a complicated problem of unnecessary and chaotic caste system such as that of India. Soldier, I will daresay that the negro under the Bill of Rights, with equal opportunities could live segregated and be perfectly content. But, the question which is so great, and is first to arise in our minds is; who shall make the laws, who shall enforce these laws and who shall fight the wars. Do you think that a segregated negro race would want a white man making his laws or vice versa.

In response to your opinion on officers, I think you are entirely wrong, because no man can understand a negro fully, but another negro. In the qualification of a competent officer for negroes, the section of the country has bearing on the officer in any way. The officer must qualify in his person traits; such as broadmindedness, and capability of good leadership. Men of all sections of our country have proven themselves possessive of the qualities.

Lest you forget, Soldier, we are fighting a war for Freedom, The Four Freedoms. Prejudice and segregation can play no part on the battlefield. In your case, Soldier, if you were so unfortunate as to be wounded on the field, would you refuse the aid of a negro comrade or refuse the surgery of a negro doctor.

Soldier, Representative Fish (he is a white man) wants to know why colored regiments are not in combat duty, that is, according to the length of their training. He did not agree on the answer he was given. The negro has fought in every war that the United States has been in, and why not, is it not their country.

Yes, Soldier, your type can keep us negroes in the ditch, but my dear friend, you will have to come down there with us to hold us there. Soldier, the races are as a revolving wheel and it is turning fast.

Respectfully,
A NEGRO

SOURCE *Homestead Daily Messenger,* 28 Feb. 1944, 8 Mar. 1944, 13 Mar. 1944. The authors are indebted to Lori Cole for bringing these documents to their attention.

131. *"Contributors" and "Statement of Policy." From the* Negro Quarterly *(Spring 1942). Express the thoughts and opinions of the leading black intellectuals of the period; offer reflections on the impact of the war on "all aspects" of African American life. Federal agencies, including the FBI, closely monitored and tried to influence the publication practices of black newspapers and journals during the war.*

Contributors

Sterling A. Brown teaches at Howard University and is the author of *Southern Road* and one of the editors of *The Negro Caravan*.

Dorothy Brewster is associate professor of English at Columbia University.

Langston Hughes is the author of *Not Without Laughter, The Weary Blues, The Big Sea,* and the forthcoming work *Shakespeare in Harlem*.

Doxey A. Wilkerson teaches at Howard University and is the author of *Special Problems of Negro Education*.

Elie Lescot is President of Haiti.

Millen Brand is the author of *The Outward Room* and other works.

Waring Cuney's poems have appeared in *Golden Slippers, The Negro Caravan* and other anthologies.

Carl G. Hill's poems have appeared in *The Negro Times*. He is also a painter of watercolors and is now working on a series of narrative poems dealing with Harlem life.

Ralph Ellison is a short story writer as well as a literary critic.

L. D. Reddick is curator of the Schomburg Collection of Negro Literature of the New York Public Library.

Herbert Aptheker is the author of *Negro Slave Revolts* and other works on Negro history.

Angelo Herndon is the author of *Let Me Live*.

Augusta V. Jackson is a former school teacher and has written a number of critical articles on Negro life.

Harcourt A. Tynes is a teacher in the public school system of Harlem, and is one of the leaders of the Harlem branch of the Association for the Study of Negro Life and History.

Statement of Policy

The Negro Quarterly makes its appearance to the public as a review of Negro thought and opinion. It will strive to reflect the true aspirations of the Negro people and their traditions of struggle for freedom.

The rapid change of life introduced by the war makes apparent the need of reflecting upon the genuine attitudes, thoughts and opinions of Negroes, and of giving direction and interpretation to certain new social and economic factors and their relation to the special problems of the Negro.

Thus the purpose of *The Negro Quarterly* is a two-fold one: to treat critically all aspects of these new changes and to aid in furthering the literary, social, and cultural advancement of the Negro people. Such a development will not only redound to the benefit of Negroes, but will strengthen immensely the democratic ideals of the nation.

Because our country is now engaged in an all-out war with the Axis forces, the full capacity of its man power must be thrown into battle in order to insure final victory. This can be done more effectively when the barriers of Jim Crow in the Army, Navy, Air Force, and other national defense bodies are removed. Negroes must share equally in the hardships of war, as well as in the victory that is to come.

Aware of the fact that the speed and tempo of present-day life permits only a cursory glance at the past, *The Negro Quarterly,* however, shall devote space and time to research into the history of the Negro people with a view toward correcting many of the falsehoods which have been spread over the years, and with a view toward interpreting the facts as they bear upon the problems of today.

The literary and artistic talents of Negro writers have for too long lain dormant. And there is much for America to gain when these have been released to blossom forth into full expression. As far as it is possible for a magazine issued only four times a year, the pages of *The Negro Quarterly* will serve as a vehicle through which such expression can be made. For the young writer it will provide a medium for training and orientation. As against the old stereotype methods of portraying Negro character, *The Negro Quarterly* will endeavor to project the life of the Negro people in terms of their true experience.

In fulfilling the aims and purposes outlined here, *The Negro Quarterly* welcomes the participation of both Negro and white writers.

Warm appreciation and gratitude to all our friends and contributors, without whose aid and support this publication could not have appeared, is hereby acknowledged.

SOURCE "Contributors" and "Statement of Policy," *Negro Quarterly*, 1, no. 1 (Spring 1942): pp. 2–4.

132. *"Editorial Comment." From the* Negro Quarterly, *1, no. 4 (Winter–Spring, 1943): 295–301. Identifies several distinct attitudes of blacks toward their wartime experiences; concludes with an emphasis on "an attitude of critical participation."*

By way of group self-examination it might be profitable to list a few of the general attitudes held by Negroes toward their war-time experiences.

First might be listed the attitude of unqualified acceptance of the limited opportunity for Negro participation in the conflict, whether in the war industries or in the armed forces. Along with this is found an acceptance of the violence and discrimination which so contradicts a war for the Four Freedoms. This attitude is justified by the theory that for Negroes to speak out in their own interests would be to follow a "narrow Negro approach" and to disrupt war-unity. This attitude (sometimes honestly held) arises, on one hand, out of a lack of group self-consciousness which precluded any confidence in the Negro people's own judgment, or in its potentialities for realizing its own will. Others who voice this attitude, however, are simply expressing what they are paid to express. Still others suffer from what might be termed a "disintegration of the sense of group personality." For these the struggle has been too difficult; in order to survive they feel that Negroes must resort to the most vicious forms of uncletomism. Its most extreme expression, to date, has been Warren Brown's plaint—in the face of the United States' glaring jim crow system—that most of the Negro press desires to be "Negro first and American second." While another striking instance of it is seen among those Negro actors who continue to accept Hollywood's anti-Negro roles.

Back of this attitude lies a fear and uncertainty that is almost psychopathic. It results in the most disgusting forms of self-abasement. The decadent Negro counterpart of American rugged individualism, it would willingly have the Negro people accept the depths of degradation rather than risk offending white men by lifting a hand in its own defense. Men who hold this attitude are comfortable only when taking orders; they are happy only when being kicked. It is this basic attitude that produces the spy, the stool pigeon, and the agent provocateur—all of which types are found today among those who call themselves Negro leaders.

A second attitude encountered is that of *unqualified rejection:* of the war; of the Allies statement of their war aims; and of the role which Negroes have been elected to play in any of its phases. Arising out of a type of Negro nationalism which, in a sense, is admirable, it would settle all problems on the simple principle that Negroes deserve equal treatment with all other free human beings. It is this which motivates those Negroes who go to jail rather than endure the Jim Crow conditions in the Armed forces. It is the basis of Negro cynicism and it views every situation which requires Negroes to struggle against fascist forces within our own country as evidence that the United States is fighting a "white man's" war.

But this is the attitude of one who, driven into a corner, sees no way of asserting his manhood except to choose his own manner of dying. And during the folk period, before the Negro masses became politically conscious, such an attitude created folk heroes and gave birth to legend and folksong. For Negroes admire men who die rather than compromise their principles. But on the day John Henry's great heart burst in his struggle against the machine, this attitude became impractical. Today we live in a political world and such an attitude is inadequate to deal with its complex problems. Not that courageous display of manhood no longer has a place in our lives, but that when asserted blindly it results only in empty, individualistic action—or worse, admiration for the ruthless and violent *action* of fascism. Feeling that so much experience by Negroes in the U.S. is tinged with fascism, some Negroes went so far as to join the pro-Japanese Pacific Movement.

Superficially, this attitude seems the direct opposite of the first; and in basic human terms it is. Yet, when expressed in action in the present political situation it is revealed as a mere *inversion* of the first. For in its blind rejection it falls over backwards into an even blinder acceptance. Unconsciously it regards all acts of aggression against Negroes as inevitable, the forces behind these acts as invincible. Being blind it does not recognize that Negroes *have their own stake in the defeat of fascism*—which would be true even if white Americans were still practicing isolationism. It conceives of positive action for the Negro people only in terms of death—or passivity, which is another form of death. Individuals who hold this attitude become conscious of themselves as *Negroes* only in terms of dying; they visualize themselves only as followers, never as leaders. Deep down they see no possibility of an allied victory being a victory for Negroes as well as for others. Refusing to see the *peoples'* aspect of the war, they conceive of victory as the triumph of "good white men" over "bad white men"; never as the triumph of the common peoples of the world over those who foster decayed political forms and systems. Should "good white men" triumph they will, perhaps, *give* Negroes a few more opportunities. Should "bad white men" win, then things will continue as before, perhaps a little worse. And since during the course of the war the sincerity of even good white men frequently appears doubtful, the Negro can expect but little in any case.

This is a political form of self-pity, and an attitude of political children. Actually it holds no desire for Negroes to assume an adult role in government. And perhaps its most naive expression is found among those who, frustrated and impotent before the complex problems of the Negro situation, would resort to a primitive form of magic and solve the whole problem by simply abolishing the word *Negro* from the American language. It never occurs to them that no matter what name they give themselves that name will mean no more than they can *make* it mean. Nor do they understand that in the process of fighting for a free America and a free world, Negro Americans (insofar as they approach it consciously) are also creating themselves as a free people and as a nation.

Fortunately there is a third attitude. Also a manifestation of Negro nationalism, it is neither an attitude of blind acceptance, nor one of unqualified rejection. It is broader and more human than the first two attitudes; and it is scientific enough to make use of both by transforming them into strategies of struggle. It is committed to life and it holds that the main task of the Negro people is to work unceasingly toward creating those democratic conditions in which it can live and recreate itself. It believes the historical role of Negroes to be that of integrating the larger American nation and compelling it untiringly toward true freedom. And while it will have none of the slavishness of the first attitude, it is imaginative and flexible enough, to die if dying is forced upon it.

This is an attitude of critical participation, based upon a sharp sense of the Negro people's group personality. Which is the basis of its self-confidence and morale in this period of confusion. Thus, while affirming the justice of the Allies' cause, it never loses sight of the Negro peoples' stake in the struggle. This for them is the point of departure, a basic guide to theory and action which allows for objectivity and guards against both the fearful acceptance of the first and the sullen rejection of the second. It regards men unsentimentally; their virtues are evaluated and cherished, their weaknesses anticipated and guarded against. This attitude holds that any action which is advantageous to the United Nations must also be advantageous for the Negro and colonial peoples. Programs which would sacrifice the Negro or any other people are considered dangerous for the United Nations; and the only honorable course for Negroes to take is first to protest and then to fight against them. And while willing to give and take in the interest of national unity, it rejects that old pattern of American thought that regards any Negro demand for justice as an assault against the state. It believes that to fail to protest the wrongs done Negroes as we fight this war is to participate in a crime, not only against Negroes, but against all true anti-Fascists. To fight against defects in our prosecution of the war is regarded as a responsibility. To remain silent simply because friends commit these wrongs is no less dangerous than if Negroes should actively aid the enemy.

Recently this attitude has led Negroes to employ the contradictory tactic of withdrawal for the purpose of closer unity. It motivated Judge William H. Hastie's resignation from the War Department, where it was expected of him to remain silent while the window-dressing air school at Tuskegee was palmed off on the American people as the real thing. For Hastie this might have been an act of courage which lost him prestige among Fascist-minded whites, but it has made his name meaningful among thousands of Negroes, bringing eligibility for that support which is the basis of true leadership. One wonders when the other members of the so-called "Black Cabinet" will learn this basic truth? As yet, however, this attitude is found implied in the sentiments of the Negro masses, rather than in the articulated programs of those who would lead them. Hastie's action is the first by a public figure.

The existence of the attitude, however, emphasizes more than ever before the need for representative Negroes to come to terms with their own group through a consideration of the major problems of our revolutionary times. First in terms of the problem of the centralization of political power. They must (1) see the Negro people realistically as a political and economic force which has, since the Civil War, figured vitally in the great contest for power between the two large economic groups within the country; that (2) despite the very real class divisions within the Negro group itself during periods of crisis—especially during periods of war—these divisions are partially suspended by outside pressures, making for a kind of group unity in which great potential political power becomes centralized—even though Negro leadership ignores its existence, or are too timid to seize and give it form and direction; that (3) although logically and historically the Negro's interests are one with those of Labor, this power is an objective force which might be channeled for Fascist ends as well as for democratic ones; and (4) that they as leaders have a responsibility in seeing to it that this vital force does not work for Fascism—either native or foreign. To the extent that Negro leadership ignores the power potential of the group, to that extent will the Negro people be exploited by others: either for the good ends of democratic groups or for the bad ends of Fascist groups. And they have the Civil War to teach them that no revolutionary situation in the United States will be carried any farther toward fulfilling the needs of Negroes than Negroes themselves are able, through a strategic application of their own power to make it go. As long as Negroes fail to centralize their power they will always play the role of a sacrificial goat; they will always be "expendable." Freedom, after all, cannot be imported or acquired through an act of philanthropy; it must be won.

In order to plan the direction of power, Negro leaders must obey the impetus toward Negro self-evaluation which the war has made a necessity. They must integrate themselves with the Negro masses; they must be constantly alert to new concepts, new techniques and new trends among other peoples and nations with an eye toward appropriating those which are valid when tested against the reality of Negro life. By the same test they must be just as alert to reject the faulty programs of their friends. When needed concepts, techniques or theories do not exist they must create them. Many new concepts will evolve when the people are closely studied in action. And it will be out of this process that true leadership will come; fortunately, the era of subsidized Negro leadership is fast pressing. Even the mild protest of a William Pickens has become too radical for those who for years have pulled the strings of Negro middle class leadership.

A second problem for Negro leadership to master is that of accurately defining the relation between the increasing innovations in technology and the Negro people's political and economic survival and advancement. During the war the mastery of hitherto unavailable techniques by Negroes is equivalent to the winning of a major military objective: after the war they will be able to give leadership to the working class; and that leadership always rests with those workers who are most skilled.

A third major problem, and one that is indispensible to the centralization and direction of power, is that of learning the meaning of the myths and symbols which abound among the Negro masses. For without this knowledge, leadership, no matter how correct its program, will fail. Much in Negro life remains a mystery; perhaps the zoot suit conceals profound political meaning; perhaps the symmetrical frenzy of the Lindy-hop conceals clues to great potential power—if only Negro leaders would solve this riddle. On this knowledge depends the effectiveness of any slogan or tactic. For instance, it is obvious that Negro resentment over their treatment at the hands of their allies is justified. This naturally makes for resistance to our stated war aims, even though these aims are essentially correct; and they will be accepted by the Negro masses only to the extent that they are helped to see the bright star of their own hopes through the fog of their daily experiences. The problem is psychological; it will be solved only by a Negro leadership that is aware of the psychological attitudes and incipient forms of action which the black masses reveal in their emotion-charged myths, symbols and war-time folklore. Only through a skillful and wise manipulation of these centers of repressed social energy will Negro resentment, self-pity and indignation be channelized to cut through temporary issues and become transformed into positive action.

This is not to make the problem simply one of words, but to recognize (as does the O.W.I. with its fumbling *Negroes and the War* pamphlet) that words have their own vital importance.

Negro participation in other groups is valuable only to the etxtent that it is objectively aggressive and aware of this problem of self-knowledge. For no matter how sincere their intentions, misunderstandings between Negroes and whites are inevitable at this period of our history. And unless these leaders are objective and aggressive they have absolutely no possibility of leading the black masses—who are thoroughly experienced with leaders who, in all crucial situations, capitulate to whites—in any direction. Thus instead of participating along with labor and other progressive groups as equals with the adult responsibility of seeing to it that all policies are formulated and coordinated with full consideration of the complexities of the Negro situation, they will have in effect, chosen simply to be subsidized by Labor rather than by Capital.

Finally, the attitudes list above must be watched, whether displayed by individuals or organizations. They take many forms; the first two being exploited by those who like the Negro best when he is unthinking or passive. The second will help only Fascism. The third contains the hope of the Negro people and is spreading; but these hopes can be used by the charlatan and agent provocateur as well as by the true leader. In this time of confusion many wild and aggressive-sounding programs will be expounded by Negroes who, seeking personal power, would lead the people along paths away from any creative action. Thus all programs must be measured coldly against reality. Both leaders and organizations must be measured not by their words, but by their actions.

SOURCE "Editorial Comment," *The Negro Quarterly,* 1, no. 4 (Winter–Spring 1943): 295–301.

133. *"What Should the Negro Story Be?: Letters from Our Readers." From Negro Story, Dec.–Jan. 1944–45. Artists, including white writers Jack Conroy and Earl Conrad, express a broad range of views seeking to define the aims and goals of Negro Story and the prospects of blacks in American society.*

Dear Editor:

As you know, I consider your periodical one of the most welcome developments in the recent period, in the sphere of Negro and white culture. I am not concerned with whether some of the stories have been better than others, and not too deeply concerned even about the "typos." I think it is excellent that the publication is launched, that it is moving forward with or without a clear "line" other than the broad, general idea of the "Negro story" itself.

It is difficult for me to see how there can be any stated literary policy at this moment, for it falls to you to learn for the first time whether there is such a thing as the "Negro story," whether there are writers who are writing "the Negro Story" and it is, after all, the writers who in the last analysis, will make up what the "Negro Story" turns out to be. That belongs to the future, with what the mails bring in, with the growing maturity of Negro and white writers.

The "Negro Story" can be literally the Negro's great, broad, personal yet universal experience itself. I think that the Negro story can and will be largely the story of a people who have an unusual experience in a land which accords them unusual (I might say at times cruel and unusual) treatment. What you have called the "imponderables" have a definite place in the pages of Negro Story, especially if one regards these imponderables, as I do, to be such conceptions as truth, freedom, justice, and love. For the Negro's experience as an individual and a group is possibly the greatest single truth in America; surely it is one of the most important political and philosophical facts of the national experience.

The universal of freedom is at the core of all human experience and of the Negro experience in particular, and I think that stories which reflect the aspiration to freedom will automatically flow out of the hearts of Negro and white writers, and these should be nurtured.

Justice, by the same token is the quest of all men and the quest of the Negro. Love? We know that the Negro's oppression gives the lie to the great universal concept of love as intended by Christ and the other prophets and here too, we are all seeking, and the story which reflects this quest should be in your pages, and I think you will find it coming to you in the mails. There is the great gamut of individual, human experience, the minute situations, some with local, some with universal meanings which the Negro experiences—all of these things are food for the writer of the *Negro Story*. As I see it, the Negro should regard the world as his province. By and large, Negro writers will write about Negro-white relations, and white writers who contribute to your pages will write about Negro-white relations, and I believe that material, in its very nature, will be of a highly social sort. Whatever it is, we need it. I would not fear if the magazine's contents in part or in whole were called "propaganda" for all literature is propaganda. But if your periodical contains also finely written stories with less serious social meanings, and if these too are part of the Negro's story then they should appear in your pages. If you want to include the individual love story then this too is part of life, part of the Negro's life, and while I personally don't care to read too many of these, especially the type that crowd up the professional "Love Story" magazines, still your pages should also tell the story of the individual romance—even if only for relief from the large flow of serious-minded stories that are bound to appear in such a magazine as *Negro Story*. The Negro's major experience is such a crucial thing, such a critical thing that Jim Crow is, by and large, bound to be a principal subject. But it would be a mistake to limit the inclusion of stories to those which will seize only upon the harshest aspects of the Negro's lot in America—his disfranchisement, lynching, Jim Crow. You don't have to worry about this type of story, and the extent to which it will appear in your pages. It is the wellspring of the Negro experience. But I would be experimental; I would look for the unusual and print it when it came in. I would be anti-Fascist, and I would consider that this world belongs to the Negro as well as to anyone else and keep the policy as that. Sincerely, Earl Conrad.

Dear Editor: When I first began editing *The Anvil* just as the depression was getting a good grip, a common complaint was: "Why can't you find something cheerful to publish?" Most of the young writers first published in *The Anvil* were preoccupied with the phenomenon of hunger in the midst of plenty—corroding idleness when there was so much work to be done. People needed new houses, more food, clothing—but could not afford to buy them. A college graduate was fortunate if he found a low-paying job as a filling station attendant. They couldn't see much to be cheerful about.

Writers were inclined to be bitter and rebellious when recording these maladjustments, and hence were frequently accused of undue pessimism or of inciting [readers] to revolution against the status quo. Those who essayed a shift from the negative to the affirmative ordinarily resorted to what came to be known unfavorably as a "conversion" ending in which the hero or heroine would fall into a demonstration of protesting workers or urge his fellow workers to come out on strike or at least be stricken with the blinding light of economic truth.

Negro writers and white writers who explore Negro life for literary material are confronted by a problem identical to this.

The war solved—temporarily at least—a great many of the more imperative questions agitating the minds of industrial workers during the dark thirties, but the Negro is still harassed by segregation and discrimination both in military and civil life. It is hardly necessary to expand here upon the Negro's peculiar problem within a problem. A truthful and fairly well-rounded portrayal of his general condition is likely to be defeatist in tone.

Just as were the "proletarian" writers who sought for hopeful portents—and indeed accomplished facts of a hopeful nature—in American life, the writers whose Negro themes may be criticized for wishful thinking if they look about them for rainbows in the cloudy sky. Yet the harbingers of better race relations—something resembling "a square deal" for the American Negro—are not entirely absent. There are the programs of such progressive and aggressive labor unions as the C.I.O. In Detroit, while some members of both races were bashing one another's skulls, white and black members of labor unions not only refused to riot but came to the rescue of fellow unionists of the other race in numerous instances. Even down South the pattern of segregation is beginning to crack a bit. In Tennessee a white soldier asked a Negro soldier on a bus to sit beside him, the Jim Crow seats being filled. "Sure!" said the black soldier, but the bus driver intervened to say that this couldn't be permitted—it was illegal.

"Is there any law to prevent us from standing together?" the white soldier then asked.

The bus driver couldn't think of any, so the white soldier arose and stood with arm thrown in comradely fashion about the shoulders of the black soldier throughout the rest of the trip.

There are many Negro names of the past which offer stirring and dramatic historical material for writers. Some of these—like that of Toussaint L'Ouverture—are fairly well-known, but there are many others. Paul Cuffee, sailor and colonist, was an adventurer and an idealist. Gabriel Prosser and Nat Turner dared everything in a hopeless but gallant cause. There is Crispus Attucks, the first American to fall in the war for independence. Dr. Carter G. Woodson's excellent *Journal of Negro History* is crammed with the stories of Negroes who never acknowledged defeat, and who in one way or another achieved either material or spiritual success. The tragic life of gifted Paul Dunbar invites the attention of a novelist. There has been some dipping into this fertile storehouse. Ralph Korngold, Arna Bontemps and others have written about Toussaint; Bontemps' "Black Thunder" is an account of Prosser's abortive rebellion, thwarted by what seemed to be an act of God. Edwin Seaver's anthology "Cross Section" contains a play on Nat Turner by Paul Peters in which Nat Turner is the principal character. The field is an inexhaustable as life itself, and the exciting thing about it is that it is almost virginal. Sincerely, Jack Conroy

SOURCE "What Should the Negro Story Be?: Letters from Our Readers," *Negro Story,* 1, no. 4 (Dec.–Jan. 1944–45): 58–60.

LIST OF
DOCUMENTS

INDEX

313

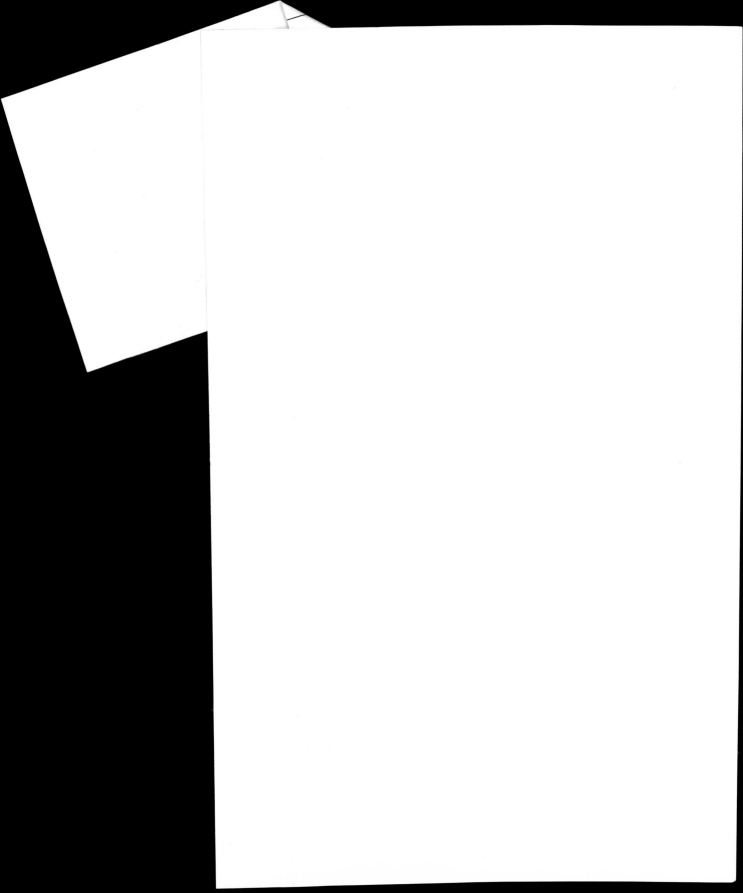

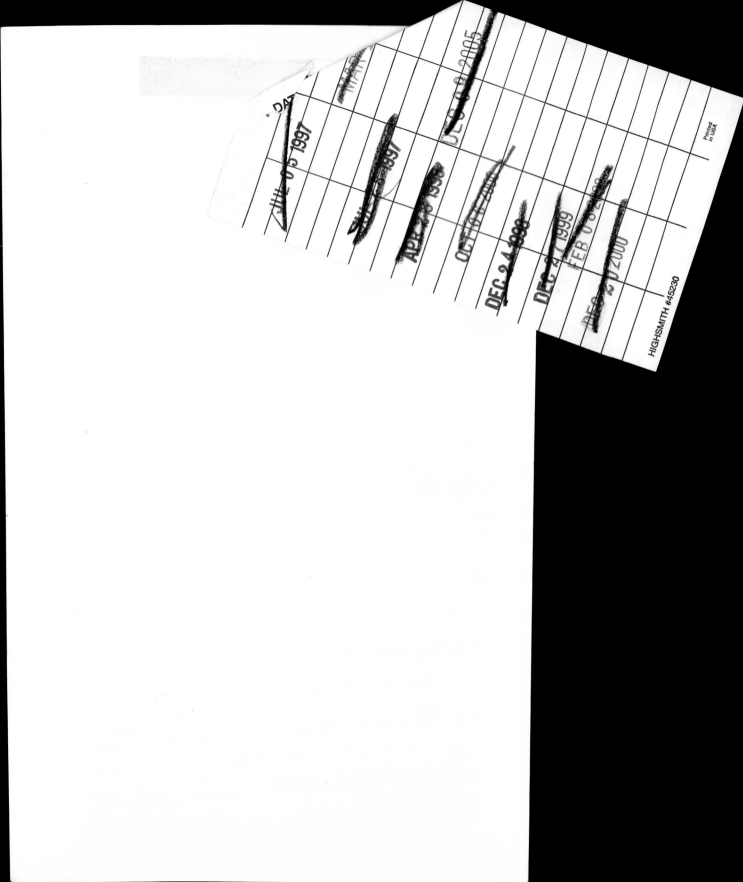